Environmental Markets

Environmental Markets explains the prospects of using markets to improve environmental quality and resource conservation. No other book focuses on a property rights approach using environmental markets to solve environmental problems. This book compares standard approaches to these problems using governmental management, regulation, taxation, and subsidization with a market-based property rights approach. This approach is applied to land, water, wildlife, fisheries, and air and is compared to governmental solutions. The book concludes by discussing tougher environmental problems, such as ocean fisheries and the global atmosphere, emphasizing that neither governmental nor market solutions are a panacea.

Terry L. Anderson is the president of the Property and Environment Research Center (PERC) and Senior Fellow at the Hoover Institution, Stanford University. His work helped launch the idea of "free market environmentalism" with the publication of his book by that title, coauthored with Donald Leal. Dr. Anderson's work emphasizes that private property rights encourage resource stewardship by harnessing the incentives of free enterprise to protect environmental quality. Anderson is the author or editor of thirty-seven books including, most recently, *Tapping Water Markets* with Brandon Scarborough and Lawrence R. Watson. He has been published widely in both professional journals and the popular press and has received many awards for his research and teaching. He received his PhD in economics from the University of Washington.

Gary D. Libecap is Professor of Corporate Environmental Management in the Donald Bren School of Environmental Science & Management and Professor of Economics at the University of California, Santa Barbara. He is also a Research Associate at the National Bureau of Economic Research in Cambridge, MA; a Research Fellow at the Hoover Institution, Stanford University; and Senior Fellow at PERC, Bozeman, Montana. His research focuses on the role of property rights institutions in addressing the tragedy of the commons. He received his PhD in economics from the University of Pennsylvania.

Cambridge Studies in Economics, Choice, and Society

Founding Editors

Timur Kuran, *Duke University*
Peter J. Boettke, *George Mason University*

This interdisciplinary series promotes original theoretical and empirical research as well as integrative syntheses involving links between individual choice, institutions, and social outcomes. Contributions are welcome from across the social sciences, particularly in the areas where economic analysis is joined with other disciplines, such as comparative political economy, new institutional economics, and behavioral economics.

Books in the Series:

Terry L. Anderson and Gary D. Libecap, *Environmental Markets: A Property Rights Approach* 2014

Morris B. Hoffman, *The Punisher's Brain: The Evolution of Judge and Jury* 2014

Peter T. Leeson, *Anarchy Unbound: Why Self-Governance Works Better Than You Think* 2014

Benjamin Powell, *Out of Poverty: Sweatshops in the Global Economy* 2014

Environmental Markets

A Property Rights Approach

TERRY L. ANDERSON

Property and Environment Research Center

GARY D. LIBECAP

University of California, Santa Barbara

CAMBRIDGE
UNIVERSITY PRESS

CAMBRIDGE
UNIVERSITY PRESS

32 Avenue of the Americas, New York, NY 10013-2473, USA

Cambridge University Press is part of the University of Cambridge.

It furthers the University's mission by disseminating knowledge in the pursuit of education, learning, and research at the highest international levels of excellence.

www.cambridge.org
Information on this title: www.cambridge.org/9780521279659

First published 2014

A catalog record for this publication is available from the British Library.

Library of Congress Cataloging in Publication Data
Anderson, Terry Lee, 1946–
Environmental markets : a property rights approach / Terry L. Anderson, Property and Environment Research Center, Gary D. Libecap, University of California, Santa Barbara.
pages cm. – (Cambridge studies in economics, choice, and society)
Includes bibliographical references and index.
ISBN 978-1-107-01022-2 (hardback) – ISBN 978-0-521-27965-9 (paperback)
1. Environmental economics. 2. Environmental quality. 3. Right of property – Environmental aspects. 4. Environmentalism – Economic aspects. I. Libecap, Gary D. II. Title.
HC79.E5A5145 2014
333.7–dc23 2013043149

ISBN 978-1-107-01022-2 Hardback
ISBN 978-0-521-27965-9 Paperback

Contents

List of Figures and Tables

FIGURES

TABLES

Preface

Environmental economics often focuses on the failure of markets to allocate and manage natural and environmental resources efficiently. Under the banner of externalities, markets fail either because private costs are less than social costs or because private benefits are less than social benefits. The former results in overuse of the environment such as overfishing, excessive air and water emissions, and overpumping of groundwater basins. The latter results in too little provision of public goods such as preservation of endangered species habitats, maintenance of adequate stream flows for recreation or pollution dilution, or investment in biodiversity.

The policy remedies for market failure include both taxes to raise private costs to social costs and regulation to hold quantities to the optimal amount. There is little discussion in the literature on the process through which taxes or regulations are devised and implemented that lead to socially beneficial improvements. Are the costs of securing tax or regulatory policies less than the benefits, or alternatively is the route one of rent seeking and interest-group politics? What motivates politicians and regulatory agencies to adopt taxes or regulations that lead to effective correction of the externality? Because taxes are rarely implemented, at least in the United States, the obvious question is why, if they are so beneficial? Is their absence an indication that political interests dominate efficiency goals? Similarly, command-and-control regulations are adopted to limit use of air, water, fisheries, forests, and other resources, but they are costly and often do not capture the incentives of resource users to engage in more optimal production. For example, in the case of fisheries, fishing season limits have been a common regulatory response to overharvest, but they generally result in twenty-four-hour fish derbies, excessive investment in capital and labor to win the derby, and a glut of fish during the season. Regulations on the number of vessels lead to larger ones with more sophisticated equipment to find and catch fish. In some cases where neither taxes nor regulations have been adopted, public ownership and management have been called on to improve resource use. For example, more than one-third of the land area of the United States is owned by the federal government as national forests, range lands, and national parks. Again, however, political considerations through interest-group politics and political and administrative-agency agendas have trumped efficiency, leaving national parks overused and underfunded and national forest management paralyzed by litigation and the demands of competing groups.

We do not claim that all regulation or tax policy has been a failure, but we do believe that environmental economics has paid too little attention to the underlying causes of the divergence between private and social costs and benefits and too little attention to institutional options.

Meanwhile, other economic subdisciplines have carefully and critically considered the importance of institutions that determine who bears the costs and reaps the benefits of efficient use of physical, human, and natural capital. Following the lead of Ronald Coase in his seminal article on "The Problem of Social Costs," institutional economists have focused on the role of property rights, the rule of law, and transaction costs in determining incentives for resource use and the costs and benefits of various responses to the losses of excessive production. As with regulation and taxes, property rights and market exchange are costly, and it may not always be the case that it is socially optimal to solve the environmental or resource problem.

This book applies an institutional approach to environmental problems in an effort to show how property rights and transaction-cost considerations can encourage efficient natural resource use through environmental markets. We do not contend that markets can solve all environmental problems or that political approaches always fail. Rather we offer a lens through which we can tackle environmental problems using property rights and markets and compare them to the regulatory and tax alternatives.

For the economist reader, the book relies heavily on Coase's insights regarding the reciprocal nature of environmental costs. We apply his logic regarding property rights and transaction costs to a variety of environmental issues ranging from local problems such as water quality and wildlife conservation to global problems such as ocean fisheries and the atmosphere.

Where private property rights and markets are difficult to define and enforce, we explore the potential for common property solutions as developed by Elinor Ostrom. We argue that in many local settings, particularly, environmental markets are an effective and often under-utilized option for improving water quality, providing habitat conservation, and encouraging investment in conservation of fish stocks. On the other hand, for broad global problems, the costs of defining property rights and use of markets may exceed the benefits. This does not necessarily imply that tax or regulatory actions are superior, but that a careful analysis of costs and benefits is necessary before implementing *any* policy.

For environmentalists, the book offers concrete solutions in the form of case studies that illustrate the importance of environmental entrepreneurship. The environmental entrepreneur identifies gains from trade and facilitates markets that improve environmental quality through profit opportunities. Whether it is a compensation fund created by environmentalists to compensate livestock owners who are harmed by the reintroduction of wolves, the riparian land owner who invests in stream reclamation in order to enhance property values, or the broker who provides information to investors for habitat or water reallocation or quality improvements, environmentalists will learn how market incentives can be harnessed to achieve environmental ends.

For policy leaders, the book goes beyond command-and-control regulations or taxes to suggest how governments at all levels can reduce transactions costs so as to encourage environmental markets and private incentives to improve and protect environmental quality. For example, we show how water markets could do more to advance water use efficiency and water quality, but they are constrained by institutions that raise the costs of defining and enforcing water rights and of allowing exchanges between willing buyers and willing sellers. In other words, government policies can help make markets where they are missing. The problem is one of *missing* markets, not market failure, and government actions can address this problem by lowering transaction costs.

Although the book is built on a foundation of economic principles, we have tried to keep the jargon to a minimum and to maximize the use of concrete environmental examples at work. As environmental economists, we cannot resist the efficiency gains that markets can provide, but we also embrace the potential of markets to go hand-in-hand with environmental improvements. In short, this book is about the environment *and* the economy, not about the environment *or* the economy.

Terry L. Anderson and Gary D. Libecap
July 2014

Acknowledgments

This project is built on a friendship that started many years ago when we were undergraduates at the University of Montana. Between then and now our careers followed parallel paths until they came together as Senior Fellows at the Hoover Institution. There, director John Raisian asked us to co-direct the Task Force on Property Rights, Freedom, and Prosperity. This book combines the property rights theme of the task force with our mutual interest in environmental economics and policy.

Our thanks go to John Raisian for affording us the opportunity to work together on this project and to members of the task force for listening to our nascent ideas and reading drafts of chapters. It is not surprising that such a group forced us to hone both the ideas and the writing.

Support for the Task Force and this project came from the generosity of John and Jean DeNault. Their willingness to invest in "ideas defining a free society" – Hoover's motto – enabled us to find the time and resources to focus on *Environmental Markets*. We also thank John and Jean DeNault and Sherm and Marge Telleen for their support of our Hoover Fellowships.

The entrepreneurship of Henry Butler, director of George Mason's Law and Economic Center, led to a conference where we received comments from the best and brightest of law and economics scholars. Our thanks go to Henry and the conference participants who read and commented on the manuscript.

Finally, we thank one another for the friendship that has endured the years and grown stronger despite our idiosyncrasies. Combining friendship and scholarship is a rare gift.

1

Who Owns the Environment?

The objective of this book is to promote greater consideration of property rights and markets in addressing environmental problems. Although there is movement toward increased use of market approaches with the adoption of cap-and-trade in controlling air emissions, fishery harvests, and land use, there have been bumps in the road. Several environmental markets are thin with few trades, in others, prices have trended toward regulatory-set floors, and many have insecure property rights that limit incentives for long-term investment and conservation. We explore why that might be the case and what options exist for, and what benefits may be derived from, expansion. We believe that more can be done to improve the efficient provision of environmental quality through the greater definition of property rights and market exchange.

THE RECIPROCAL NATURE OF THE PROBLEM: NORMATIVE AND POSITIVE ANALYSIS

The manner in which our approach differs from standard presentations is that we recognize environmental problems as ones of reciprocal costs. Natural resource and environmental problems arise when people with diverse demands compete for the use of environmental goods. For example, the policy debate over air pollution levels reveals competition between those who want to use the air for low-cost waste disposal or to facilitate use of certain fossil fuels and those who want to breathe clean air, avoid the health effects of ingesting contaminants, have clear views of the surrounding terrain, or mitigate potential climate change. Debates over clear-cut forests reflect competition between those who demand wood products at low cost and seek maintenance of timber-based industries and communities and those who prefer forests for hiking trails, wildlife habitat, or carbon sequestration and the expansion of ecotourism.[1] Concerns about overfishing indicate competition between those who want fish now, regardless of stock impacts, and those who want a sustainable yield into the future. In a positive sense, these are competing and conflicting demands.[2] The different effects on welfare if one use dominates the other often are not obvious, although advocates on both sides have clear opinions. The ultimate answer depends upon the benefits and costs of each alternative and their distribution across society.

THE CENTRALITY OF OPEN ACCESS

Before turning to a discussion of various institutions that can help resolve competing demands, it is important to understand that competition and conflict are at their worst when access is open to all – when there are no clear property rights to limit access or moderate use. Economists describe the results of such open access as a "tragedy of the commons."[3] The term is often associated with an article by ecologist Garrett Hardin (1968) about global population growth and individual decisions underlying it, but the idea was first applied to fisheries by economist H. Scott Gordon in 1954. He described the tragedy this way:

As long as the user of a fishery is sure that he will have property rights over the fishery for a series of periods in the future, he can plan the use of the fishery in such a way as to maximize the present value (future net returns discounted to the present) of his enterprise. From the social point of view it can be said

---

[1] We recognize that there are other issues, such as erosion from clear-cut areas on down-slope parties, or that clear-cut areas may slow the advance of wildfires and the spread of insect infestation. Addressing these issues does not change our basic point.

[2] Notice that we are not emphasizing "externalities" that by definition arise from incomplete property rights. In our view, addressing externalities occurs when property rights are more completely defined so that all costs and benefits are captured in decision making by resource users.

[3] Garrett Hardin (1968), "The Tragedy of the Commons," *Science* 162: 1243–1248.

that he will bring about the "best" use of the fishery and of all other factors invested in it over future periods by thus allocating outputs and outlays over time in accordance with the current rate of discount.[4]

In 2000, Anthony Scott further clarified the problem of overfishing:

Consider the fisherman in his role as the owner of a fishing vessel. He has all three powers over it: he can run it, sell it and take the profit from doing these things. But now consider the same fisherman in his role as occupier of the fishery itself. This role does not give him powers to manage it or dispose of it. All he has is the third power, the law of capture: the power to take and keep the fish he catches. The absence of the first two powers deprives him of any incentive to look after the fishery. To illustrate, if he were the kind of fisherman who tried to manage and exploit the fishery with care and prudence, he would not be rewarded. Although his care might have made the fishery more valuable, he would never have the powers needed to capture this extra value. His efforts would have a near-zero yield to him. That is why, lacking the necessary ownership powers, almost everyone in an offshore fishery finds it not worthwhile to look after it.[5]

Open access to a groundwater aquifer produces a similar result. Groundwater supplies more than 50 percent of the drinking water in the United States and is a major source for irrigation.[6] In most cases, water is pumped from a common aquifer under the rule of capture, in this case through pumping. The result of competitive pumping is analogous to several children with their straws in a cold soda on a hot day. Each might have an incentive to savor the flavor and avoid drinking so fast as to get a headache. However, without constraints on drinking, any restraint by one will be met by faster drinking by another to capture more of the cool drink. In the same way, multiple pumpers from the same aquifer can overpump. Similarly, water left in the aquifer will cost less to lift, will be available for future use, and will continue to support the ground above, thereby limiting subsidence. However,

[4] H. Scott Gordon (1954), "The Economic Theory of a Common-Property Resource: The Fishery," *Journal of Political Economy* 62(2): 124–142; Anthony Scott (1955), "The Fishery: The Objectives of Sole Ownership," *Journal of Political Economy* 63(2): 116–124.

[5] Anthony Scott (2000), "Introducing Property in Fishery Management," Section 3.2 in Ross Shotton, ed., *Use of Property Rights in Fisheries Management*, Rome: FAO Fisheries Technical Paper 404/1 http://www.fao.org/docrep/003/X7579E/x7579e03.htm.

[6] The Groundwater Foundation, http://www.groundwater.org/gi/whatisgw.html.

if access to pumping is open to all, any water left by one pumper is available to another, thus creating a race to the pump house.

Currently, the major approach for achieving environmental quality and natural resource conservation is the use of government regulations and, to a far lesser extent, tax policies. Part of the motivation for reliance on government regulations or taxes is the notion that providing environmental benefits and avoiding the depletion of natural resources are public goods. It is well known that markets may not provide enough public goods, and that this so-called market failure is a reason for government intervention. As we argue, however, regulation and tax policies are not always the most efficient or timely alternatives. There can be government failure as well when policies are molded by interest-group politics and by political and regulatory agendas that may do little for the environment or the provision of public goods. Regulations often include uniform standards that do not reflect differences in abatement costs, subsidies that distort incentives for efficient exploitation and production, and mandates for product characteristics and energy sources that have little consumer appeal or long-term environmental protection potential.[7] In fact, most of the recent market innovations in providing environmental quality or natural resource conservation have resulted from either the high cost of government regulation or its ineffectiveness.[8]

In either case, however, when comparing government regulations and environmental markets, we will be considering imperfect arrangements or second-best solutions. Transaction costs make all responses to

---

[7] CAFE standards that require minimum vehicle fleet mileage mandates not only have many exemptions that subvert the goal of improving fuel efficiency and reducing oil imports, but also lead to costly investment in vehicles that may have little demand, at least in the short run. The slow sales of the Chevy Volt and Nissan Leaf are an example with high up-front costs and long payback periods for consumers. http://www.nydailynews.com/autos/electric-vehicle-market-struggles-slow-sales-article-1.1178155.

[8] This was a major reason for the 1990 Clean Air Act amendments that allowed for the establishment of the SO_2 emissions market. More broadly, the costs of regulation with regard to fisheries are addressed by Frances R. Homans and James E. Wilen (1997), "A Model of Regulated Open Access Resource Use," *Journal of Environmental Economics and Management* 32: 1–27 in their discussion of fishery regulation and rent dissipation.

environmental and natural resource concerns incomplete.[9] The issue at hand is which approach can bring the greatest environmental and natural resource benefits at least cost. The answer will be determined on a case-by-case basis, and we provide many examples of market opportunities and limits in this volume.

In our discussion we distinguish between positive analysis (what is factual) and normative analysis (what policies should be, on the basis of political or value judgments). Within the realm of environmental and natural resource policies, it is very easy to cross the line between positive and normative analysis and believe that what is self-evidently preferable to one party is the social optimum. It may or may not be, but these beliefs are strongly held, and this is one reason why environmental policies often are so contentious.[10] Another related reason for disagreement is the distributional impact of environmental policy. Although environmental justice can be portrayed as an effort to provide improved conditions for poor and underserved populations, environmental regulations themselves raise costs and are often regressive.[11] Although many of the policy suggestions made in this volume are normative, our analysis of the underlying reciprocal source of any environmental problem and the potential for secure property rights to address it reflects positive assessment. We hasten to add that the transaction costs of defining and enforcing property rights that are critical for markets may be too costly relative to the benefits,

[9] Ronald Coase (1960), "The Problem of Social Cost," *Journal of Law and Economics* 3: 1–44. Transaction costs are more precisely defined in Douglas W. Allen (1991), "What Are Transaction Costs?" *Research in Law and Economics* 14: 1–18 and Douglas W. Allen (2000), "Transaction Costs," in Boudewijn Bouckaert and Gerrit De Geest, eds., *The Encyclopaedia of Law and Economics*, Vol. 1. Cheltenham: Edward Elgar, 893–926.

[10] For a discussion of positive and normative analysis, see Charles D. Kolstad (2011), *Environmental Economics*, 2nd edition, New York: Oxford University Press, 30–42.

[11] There is the notion of a "double dividend," that environmental policies can provide improvements and at the same time encourage development of new technologies and economic growth. Assessing whether this is an outcome requires empirical investigation, and the results are likely to vary case-by-case. There clearly will be temporal differences, with costs rising initially and any economic benefits being generated later. See Kolstad (2011, 255–259). The effects of macroeconomic conditions on environmental demand are discussed by Matthew E. Kahn and Matthew J. Kotchen (2010), "Environmental Concern and the Business Cycle: The Chilling Effect of Recession," NBER working paper 16241, July.

and if so, a regulatory alternative may be more cost-effective. Or it might not be, depending on the transaction costs of lobbying to mold public policy and enforcement.

In most cases, environmental problems arise from overproduction so that constraints are required to achieve more optimal output levels, and some parties potentially will be made worse off unless compensated. In government regulation, distributional implications can be obscured because interest group politics reward groups that are well-organized and wealthy relative to other groups.[12] To be sure, the assignment of property rights and the use of markets also have distributional consequences. This is what makes the use of property rights controversial. Nevertheless, the process can be far more transparent, and if environmental markets are more cost-effective, there are greater surpluses to compensate those who are harmed by the policy.

To continue, environmental and natural resource problems often are portrayed in a normative sense – the polluter must pay; natural resources should be exploited sustainably; fossil fuel use should stop in order to halt greenhouse gas (GHG) emissions and possible global climate change. The trade-offs involved in confronting these challenges in a positive sense generally are not made clear by advocates. Consider the conflict between developing oil and gas deposits in Alaska and environmental quality. Tapping oil and gas reserves in the Arctic helps supply U.S. energy demands that are inherent in a growing economy that provides for goods and services, employment, and opportunities for citizens. At the same time, oil and gas extraction has its costs. To mention a few, there are risks of oil spills damaging fisheries, increased air emissions including carbon, and fewer pristine places. Disallowing oil and gas development in Alaska will eliminate the environmental costs, but will come with possibly higher energy charges, more dependence on foreign oil supplies, and perhaps slower economic growth, at least in some areas.[13] In short, environmental problems are inherently wrought with trade-offs. The question is: How

---

[12] Sam Peltzman (1976), "Toward a More General Theory of Regulation," *Journal of Law and Economics* 19(2): 211–240.

[13] Matthew J. Kotchen and Nicholas E. Burger (2007), "Should We Drill in the Arctic National Wildlife Refuge? An Economic Perspective," *Energy Policy* 35: 4720–4729.

can these trade-offs be weighed against one another to promote efficient provision of environmental quality?

To further illustrate, the Ogallala aquifer system, which underlies 174,000 square miles from South Dakota to Texas and supplies irrigation water to 27 percent of the irrigated land in the United States and drinking water to 82 percent of the population living above it, is a poignant example of groundwater overdraft. Thousands of pumpers extract from the aquifer across the Great Plains. Their uncoordinated withdrawals and increasing demands on the Ogallala aquifer have outstripped the recharge rate, causing water levels to fall. Since pumping intensified in the 1940s, water levels have declined more than 100 feet in parts of Kansas, New Mexico, Oklahoma, and Texas, making irrigation impossible or cost-prohibitive in some areas. Total storage has also declined significantly. The United States Geological Survey (USGS) estimated that total water storage in the aquifer was about 3,178 million acre-feet in the 1950s. By 2005, it had declined by 9 percent to about 2,925 million acre-feet. Unfortunately, these results are mirrored around the world, where groundwater is an open-access resource, but is also a critical source for water.[14]

Subsurface oil and natural gas provide yet another example. Since the first discovery of oil in the United States in 1859, competitive pumping has generated enormous waste. Oil and gas are found in subterranean hydrocarbon formations through which the minerals migrate at faster or slower rates depending on subsurface pressure, oil viscosity, and the rock formation's porosity. As pumpers puncture the formations, the oil and gas migrate to the pumping source, making it more costly for others to pump. Recognizing this, all pumpers have an incentive to drill and drain as fast as they can. In other words, the incentive is to get the oil before someone else does. Not only does excessive pumping reduce subsurface pressures, making it more difficult to release trapped oil from the rock, it can also cause a glut on the market resulting in price volatility and increase surface storage costs, where oil is less vulnerable to drainage than underground, and reduce overall oil recovery. An estimate of the magnitude of the

---

[14] See Terry L. Anderson, Brandon Scarborough, and Lawrence R. Watson (2012), *Tapping Water Markets*, Washington D.C.: Resources for the Future; Chapter 9 for a discussion of these issues.

overpumping waste was provided by a 1914 U.S. Bureau of Mines study placing the costs of excessive wells alone at one quarter of the value of total annual U.S. production.[15]

In all of these cases, property rights to the resource are either absent or very incomplete so that users inflict costs on one another (and the resource) and do not consider those effects in their decisions. The tragedy of the commons as it relates to the atmosphere is even more complex than it is for fisheries, groundwater, or oil. With resources where impacts occur in the vicinity of the nets, groundwater pumps, or oil wells, the parties can observe one another and potentially take collective action for mitigation. With broad-based pollution, however, both users and their effects on each other are separated by long distances (and in some cases, long time periods, perhaps generations). Accordingly, competing parties do not see their impacts on others or may not believe they are significant – especially when there are many confounding factors in large natural systems that can affect the status of the resource – and therefore have less incentive to adjust their behavior. Those who demand and receive cleaner air (perhaps through regulation) raise the cost for those who use it for the disposal of waste. And it works the other way. As we illustrate, if those who advocate for cleaner air do not bear the costs involved, they can demand air quality standards that are too high. Similarly, those who emit and do not bear the costs will overpollute. Both are examples of the tragedy of the commons. In a positive sense, it is a reciprocal problem. To return to the importance of spatial distribution, in cases where emissions are concentrated in particular areas, such as in the Los Angeles basin, they can create significant health hazards, and the problem may generate action, through either regulation or markets. CO_2 emissions, on the other hand, intermix all around the planet, making the entire Earth's atmosphere a commons. In this case the solution requires multilateral cooperation across the globe, and therefore is far more complicated.

Open access then is the source of environmental and resource problems. When it exists, decisions on use are made that do not reflect the full social benefits and costs involved, but rather are molded by

---

[15] Gary D. Libecap and James L. Smith (2002), "The Economic Evolution of Petroleum Property Rights in the United States," *Journal of Legal Studies* 31 (2, Pt. 2): S589–S608, S592.

private net-benefit considerations. This setting leads to overfishing, overextraction of groundwater or oil and gas deposits, overgrazing, too-rapid deforestation, depletion of habitat critical for biodiversity, and too much air pollution. Given the explanation of a common or open resource provided some time ago by Scott, Gordon, and Hardin and the potential size of the losses involved (rents dissipated), one might think that the tragedy of the commons would have been solved by now, but solutions have been elusive. The main reason that open-access problems persist is that it is costly to define and enforce rules via regulation or environmental markets regarding who has access, who bears the costs and benefits of decision making, and who can capture the value of scarce environmental resources.

The central question addressed in this book is how competition over scarce environmental resources can be resolved in a civil, timely, and cost-effective way so that more of the costs and benefits are incorporated in decision making. Accounting for all of the costs and benefits of any resource use is very costly, and it is not clear a priori whether regulation or greater definition of property rights and use of markets will be the better solution. We can say that neither will be ideal. What is important is to explore the transaction costs of both options to determine which is more likely to address the environmental challenge in the most complete way at least cost.

When we are comparing the outcomes of government regulation and environmental market alternatives, we are not contrasting a situation where government plays a role to one where it does not. It is a question of the degree of government involvement and who the ultimate decision makers are. As we describe in Chapter 2, with regulation, politicians, regulatory officials, and judges determine the range of resource uses to achieve political goals, usually as defined by interest-group politics. Once regulatory legislation is enacted by politicians, agency officials who implement it typically set uniform performance or technology standards for the industry and then monitor compliance. Adjustments in standards and other regulatory discretion depend on the nature of the enacting legislation and the position of parties who have adjusted to the rules. Judges may intervene if some parties believe that the law is not being implemented or administered as required by statute. New rounds of political action stimulated by additional benefits and costs perceived by interest groups – industry, labor unions, environmental nongovernmental organizations, regional and state governments, professional associations, and so on – can result in changes in the law. These are characteristics of the legislative histories of the major federal environmental regulations: the Clean Air and Clean Water acts, CAFE (Corporate Average Fuel Economy) or fleet standards, renewable fuel standards, renewable energy portfolio standards, and the Endangered Species Act.[16]

As we describe in Chapter 3, with environmental markets, politicians enact legislation recognizing property rights of existing users of land, water, or other natural resources through grandfathering or use of prior possession rules.[17] They may also distribute property rights through lotteries, auctions, or other mechanisms, especially if there are no present claimants. Finally, politicians may create property rights by setting total allowable harvests, emissions, or habitat removal as an annual cap, and distribute shares in that cap. This is the basis for cap-and-trade regimes for fisheries, air quality, and land use.[18] Regulatory agencies and courts may monitor resource use to ensure that it complies with the property rights authorized. Once the rights are defined, the locus of decision makings lies with users, rather than regulators. The principal mechanism for achieving environmental quality or protecting the natural resource lies in the incentives of owners and the exchange of assets in markets. As we explore in Chapters 6 and 7, property rights can be exchanged to provide instream flows, habitat conservation, water quality, fish stock improvements, and reductions in air pollution at the lowest mitigation cost.

The question that arises, then, is whether regulation or markets more efficiently addresses the environmental or natural resource

---

[16] Clean Air Act Extension of 1970 (84 Stat. 1676, P.L. 91–604); Clean Water Act of 1972 (86 Stat. 816, P.L. 92–500); CAFE Standards (89 Stat. 871, P. L.94–163), Endangered Species Act (87 Stat. 884, P.L. 93–205). Renewable Energy Portfolio Standards vary by state.

[17] For examples of this process, see Gary D. Libecap (2007), "The Assignment of Property Rights on the Western Frontier: Lessons for Contemporary Environmental and Resource Policy," *Journal of Economic History* 67(2): 257–291. Prior possession is discussed by Dean Lueck (1995), "The Rule of First Possession and the Design of the Law," *The Journal of Law and Economics* 38(2): 393–436.

[18] Tom Tietenberg (2007), "Tradable Permits in Principle and Practice," in Jody Freeman and Charles D. Kolstad, eds., *Moving to Markets in Environmental Regulation: Lessons from Twenty Years of Experience*, New York: Oxford University Press, 63–94.

problem? The answer to this question lies with the transaction costs of defining, implementing, and using each of these options and the completeness of the property rights that are assigned.

Because regulation maintains the authority of politicians and agency officials over the resource, how it is designed and put into practice can have enormous competitive and welfare implications for firms, regional political representatives, consumers, and other interests. As a result, crafting regulation is subject to political maneuvering, coalition building, and log-rolling. Accordingly, there is considerable rent-seeking in the regulatory process. Regulation invites investment by interest groups in lobby expertise and investigation into the levers through which politicians and agencies can reward favored constituents.[19]

The high costs from promotion of high-sulfur coal under the Clean Air Act Amendments of 1977,[20] contemporary questions about environmental mandates and rising energy costs,[21] the near-collapse of many regulated fisheries prior to recent rights-based

---

[19] Note how difficult it is to eliminate the U.S. ethanol renewable fuels mandate, despite criticism from many quarters that it is inefficient. For a discussion see Randy Schnepf and Brent D. Yacobucci (2012), *Renewable Fuel Standard (RFS): Overview and Issues*, Washington D.C. Congressional Research Service, January 23. More broadly, see James M. Buchanan and Gordon Tullock (1962), *The Calculus of Consent*, Ann Arbor: University of Michigan Press; George Stigler (1971), "The Theory of Economic Regulation," *Bell Journal of Economics and Management Science* 2: 3–21; J.J. Laffont and J. Tirole (1991), "The Politics of Government Decision Making. A Theory of Regulatory Capture," *Quarterly Journal of Economics* 106(4): 1089–1127; Peltzman (1976), (1998), *Political Participation and Government Regulation*, Chicago: University of Chicago Press; Anne O. Krueger (1974), "The Political Economy of the Rent-Seeking Society," *American Economic Review* 64(3): 291–303; Gordon Tullock (1967), "The Welfare Costs of Tariffs, Monopolies, and Theft," *Western Economic Journal* 5(3): 224–232; Ronald N. Johnson and Gary D. Libecap (2001), "Information Distortion and Competitive Remedies in Government Transfer Policies: The Case of Ethanol," *Economics of Governance* 2(2): 101–134.

[20] Bruce Ackerman and William T. Hassler (1981), *Clean Coal/Dirty Air: or How the Clean Air Act Became a Multibillion-Dollar Bail-Out for High-Sulfur Coal Producers*, New Haven: Yale University Press; Peter B. Pashigian (1985), "Environmental Regulation: Whose Self-Interests are Being Protected?" *Economic Inquiry* 23(4): 551–584; Indur M. Goklany (1999), *Clearing the Air: The Real Story of the War on Air Pollution*, Washington D.C.: The Cato Institute; Paul L. Joskow and Richard Schmalensee (1998), "The Political Economy of Market-Based Environmental Policy: The U.S. Acid Rain Program," *Journal of Law and Economics* 41(April): 37–83.

[21] http://www.gallup.com/poll/153404/americans-split-energy-environment-trade-off .aspx.

reforms,[22] and ongoing contention over the Endangered Species Act reveal that regulation is controversial and may not always be the low-cost solution.[23]

Although environmental economists often are critical of environmental regulation, they generally are uniform in their support of environmental taxes. In the tradition of A. C. Pigou (1932), taxes can be a method of imposing the full social costs of resource use.[24] This approach contends that private costs to users, such as a groundwater pumpers, are less than social costs when costs to other pumpers are included. Accordingly, taxes could be levied to equalize social and private costs. Although there is much theoretical merit in this argument, Pigouvian taxes require considerable information regarding the optimal tax, and users have little incentive to provide this information.[25] A question then that arises is whether any tax is better than no tax.? If the tax is set too high, too little production will take place; and if it is set too low, too much production will result. Whether or how regulators will acquire sufficiently-accurate information to set the tax properly requires more attention in the literature than it has received. Additionally, a tax raises private costs (as it is supposed to do) to provide a public good. Few users find this to be an attractive option, and such taxes are almost never politically palatable.

---

[22] Rögnvaldur Hannesson (2004), *The Privatization of the Oceans*, Cambridge, MIT Press, 61–62; Frances R. Homans and James E. Wilen (1997), "A Model of Regulated Open Access Resource Use," *Journal of Environmental Economics and Management* 32: 1–27.

[23] Amy Whritenour Ando (2003), "Do Interest Groups Compete? An Application to Endangered Species," *Public Choice* 114(1–2): 137–159 and Amy Whritenour Ando (1999), "Waiting to be Protected under the Endangered Species Act: The Political Economy of Regulatory Delay," *Journal of Law and Economics* 42(1): 29–60; Richard L. Stroup (1995), "The Endangered Species Act: Making Innocent Species the Enemy, *PERC Policy Series*: April; Dean Lueck and Jeffrey A. Michael (2003), "Preemptive Habitat Destruction under the Endangered Species Act," *Journal of Law and Economics* 46(1): 27–60.

[24] A. C. Pigou (1932), *The Economics of Welfare*, 4th edition, London: Macmillan.

[25] James M. Acheson (2003), *Capturing the Commons: Devising Institutions to Manage the Maine Lobster Industry*, Hanover: University Press of New England discusses how differences in resource stock assessment and scientific methods can lead to very different views of the need for or nature of regulation. His analysis is not directed at taxes but addresses the broader issue of the generation and communication of scientific knowledge in regulation.

In contrast, property rights restrict entry and encourage rent maximization, rather than dissipation. Well-defined and enforced property rights, whether informal or formal, private or collective, make owners the residual claimants and create incentives for owners to consider the costs and benefits of using a resource in one way or another. Owners have the ability to use the resource for themselves, to deny access to others, to modify and improve the asset, and to capture the associated returns and bear the costs of those actions as well as the net benefits of trade. Owners may be individuals, a family, a club or association, or the state. Each of these ownership arrangements embodies different decision-making and enforcement costs, different incentives, and different distributional consequences. In all cases if property rights are secure and perpetual, owners have an incentive to consider future values of the resource across a variety of applications.

Because property rights assign the flow of net rents to owners, they instill incentives for stewardship of the environmental resource. The owner who leaves juvenile fish to mature and reproduce, captures the increased value of the stock. The irrigator who conserves water and sells it to instream flow demanders to protect habitat and fish-spawning areas captures a return for conservation. Property rights encourage innovation and entrepreneurial vision for discovering new rents when they are appropriable. Resources are discovered and, protected, and new uses are identified. Innovative management techniques are found and applied. New exchange possibilities are developed. This process makes new environmental objectives feasible.[26] Entrepreneurship is especially critical in responding to new challenges involving potential global warming and methods of adapting to it through the development of drought-resistant crops, new energy sources, and new energy distribution methods.

Property rights also are the basis for environmental markets. Environmental markets transfer resources to new users and uses in response to new information and values. Transferability encourages existing owners to consider demands made by others and to engage in trade when the alternative involves higher values. Such trades generate

---

[26] For a discussion, see Terry Anderson, Ragnar Arnason, and Gary D. Libecap (2011), "Efficiency Advantages of Grandfathering in Rights-Based Fisheries Management," *Annual Review of Resource Economics* 3: 159–180.

prices, which, in turn, provide information about the value of environmental assets across a variety of applications. Moreover, such exchanges, as Ronald Coase argued, can be achieved smoothly and without controversy when transaction costs are low.[27] How transaction costs might be lowered is examined in Chapter 3. Markets often can work more rapidly and adjust to new information and new values more quickly than can political and regulatory processes where many constituent demands have to be addressed and the size and distribution of the benefits and costs of regulation are unclear. Outcomes are determined by lobbying expertise, rather than by ownership and market exchange. As we discuss in Chapter 5, the long, contentious, and costly battle over Los Angeles' rights to the tributary waters to Mono Lake might have been avoided if the city's water rights had been recognized and purchased.[28]

In order for property rights to effectively assign responsibility for environmental assets and generate incentives for stewardship, the owner must be able to measure and bound the asset, to exclude others, and to transfer rights via market exchange. If the costs of these activities are too high, relative to the expected value of the asset, it is not efficient to define property rights. Under this condition, we would expect assets to remain open to access by all.[29] Accordingly, as we describe in Chapter 3, whether property rights can be defined and enforced depends on the physical nature of the resource and its expected value in alternative uses. Property rights solutions for environmental problems associated with stationary, observable, and boundable resources, such as land, are more feasible than they are for

---

[27] Ronald Coase (1960), "The Problem of Social Cost," *Journal of Law and Economics* 3: 1–44.

[28] See Gary D. Libecap (2007), *Owens Valley Revisited: A Reassessment of the West's First Great Water Transfer*, Palo Alto: Stanford University Press and Jedidiah Brewer and Gary D. Libecap (2009), "Property Rights and The Public Trust Doctrine in Environmental Protection and Natural Resource Conservation," *Australian Journal of Agricultural and Resource Economics* 53: 1–17.

[29] Thomas W. Merrill and Henry E. Smith (2010), *Property*, New York: Oxford University Press; Dean Lueck and Thomas J. Miceli (2007), "Property Law," in A. Mitchell Polinsky and Steven Shavell, eds., *Handbook of Law and Economics*, Vol 2, Elsevier, Chapter 3, 184–257; Gary D. Libecap (1989), *Contracting for Property Rights*, New York: Cambridge University Press, 1–28; Harold Demsetz (1967), "Toward a Theory of Property Rights," *American Economic Review* 57(2): 347–359.

other, more mobile, less observable resources, such as groundwater.[30] And non-excludable resources such as the atmosphere and migratory ocean fisheries offer the greatest challenges for the use of property rights. In this case, governments can create the right to use an asset as we have noted, rather than a property right to the asset itself. These use privileges can be traded and thereby take advantage of differences in productivity, valuation, or mitigation costs.

These notions are the basis for cap-and-trade. In the case of fisheries, the right to fish as a share of a total allowable catch changes private harvest incentives relative to either open access or regulation. With tradable shares, fishers become residual claimants of the larger rents generated from reduced pressure on the stock, higher prices, and lower costs. In many cases, such as in the Iceland and New Zealand, the results have been spectacular.[31] In the case of air pollution and water quality controls or preservation of open spaces and species habitat, the process is similar. The right to pollute, discharge, or use habitat is a share of total emissions, discharges, or required habitat in a region. Users surrender their shares as they produce. If they can abate pollution or provide habitat at lower cost than others, they do so and trade excess shares to those with higher compliance costs. As they continue, their costs are driven up until they no longer have a cost advantage vis-a-vis others. In this manner, marginal abatement costs are equalized and the environmental target is achieved at the lowest cost.

---

[30] Robert Glennon (2002), *Water Follies: Groundwater Pumping and the Fate of America's Fresh Waters*, Washington DC: Island Press; William Blomquist (1991), *Dividing the Waters: Governing Groundwater in Southern California*, San Francisco: ICS Press. In California, the formal designation of water rights can occur through court-assisted adjudication. See S. Bachman, C. Hauge, R. McGlothlin, T. K. Parker, A. M. Saracino, and S. S. Slater (2005), *California Groundwater Management*, Sacramento: Groundwater Resources Association of California; Jedidiah R. Brewer, Robert Glennon, Alan Ker, and Gary D. Libecap (2008), "Water Markets in the West: Prices, Trading, and Contractual Flows," *Economic Inquiry* 46(2): 91–112; Brandon Scarborough and Hertha Lund (2007), *Saving Our Streams: Harnessing Water Markets*, Bozeman, MT: PERC; and Anderson, Scarborough, and Watson (2012), 102–106.

[31] See Ragnar Arnason (2002), "A Review of International Experiences with ITQ," in *Annex to Future Options for UK Fishing Management, Report to the Department for the Environment, Food and Rural Affairs, CEMARE*, Portsmouth UK: University of Portsmouth and Ross Shotton (2000), "Current Property Rights Systems in Fisheries Management," in Ross Shotton, ed. *Use of Property Rights in Fisheries Management, Proceedings of the FishRights99 Conference*, Fremantle Western Australia, Rome: FAO, Fisheries Technical Paper 404/1, 45–50.

There is, however, a fundamental difference between shares of a cap in renewable resources relative to shares in a cap over air and water pollution emissions and habitat use. As we discuss in Chapter 8, in the first case, users capture rents and hence have incentive to police and monitor one another and preserve the stock. They also have incentive to gather information on the stock's condition and to invest in its rebound. Indeed, there may be little role for the regulatory agency if the group can voluntarily agree on an overall cap. In the second case, users provide a public good and do not directly capture rents, except for their share of the public good and lower abatement costs. Public goods are not excludable and hence there are fewer private rents to capture, changing incentives for private information provision and participation in the arrangement. Regulators retain a central role because they adjust the total cap in order to meet regulatory objectives; may have more information about the overall pollution problem, especially if the problem is widespread; and they have greater latitude in adjusting shares. With less anticipated rents, share holders in these cap-and-trade schemes may be a less cohesive group for protecting their use privileges from political infringement. For this reason, as we will see, emission permits, for example, appear to be a less secure property right than are fishery shares or quotas. These markets seem to be far more subject to political and agency manipulation of the cap and of the shares provided. As a result, even highly-advertised emissions trading markets generally have performed less well over the long term than environmental economists have had hoped.[32] This may also explain why markets for conservation credits, tradable development rights, and habitat mitigation banks tied to land have remained quite limited as compared to the spread of fishery use rights.

Property rights as we view them are whole; they are ownership of an asset and the ability to make decisions about it while internalizinge the resulting costs and benefits. They are not a bundle of sticks, whereby

---

[32] For instance, the European Union Emission Trading Scheme that we discuss in Chapter 7 faces growing internal disputes among member countries regarding the cap and the number of emission allowances provided. See Sean Carney, "Allowance prices have fallen. Europe's Emissions Plan Hits Turbulence: Crisis Hampers Program Aimed at Fighting Global Warming, as Economic Recovery Efforts and Environmental Goals Clash," *Wall Street Journal* February 20, 2013, A10, http://online.wsj.com/article/SB10001424127887323764804578314130143612990.html.

each stick is a specific attribute of property rights, such as transfer-ability, modification, investment, storage, appropriation of financial benefits and costs, and so on. Viewing property as a bundle of sticks suggests that each one can be removed from the bundle by regulation or tax policies without affecting the underlying property right and its ability to enlist the incentives of owners in making efficient use deci-sions. Attenuation of property rights by removal of "sticks" weaken their ability to promote efficiency in the provision of environmental quality or protection of natural resources. This issue is underappre-ciated, surprisingly, among environmental economists who advocate the use of market-based approaches, such as cap-and-trade in emission permits.[33]

If markets and exchange are to be effective in meeting environ-mental demands, they must reallocate resources from lower-valued to higher-valued uses and generate information about alternatives (opportunity costs). For this to happen, those who determine resource use must account for the benefits and costs in their decisions. This connection is most complete when decision makers capture the differ-ence between the value added and the costs created. Environmental markets are most likely to be effective when involving cooperation among local parties and organizations that are closest to the problem and have the best information about resolving it.[34] When actual users are involved in the design of solutions, the mechanisms are far more likely to be incentive-compatible and encourage compliance, invest-ment, and experimentation.

GOVERNMENT REGULATION

The most common response to open access has been command-and-control regulation that prescribes inputs and production methods,

---

[33] Merrill and Smith (2010, 1–13) argue that property rights are not a bundle of sticks, but full ownership of the asset. Richard Schmalensee and Robert N. Stavins (2013), "The SO_2 Allowance Trading System: The Ironic History of a Grand Policy Experi-ment," *Journal of Economic Perspectives* 27(1): 103–122, 110–112, for example, point out that what government gives (pollution allowances), it can take away, but do not address the underlying problem for cap-and-trade systems in promoting long-term investment and use decisions in a cost-effective manner.

[34] F.A. Hayek (1945), "The Use of Knowledge in Society," *American Economic Review* 35(4): 519–530.

controls entry and output, grants subsidies, or imposes taxes.[35] Regulation is efficient when the costs of defining and enforcing property rights and implementing markets are higher than a regulatory alternative at a particular point in time.[36] In the case of overfishing, catch quotas, season controls, and equipment limits are imposed as means of reducing harvests and pressure on the stock. In the case of groundwater, permits are required to drill wells, limit access, and in some cases, constrain the amounts of water withdrawn to be consistent with "reasonable use." In the case of air pollution, emissions are regulated under federal and state laws such as the Clean Air Act to reduce the amounts of pollutants, such as lead, NO_x, particulates, and SO_2, released into the atmosphere. These regulations define the legal parameters that must be considered in using the environment and natural resources. There is, however, an implicit assignment of use privileges in regulation. Those who have a fishing license or a drilling permit, or who emit within existing standards, have legal permission to perform these activities. Those who do not have such permits or licenses or who do not meet the emission standards cannot produce. These privileges, however, are not thought of as a real property right, nor are they tradable independent of the productive activity. Whether the regulations effectively address the environmental problem depends on how the implicit property rights assign the social costs and benefits in use decisions. Given interest-group politics, short-time political horizons, and bureaucratic incentives, there is no reason to believe that the property rights assigned via regulation will more completely result in the optimal provision of public goods, such as environmental quality, relative to markets and more voluntary approaches to the problem. To emphasize the point, the case has to be made by comparing the transactions of each on a situation-by-situation basis.

---

[35] Robert N. Stavins (2007), "Market-Based Environmental Policies: What Can We Learn from U.S. Experience (and Related Research)?" in Jody Freeman and Charles D. Kolstad, eds., *Moving to Markets in Environmental Regulation*, New York: Oxford University Press, 25, 30–32; Nathaniel O. Keohane, Richard L. Revesz, and Robert N. Stavins (1998), "The Choice of Regulatory Instruments in Environmental Policy," *Harvard Environmental Law Review* 22: 313–345; and Kolstad (2011, 219–240).

[36] Gary D. Libecap (2008), "Open-Access Losses and Delay in the Assignment of Property Rights," *Arizona Law Review* 50(2): 379–408.

PROPERTY RIGHTS AND ENVIRONMENTAL MARKETS

Property rights define expectations regarding the range of uses permitted to owners, including the right to sell or trade, time lines, the stream of benefits resulting from those decisions, and the stream of costs that are incurred. If the rights are *fully* defined to a resource, by definition, all benefits and costs are borne by decision makers. Their decisions are efficient, and there is no open-access problem.

WHY ENVIRONMENTAL MARKETS?

The list of environmental goods and services has grown rapidly in recent years to include clean air and water, biodiversity, habitat, open spaces, protection of wild species, free-flowing streams, pristine vistas, healthy fish stocks, well-managed oil pools and other valuable mineral resources, and extensive temperate and tropical forests, and the list keeps growing. With such multiplicity of environmental demands, institutional variety for responding to environmental challenges is essential.

THE ROAD AHEAD

Environmental Markets provides a framework for analyzing natural resource and environmental problems through the lens of property rights and incentives. If property rights can be defined and enforced at low-enough cost, environmental markets or common property regimes will follow.[37] There will always be transaction costs in the definition, enforcement, and exchange processes. Reducing transaction costs is the domain of entrepreneurs motivated by market incentives. If the costs of definition, enforcement, and exchange exceed the rents to be had from market exchange, environmental markets will not evolve. This creates the potential for governmental action to generate natural resource and environmental rents through regulation. There is no simple analysis, however, that can tell us whether markets are better than

---

[37] Elinor Ostrom (1990), *Governing the Commons: The Evolution of Institutions for Collective Action*, New York: Cambridge University Press.

regulation or vice versa. The answer depends on the relative costs and benefits of alternative institutions. In this volume we outline the factors that determine how alternative solutions work. The examples we consider suggest that there is more potential for environmental markets than is generally acknowledged, but environmental markets are no panacea. Ultimately, whether property rights and markets or governmental regulation can improve environmental quality is an empirical question. This book provides the framework for answering that question.

2

Is Government Regulation the Solution?

As discussed in Chapter 1, we have a multitude of demands for environmental goods and services.[1] Whether it is clean air and water, tropical rainforests, habitat for polar bears, open spaces, controls on carbon emissions, whales, or energy conservation, we are willing to spend time and money on getting more of the environmental goods we want. The problems we face are how to respond to changing demands, how to tradeoff competing demands against one another, and how to balance these with the desires for other goods and services in the economy. Addressing these questions requires that environmental policies be efficient or as cost-effective as possible. This chapter examines the role of government regulations as a way of improving environmental quality – which is the traditional approach – and compares it to environmental markets.

There are many different ways to produce environmental goods, ranging from markets with well-specified private property rights, the subject of Chapter 3, to governmental regulation, the solution considered in detail here. One reason for choosing government rather than markets is the potential for markets to fail in fully accounting for social costs and benefits.[2]

---

[1] For example, see this Gallup Poll at http://www.gallup.com/poll/146810/water-issues-worry-americans-global-warming-least.aspx.

[2] For a discussion of market failure in the provision of environmental goods and the problems of high transaction costs, see Nathaniel O. Keohane and Sheila M. Olmstead (2007), *Markets and the Environment*, Washington D.C.: Island Press, 65–83, 127–128. Jean-Marie Baland and Jean-Philippe Platteau (1996), *Halting Degradation of Natural Resources: Is there a Role for Rural Communities?* New York: Oxford

Generally government policies come in the form of regulations that specify what the environmental objectives are and define how those objectives are to be met using the government's authority to enforce regulation.[3] Examples of governmental actions to produce environmental goods include directives that specify amounts emissions into the air and water (such as mercury and air toxic release standards), restrictions on access and use (fishing licenses and seasons), or prescribed methods and equipment (electric utility flue-gas sulfur scrubbers). Other government interventions include information provision (Toxic Release Inventory), subsidies (fish hatcheries and solar power and wind power grants and tax credits), taxes (charges for solid waste disposal and user fees), and the creation of use rights where they did not exist before (fishery shares or quotas or pollution emission allowances). These follow from the framework of cap-and-trade, where government sets the cap and allocates a limited number of use rights.

Cap-and-trade differs from traditional regulation in that it provides more discretion to parties regarding how environmental objectives will be achieved. Because trading is the centerpiece, mitigation can be undertaken by the low-cost provider. Those with high mitigation costs buy permits or allowances from those with lower costs, and overall expenses are lowered through voluntary exchange. Therefore, cap-and-trade markets can be more rapid, more flexible, and less costly than strict regulatory standards in meeting environmental objectives. Further, by enlisting the incentives of users, they can produce information about and promote the adoption of new technologies that reduce

---

University Press stress the transaction costs of market trading and especially the role of private information in undermining bargaining, 52–56. Because they are interested in community responses to open access problems, they do not explore the transaction costs of government intervention. Accordingly, their game-theoretic framework does not address the tradeoff between a second-best market approach versus a second-best government response.

[3] For a discussion of the prevalence of regulation in addressing environmental and natural resource problems, see Robert N. Stavins (2007), "Market-Based Environmental Policies: What Can We Learn from U.S. Experience (and Related Research)?" in Jody Freeman and Charles D. Kolstad, eds., *Moving to Markets in Environmental Regulation*, New York: Oxford University Press, 25, 3–32, and Charles D. Kolstad (2011), *Environmental Economics*, 2nd Edition, New York: Oxford University Press, 223.

the cost of compliance with regulations and enhance the likelihood of achieving environmental objectives in the least-cost manner.[4]

Although alleged market failure is an argument for government regulation, government regulations also may not necessarily improve economic efficiency or environmental quality. Just as there can be market failure, there can be political failure. Therefore, the use of regulation begs several critical questions. To mention a few: What information goes into decisions regarding what environmental goods to produce and how to produce them? How is the public interest measured and weighed against special interests? How does the potential for government failure compare to the potential for market failure in meeting environmental demands? What are the incentives for politicians and bureaucratic officials to respond to environmental demands? How flexible are government regulations to dynamic conditions and new information about problems?[5]

In short, government regulation has many of the same costs inherent to markets. Hence, determining which is preferable requires weighing the costs and benefits of each to find second-best solutions. Regulatory costs cannot be ignored any more than bargaining costs in markets can be. There certainly are costs in defining and enforcing property rights and costs of bargaining among demanders and suppliers, the subjects of Chapter 3. The point we emphasize here is that these costs should be considered against the cost of using command-and-control regulation to achieve environmental outcomes.[6] The benchmarks for each must be made clear in comparing the effectiveness of the two alternatives.

Economic arguments for government regulation of environmental goods center on two factors. First, many environmental goods are public goods, meaning that once produced, they can be consumed by a large number of people at no extra cost. In other words, consumption or use is non-rivalrous because consumption or use by one person

---

[4] For a discussion of market advantages relative to command-and-control regulation in certain contexts, see Stavins (2007, 25–30).

[5] The complex political economy of regulation is illustrated in Kolstad (2011, 221).

[6] As Kolstad (2011, 267–272) argues, there may be cases in which a bargaining solution is too costly relative to government intervention, and that therefore the choice must be made among different governmental policies. Before asserting that bargaining costs are too high, however, we argue that the real costs of government regulation must be compared to the real costs of market solutions.

does not preclude that by another. If those enjoying the benefits of such goods cannot be excluded for not paying, non-payers may get a free ride from those who do pay. This can lead to under-production of the good or service. Second, many natural resources necessary to produce environmental goods are subject to the tragedy of the commons. There are no property rights and wasteful open-access conditions prevail.[7] In this chapter, we consider each of these factors in detail. We then discuss the problems inherent in implementing government regulation through the lens of public choice economics and in the context of several examples.

THE ENVIRONMENT AS A PUBLIC GOOD

Consider air quality. If a factory reduces its emissions of waste into air, everyone in the airshed enjoys the benefits of improved air quality, although each person may value the improvements differently. Another person moving into the airshed can also enjoy the benefits at no extra cost to the factory or to other citizens. Economists therefore call this type of good non-rivalrous in consumption because one consumer's enjoyment of the good does not reduce or rival the consumption of another.

The important implication of this characteristic of environmental goods is that the aggregate demand for such goods is vertically additive. That is to say, if person A values an extra unit of air quality at $10 and person B values it at $5, the total value of the extra unit is $15. In contrast, if a good is rivalrous in consumption, as in the case of a hamburger, consumption by one person precludes consumption by another. Hence, if person A values the hamburger at $10 and person B at $5, the value of the hamburger will be determined by the one who consumes it – either $10 if person A or $5 if person B, but not the sum of the two.

The standard economic argument that follows from this discussion is that the free-rider problem associated with non-rivalrous goods creates a market failure because too little or perhaps even none of the good will be produced privately. There is no ability for producers to exclude non-payers. This analysis, however, is not sufficient to

---

[7] Garrett Hardin (1968), "The Tragedy of the Commons," *Science* 162: 1243–1248.

conclude that markets would fail to provide the optimal amount of the public good without more focus on various options for exclusion and the marginal cost of supplying the public good relative to marginal demand. Ownership of a complementary input can provide a means for exclusion and hence, the ability of the owner to deny access to those who do not pay. In this circumstance, market provision of the public good is possible.[8] The public good may also be privately provided if the supplier extracts sufficient private value to cover the costs of supply or obtains returns from the sale of complementary products.[9] For the reasons we make clear in this volume, both government and markets may provide some quantity of the public good of environmental quality. The issue is which will provide an efficient quantity? Both private and government provision are costly.

Consider a movie theater. Once the movie is showing, it can be viewed by additional people up to the seating capacity of the theater, with each additional viewer getting added value from the showing.[10] The large number of private theaters tells us that the market can supply a non-rivalrous public good. Alternatively, consider flower beds, which beautify the owner's house and, at the same time, the neighborhood. Assume that the value of additional flowers to each neighbor or passersby is quite low, which is likely, so that an additional flower does not add much benefit. Further assume that the homeowner captures most of the additional value from flowers, which is also likely. If the marginal cost of additional flowers is low, the homeowner will provide the optimal amount of flowers while generating surplus value for neighbors and passersby. In this circumstance there also is no market failure even if excludability is costly.

Further, think about the provision of habitat for wildlife, such as bison, which are valued either because people enjoy knowing the

---

[8] In a similar manner Ronald Coase illustrated the private provision of public goods through private lighthouses in Britain, see Ronald H. Coase (1974), "The Lighthouse in Economics," *Journal of Law and Economics* 17(2): 357–376.

[9] This discussion follows that of David D. Haddock (2007), "Irrelevant Externality Angst," *Journal of Interdisciplinary Economics* 19(1): 3–18. This is also the standard problem facing firms in the social responsibility of business debate. See Bruce Hay, Robert Stavins, and Richard H.K. Vietor, eds. (2005), *Environmental Protection and the Social Responsibility of Firms*, Washington D.C.: Resources for the Future.

[10] This assumes that one viewer does not distract another by blocking the view, say with a big hat, or by making noise, say with a ringing cell phone.

animals exist or because people can view them, or both.[11] Clearly existence values are non-rivalrous because one person takes pleasure in their survival at the same time that another does. Neither actually has to see the animals. It is impossible to imagine how the person providing bison habitat could identify each existence demander and collect from that person to help pay for the habitat. In other words, demanders would be able to free ride on the supplier who bears the cost of provision. But the public good may still be provided if there are sufficient private benefits from doing so.

Examination of Ted Turner's Flying D ranch in Montana helps to make this clear. A public road runs through the ranch en route to a national forest campground and trailheads, and Mr. Turner has no ability to put up a toll booth to charge people driving on the road. Motorists see bison in a spectacular setting, undoubtedly generating significant value for them. The marginal cost of providing these bison for viewers may not be low, but the marginal value to Mr. Turner is high as evidenced by his ownership of several bison ranches and by the revenue he earns from selling bison meat in his restaurants. Although bison on the Flying D are non-rivalrous goods for people seeing them along the public road, they are not necessarily under-supplied by the private owner, Mr. Turner.

We do not know if Mr. Turner provides the optimal viewing of bison, nor do we know if public provision of bison viewing, such as in Yellowstone Park, is the optimal amount. Standard economic theory suggests that Mr. Turner will decide based on his private benefits and costs and as a result, public goods will be under-supplied, but compared to what alternative?[12] The political economy of regulation and government provision of public goods points to the roles of rent-seeking, lobbying, and interest group politics.[13] These factors can lead to non-optimal over-or under-supply by governments. Private considerations

---

[11] See John Krutilla (1967), "Conservation Reconsidered," *American Economic Review*, Volume 57(4): 777–786.

[12] For a discussion of the nirvana fallacy, see Harold Demsetz (1969), "Information and Efficiency: Another Viewpoint," *Journal of Law and Economics* 12(1): 1–22.

[13] See James M. Buchanan and Gordon Tullock (1962), *The Calculus of Consent*, Ann Arbor: University of Michigan Press and Craig Volden and Alan E. Wiseman (2007), "Bargaining in Legislatures over Particularistic and Collective Goods," *American Political Science Review*, 101(1): 79–92.

play an important role in the political process as well. Without greater specificity in defining the conditions under which governments will supply public goods, it is not possible to predict whether private actors will necessarily under provide relative to the government option. The details will matter in each case. The lesson from this discussion is that governmental regulation is not necessarily required to supply public goods. As we argue throughout this book, determining whether government or market provision of environmental goods is superior is an empirical issue on a case-by-case basis.

ENVIRONMENTAL GOODS AND THE TRAGEDY OF THE COMMONS

The second argument for governmental regulation for the provision of environmental goods is that the inputs for producing them are subject to the tragedy of the commons.[14] The tragedy is that resources are over-exploited because property rights (informal or formal, group or individual) are lacking, thus allowing open access to all. Simply put, open access is the bane of natural resource and environmental stewardship. As long as access is open, parties who use it will not bear the full costs of their actions, and in the absence of trading, there will be no price signals to reveal the opportunity costs of current or future uses. As a result, aggregate production or use levels are too high and investment in the resource is too low, compared to what would be expected if an owner took account of the resource's value now and into the future. Without property rights to limit and define who has access to the resource and the right to derive value from it, parties cannot bargain with one another to constrain use, to invest in it, or to re-allocate it to higher-valued activities.[15] And even if a group of existing

---

[14] Hardin (1968) was not the first to outline the logic and losses in the tragedy of the commons. More than a decade before his article, H. Scott Gordon (1954), "The Economic Theory of A Common-Property Resource: The Fishery," *Journal of Political Economy* 62(2): 124–142 clearly described a similar process. Gordon's analysis was extended by Anthony Scott (1955), "The Fishery: The Objectives of Sole Ownership," *Journal of Political Economy* 63(2): 116–124, and others.

[15] Bargaining of the kind discussed by Ronald Coase (1960), "The Problem of Social Cost," *Journal of Law and Economics* 3: 1–44, is not possible. Steven N.S. Cheung (1970), "The Structure of a Contract and the Theory of a Non-Exclusive Resource," *Journal of Law and Economics* 13(1): 49–70, emphasized the inability of parties to contract for more socially-optimal outcomes.

users could agree to control use of the resource, new entrants could undermine the agreement. This problem would be even greater if the first group enhanced its value and made it more attractive to entry by others. There will be competitive rush to exploit the resource and to neglect its long-term viability. That rush and potential violence are not only costly in terms of labor and capital diverted from production to predation and defense, but they shorten time horizons and discourage investment.[16]

Two examples illustrate this tragedy. In a non-exclusive fishery, any fisher with a boat can cast a line or net and catch as many fish as he or she desires. With abundant fish stocks, the catch by one fisher does not affect the catch by another. However, so long as there are profits (economic rents) to be had from fishing and no limits on entry, more fishers will be attracted, harvests will increase, and eventually, the stock will be driven down and fishing costs driven up until the value of the resource is zero. And in the rush for fish, fishers take increasingly risky actions, such as fishing in rough seas, or violently confronting their competitors. This unhappy outcome affects far too many fisheries which are the source of 25 percent of animal protein in the world.[17] We explore the problem of regulation as a solution and the important potential role of property rights in fisheries in more detail later in this chapter and in Chapter 5.

Another example is the national parks. Although access is restricted to those who can travel to a park and pay the entry fee, such costs are sufficiently low and kept low by political demand so that too many visitors create congestion. This situation diminishes the value of the experience to all and places some of the natural habitat in jeopardy. "Bear jams" (cars brought to a standstill as people observe bears and other wildlife) in Yellowstone National Park are a prime example. People also race to get camp sites during the busy summer season.

---

[16] For a classic study in the early California gold rush, see John Umbeck (1981), "Might Makes Right: A Theory of the Foundation and Initial Distribution of Property Rights," *Economic Inquiry* 19(1): 38–59. See also the historical use of violence to protect informal claims in the Maine lobster fishery, James M. Acheson and Roy J. Gardner (2005), "Spatial Strategies and Territoriality in the Maine Lobster Industry," *Rationality and Society* 17(3): 309–341.

[17] United Nations, Food and Agriculture Organization (2009), *FAO Yearbook; Fishery and Aquaculture Statistics 2007*.

Figure 2.1. National Park Congestion.
Source: Google Images: http://yellowstone.net/wp-content/uploads/2012/10/
old-faithful-geyser.jpg. Bearjam: http://www.flickr.com/photos/chickadeetrails/
3386045027/.

In Yosemite National Park with its towering granite rock walls, there
are even queues to climb the seemingly impossible 3,000-foot vertical
face of El Capitan. On the Serengeti Plain in Kenya and Tanzania,
wildlife migrations attract so many people that the roads are clogged
with minivans and the sky filled with airplanes and hot air balloons.
This is not the outcome that most park visitors wanted, or predicted,
but it is the natural result of open access.

On the opposite side of the tragedy-of-the-commons coin are individual actions that generate benefits to others for which the producers
of benefits receive no compensation. When an individual refrains from
clear cutting a hillside forest, which can be viewed from afar, individuals in the viewshed capture some of the value – perhaps in the form
of higher property values – without having to pay the party who for-
goes logging revenues. Similarly, when an environmental group purchases land for endangered species habitat or open space, it provides a
non-rivalrous public good. Farmers whose land management practices
improve the quality of water flowing downstream to municipalities,
which in turn lowers water treatment costs, are producing benefits for
which they are not compensated.

The loss from the tragedy of the commons or from the free-rider
problem provides incentives to correct the situation. This begs the
question of how this is best accomplished. In the case of the national
parks, private property rights could be defined and enforced and access
allocated through prices, but there is little political possibility for such

a dramatic shift.[18] In the case of fisheries, fish stocks are being driven to critical lows because of overfishing, and the wealth losses can be large. Establishing property rights to such mobile resources is costly, making regulation a possible remedy where governments have jurisdiction as they do in their exclusive economic zones.[19] In the case of wild-ocean fisheries where there is no overriding sovereign political authority, neither regulation nor property rights may be feasible without international collective action, which may or may not be forthcoming. In the case of beautiful land views, fences can be constructed to keep out free riders, but such fencing is costly. We examine the political and resource costs of defining property rights and closing open access throughout the volume.

THE SIMPLE ANALYTICS OF MARKET FAILURE

The standard economic analysis of the tragedy of the commons focuses on whether users bear the full costs of resource use and on the free-rider problem of whether the producer reaps the benefits from goods produced.[20] When people can free ride, the costs of provision are born by others. In the first case there is too much production and in the latter too much demand. Individual fishers with unrestrained access to a fishery face only part of the social costs of catching fish. They bear

---

[18] To be sure, the political issues are complex, given the competing objectives of providing low-cost access to parks, as part of the country's heritage, and of protecting their unique natural habitats. For the politics of raising fees, see the tentative manner in which modest fee increases were introduced in 2007, http://www.nytimes.com/2007/05/07/washington/07parks.htm. More fundamental problems in the fee structure and management of the National Parks are discussed by Brian Yablonski (2009), "The National Parks: *America's Best Idea*" *PERC Reports* 27(3), Fall.

[19] The World Bank (2008) in *The Sunken Billions: The Economic Justification for Fisheries Reform* estimated that $50 billion annually was lost in fishery mismanagement (www.fao.org/newsroom/en/news/2008/1000931/index.html). Many fisheries are either open access or subject to ineffective government regulation. Rights based systems are gaining traction, however. See Christopher Costello, Steven Gaines, and John Lynham, 2008, "Can Catch Shares Prevent Fisheries from Collapse?" *Science* 321, September 19: 1677–1678.

[20] When private and social costs (benefits) diverge, there is said to be an externality or third-party effect. A clear discussion is provided in Kolstad (2011): 89–95. Because we view the diversion of private and social costs (benefits) as one of incomplete property rights we do not use the term. Cheung (1970) also takes a similar approach. As we describe in Chapter 3, by focusing on incomplete property rights rather than diversions between private and social costs we can direct attention to the fundamental problem at hand.

the costs of labor and capital – boat, nets, and fuel – but the costs of forgone fish growth and reproduction and the higher cost of catching fish once the stock is reduced and dispersed are ignored. If access is open to all, fish left to grow and reproduce will be caught by someone else, added reproductive capacity will be shared by all who exploit the fishery, and the lower costs of catching fish if the stock is larger and more condensed will benefit all fishers.

Similarly, people pumping from an open-access groundwater basin will consider the costs of drilling and pumping but will have little reason, other than community norms or local rules (see Chapter 4), to consider how depletion of the aquifer affects others.[21] Over-pumping can raise the cost for everyone of lifting water from greater depths, create cones of depression around an individual well that literally suck water from nearby wells,[22] cause sink holes when the underlying earth structure collapses because of the withdrawal of groundwater, or allow for salt water intrusion when fresh water is extracted from an aquifer near the ocean. The result will be a race to the pump house wherein too much water will be pumped too soon.

If the private costs to resources users are less than the social costs, resources will be over used, and if the private benefits of resource improvements are less than the social benefits, environmental goods will be underproduced.[23] The implications of a setting where not all costs are considered in decision making by users can be seen in Figure 2.2 where we use a fishery as an example.

MPC shows the marginal private costs faced by each party; MSC shows the marginal social cost; MPB and MSB show the marginal private and social benefits, which are assumed to be equal in this example.

---

[21] For a discussion of the losses of unrestrained pumping, see Robert Glennon (2002), *Water Follies: Groundwater Pumping and the Fate of America's Fresh Waters* Washington DC: Island Press. For a discussion of the role of common property institutions in groundwater management, see Elinor Ostrom (1990), *Governing the Commons: The Evolution of Institutions for Collective Action*, New York: Cambridge University Press, 104–139.

[22] The cone of depression results from differential pressures between the well head and the surrounding rocks surrounding it. Pumping reduces pressure at the well head and, in essence, sucks water from nearby rocks. This can raise the cost to others pumpers as they struggle to access the resource for their wells and can deplete the resource that lies below their surface properties.

[23] Here we focus on the divergence between private and social costs, but the reader should recognize that a divergence between private and social benefits can be analyzed in the same way.

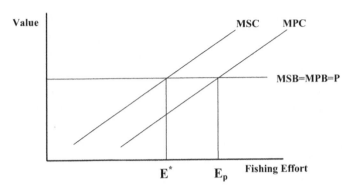

Figure 2.2. The Simple Analytics of Market Failure.

With open access and hence, no property rights to the resource, there is no way for user A to force user B to pay for his or her effect on the overall costs of production. One fisher cannot demand and receive compensation for any additional catch costs arising from fishing or congestion by others, nor can a groundwater pumper charge another well owner for causing higher lift costs from unrestricted aquifers.[24] Indeed, quite the opposite. When private costs are less than the private benefits, it is worthwhile for each individual to combine additional labor and capital with the resource to capture more of the rents. The resulting competition leads to more investment in extraction, driving up total costs, driving down total value and dissipating long-run resource rents. For non-renewable resources, the tragedy of the commons is economically-premature exhaustion and for renewable resources it is lower long-run recovery rates.[25]

[24] This point is implicit in the analysis of unrestricted fisheries by Gordon (1954) and Scott (1955). The problem of interconnected costs of groundwater pumping is described in J. Herbert Snyder (1954), "The Economics of Groundwater Mining," *Journal of Farm Economics* 36(4): 600–610.

[25] The classic article on the economics of resource extraction is Harold Hotelling (1931), "The Economics of Exhaustible Resources." *Journal of Political Economy* 39(2): 137–175. It is worth pointing out that for all the cyclical worry about non-renewable resource exhaustion, there is not one solid historical example of society running out of such a resource. In contrast, exhaustion of renewables has happened quite frequently (species extinction). This is why it is illogical to refer to non-renewables as "exhaustible" and renewables as "inexhaustible" resources. A major reason for this outcome is the property rights structure. Non-renewables tend to be privately owned and exploited, whereas renewables tend to be open-access either because of the high costs of bounding or by law. We explore the transaction costs of defining property rights throughout the volume.

With open access MPC is below MSC, and assuming that the catch is sold in a competitive market where the price reflects additional benefits of fishing effort to the fisher and to the consumers of fish, MPB = MSB. The individual optimal fishing effort is E_p, compared to the socially optimal effort of E^*. Beyond this static analysis, harvest practices have dynamic effects as new entry and overfishing drive fish stocks down thus raising private and social costs. Gradually with stock depletion, individual and aggregate effort levels decline as the rents from the fishery are depleted.[26] If markets or regulations can make the private costs reflect the social costs, efficiency will be improved.

THE LEGACY OF PIGOU

The underpinning of this analysis comes from British economist Arthur Cecil Pigou, who argued that the divergence between private and social costs calls for regulatory action to correct the problem. As he put it, the divergence in costs occurs "owing to the technical difficulty of enforcing compensation for incidental disservices" (Pigou 1932, 185).[27] In effect, Pigou was referring to the costs of defining property rights and promoting exchange. He called the resulting efficiency loss a reduction in the "national dividend."

The general problem described by Pigou is referred to as market failure because autonomous actors fail to reach the optimal level of resource use and maximize resource rents. In actuality, however, the problem is more appropriately referred to as a missing market rather than a failing market. The absence of property rights due to "technical difficulties" precludes contracts that constrain access and output and that promote trade to generate price signals about opportunity costs. In other words, "technical difficulties" prevent a market from occurring. Rather than determining what causes the impediments to establishing

---

[26] In the case of property rights and differential responses across resources, see Gary D. Libecap (1989), *Contracting for Property Rights*, New York: Cambridge University Press.

[27] On the benefit side, underproduction of valuable services occurs because marginal private benefits are less than marginal social benefits "because incidental services are performed to third parties from whom it is technically difficult to exact payment" A. C. Pigou (1932), *The Economics of Welfare*, 4th edition, London: Macmillan: 183–184.

Figure 2.3. Arthur Cecil Pigou, 1877–1959.
Source: Pigou.ipg. http://www.hetwebsite.org/het/profiles/pigou.htm.

rights and bargaining over them, Pigou's focus was on how taxes could raise private costs to the level of social costs, MPC + Tax = MSC, and thereby induce the optimal level of fishing effort.[28] Once the tax is set, firms decide their desired production levels according to marginal private costs including the tax.[29] In the case of unaccounted for benefits, Pigou's logic calls for a subsidy to equate private and social benefits and increase private production of the good.

Alternatively, government could directly constrain production or output to optimal levels, E*, in the fishing effort example through performance and technology standards, such as catch limits, short fishing seasons, harvest area restrictions, specialized gear requirements, and vessel size controls.[30] Performance standards leave some discretion with the agent for compliance with a fixed target, although as we will see the adjustments margins chosen drive up costs. In the fishery case,

[28] Carl Dahlman (1979), "The Problem of Externality," *Journal of Law and Economics*, 22(1): 141–162, 158–160) discusses the importance of directing attention to how the transaction costs of bargaining might be lowered rather than focusing solely on a perceived distinction between private and social costs. Doing so would more likely result in improved environmental and natural resource policies.

[29] See Keohane and Olmstead (2007, 134–137) among others for a discussion of Pigouvian taxes.

[30] Prescriptive regulation, particularly with regard to air pollution control, is described by Kolstad (2011, 223–240) with an extensive discussion of the direct costs involved.

more and more fishing vessels and crews are added as fishing seasons are shortened to meet a particular total allowable harvest. Technology requirements are easier to verify because inspectors can see whether the authorized equipment is being used, but they may not be the most efficient way of achieving the desired level of environmental good production.

Though described by Francis Bator as the "simple analytics of welfare maximization,"[31] transitioning from the analytics of regulation or taxation to the implementation of such policies is more complex in the political context. The transaction costs of implementation include information costs, distributional effects, and special interest lobbying. The total costs can be high and exceed the alternative of defining property rights and relying upon markets.

INFORMATION COSTS

Setting the appropriate tax or production rate requires having knowledge of the private and social costs and benefits implicit in the simple analytics. Regulators may not be in the best position to secure this information.[32] As Hayek (1945, 519–520) noted, "the economic problem of society is... not merely a problem of how to allocate 'given resources' if 'given' is taken to mean given to a single mind which deliberately solves the problem set by these 'data.'" The "use of knowledge in society," as Hayek described it, requires obtaining information on benefits and costs – information that often is not well-known or is controversial because it is specialized and diffused and is generated dynamically over time. For Hayek, prices generated by trading in decentralized markets produced this knowledge.[33] Regulation, unless it allows for exchange, does not generate such information.

For efficiency, Pigouvian regulation would be set equal to the difference between marginal private and social costs at the optimal level of production, but knowing what this difference is as well as optimal pollution levels requires collaboration between users and regulators. The

[31] Francis M. Bator (1957), "The Simple Analytics of Welfare Maximization," *American Economic Review* 47(1): 22–59.
[32] The information problem also is discussed by Stavins (2007, 21).
[33] F.A. Hayek (1945), "The Use of Knowledge in Society, *American Economic Review* 35(4): 519–530.

former have little incentive to cooperate because they will pay the fee and bear the costs of adjusting to the regulatory constraint. Collecting sufficient abatement cost and pollution-control benefit information in order to set an optimal tax is a huge challenge, and just how the political process would assemble such information without objectives being hijacked by special interests is not clear. At the same time, setting a pollution cap and its use in cap-and-trade systems, which we describe later, also requires similar information, but in the latter case there could be more flexibility as new information on the value of pollution reductions becomes available. The cap could be adjusted. Taxes, which are fairly transparent, may not be so easily modified in the political process, especially if increases are required.[34]

In theory, implementation of a Pigouvian tax would equate marginal control costs across firms. Those firms with lower compliance costs would cut back more and those with higher costs less. But obtaining firm-specific information is difficult, and uniform standards that are commonly used typically do not allow for exchanges between firms in responding to regulatory controls.[35] Of course, producers utilizing the open-access resources – be it a fishery or the atmosphere – will have their own assessments of the size and characteristics of the resource and extent of the open-access problem. These users, however, are likely to be reluctant to reveal their private information, preferring to act strategically in the political process so as to secure the most

---

[34] In a similar case, the Colorado Big Thompson Water Project in north central Colorado assigns owners of water rights a share in the total allowable amount of water that can be withdrawn each year. In dry years the cap is tightened and in wet ones, loosened. The shares remain constant, but the amounts vary and all rights owners understand this process. We examine the Colorado Big Thompson later in the volume.

[35] Point sources of pollution are more easily observed and generate more information than nonpoint sources, which is why the former are usually the focus of regulation, as with discharge controls under the Clean Water Act. Nonpoint pollution, however, may be a greater problem. Methods of addressing nonpoint pollution are examined in Kathleen Segerson (1988), "Uncertainty and Incentives for Nonpoint Pollution Control," *Journal of Environmental Economics and Management* 15: 87–98; A.P. Xepapadeas (1992), "Environmental Policy Design and Dynamic Nonpoint-Source Pollution," *Journal of Environmental Economics and Management* 23: 22–39; and Richard D. Horan, James S. Shortle, and David G. Abler (1998), "Ambient Taxes When Polluters have Multiple Choices," *Journal of Environmental Economics and Management* 36: 186–199.

favorable regulation or tax and to avoid penalties for the failure to comply.[36]

DISTRIBUTIONAL EFFECTS

Any regulation or tax will have differential effects on resource users depending on the value they capture from its use. At the margin, rents under open access will be driven to zero, but inframarginal users, who have more knowledge of the resource or who have made physical and human capital investments specific to it, may still be capturing some rents. A tax will reduce their returns even if it increases overall rents, giving them reason to oppose the tax.[37]

Such distributional effects make it difficult to create the political coalitions necessary to implement efficiency-enhancing policies.[38] In the fishery example, those fishers earning rents even with open access might support a tax if it were placed on the marginal entrants.[39] But the politician or bureaucratic official proposing such a tax will undoubtedly face opposition from those entrants who are now forced to move their labor and capital to other sectors. Although a tax could increase the "national dividend" as it was called by Pigou, the increase will accrue to some, while the costs are borne by others.

Similarly, a carbon tax proposed to limit CO_2 emissions may provide general benefits to the global population and generate large

---

[36] Strategic behavior also is possible in the allocation of property rights, such as catch shares or emission allocations. But with subsequent exchange, reallocation of rights is possible. Regulation is rarely so flexible.

[37] Ronald N. Johnson and Gary D. Libecap (1982), "Contracting Problems and Regulation: The Case of the Fishery," *American Economic Review* 72(5): 1005–1022 discusses why certain fishers in an open access fishery would earn rents and why they would resist uniform restrictions. For further analysis of differential rents in an open-access fishery, see Corbett Grainger and Christopher Costello (2012), "Resource Rents, Inframarginal Rents, and the Transition to Property Rights in a Common Pool Resource," working paper, Department of Agricultural and Resource Economics, University of Wisconsin, Madison.

[38] Mancur Olson (1965), *The Logic of Collective Action: Public Goods and the Theory of Groups.* Cambridge, MA: Harvard University Press. Kolstad (2011, 230) and Stavins (2007, 21) discuss opposition to the use of taxes and their relatively limited use in environmental policy.

[39] See Terry L. Anderson, Ragnar Arnason, and Gary D. Libecap (2011), "Efficiency Advantages of Grandfathering in Rights-Based Fisheries Management," *Annual Review of Resource Economics.* www.resource.annualreview.org.

revenues for governments, but it will impose specific costs on local carbon producers, such as electric utilities and consumers. There then is the potential for migration of regulated entities to less-regulated settings, with the corresponding loss of production, employment and economic growth. This phenomenon is called leakage in climate change regulation, and it is a major concern of politicians and their constituents.[40] These issues explain why taxes are not politically popular and are rarely used by politicians or agencies to solve the open-access problem.

If restrictions to an open-access resource increase overall rents, it is conceivable that losers could be compensated from the gains. Even then, there remains the question of who gets access and who should pay whom.[41] Making transfer payments is politically complex because it requires building a consensus on how much to pay, who should be paid, and who should pay. Compensation is critical because the impact of the tax must be weighed against the environmental benefit. Fullerton and Metcalf (1997) argue that the literature on Pigouvian taxes has focused too heavily on the revenue generated and too little on the environmental outcome. Because all taxes impose costs on someone, the tax burden could outweigh the environmental benefit. Thus, the government must use Pigouvian tax revenue to lower other taxes, but the theory by which politicians would credibly commit to such reductions is not spelled out. Fullerton and Metcalf also argue that the effectiveness of any Pigouvian tax depends on whether it supplements or replaces existing regulation. If the tax replaces command-and-control regulation, it might be environmentally beneficial at least in terms of cost effectiveness. If it adds to existing regulation, the environmental and efficiency effects are not obviously

---

[40] The problem of leakage applies to any unilateral regulation in addressing a global problem. See Jonathan Baert Wiener (2007), "Think Globally, Act Globally; The Limits of Local Climate Change Policies." *University of Pennsylvania Law Review*, 155: 101–119; James B. Bushnell, and Erin J. Mansur (2011), "Vertical Targeting and Leakage in Carbon Policy," *American Economic Review, Papers and Proceedings* 10(3): 263–267.

[41] For a discussion of the allocation of emission permits for SO_2 see Paul L. Joskow and Richard Schmalensee (1998), "The Political Economy of Market-Based Environmental Policy: The U.S. Acid Rain Program," *Journal of Law and Economics* 41(April): 37–83.

beneficial. The baseline on which the tax is considered affects its outcome significantly.[42]

Regulation and tax policies are the results of the political process,
where outcomes are determined by interest group politics. In the
political arena, outcomes diverge from the public interest as a result
of lobbying, log rolling, agency delegation and discretion, executive
authority, and litigation.[43] In this political process, benefits are concentrated on special interests while costs are diffused to the general
population, and voters remain rationally ignorant, meaning they typically are well informed about narrow issues of concern to them, and
ill-informed about broader issues outside their coalition.[44]

On the political economy of regulation and taxation or subsidies,
Pigou was not naïve. As he put it, "It is not sufficient to contrast
imperfect adjustments of unfettered private enterprise with the best
adjustment that economists in their studies can imagine. We cannot expect that any public authority will attain, or will even whole-
heartedly seek, that ideal."[45] In a sense, Pigou presages the public
choice revolution by recognizing the importance of the "quality" of the

---

[42] Don Fullerton and Gilbert E. Metcalf (1997), "Environmental Taxes and the Double-
Dividend Hypothesis: Did You Really Expect Something for Nothing?" Cambridge,
MA: *NBER Working Paper* w6199.

[43] Transactions costs and coalition formation and stability are discussed in Ronald N.
Johnson and Gary D. Libecap (2003), "Transaction Costs and Coalition Stability
under Majority Rule," *Economic Inquiry* 41(2): 193–207, with references to key
literatures.

[44] See Gordon Tullock (2008), "Public Choice," in Steven N. Durlauf and Lawrence E.
Blume, eds., *The New Palgrave Dictionary of Economics*, 2nd Edition, New York:
Palgrave Macmillan <http://www.dictionaryofeconomics.com/article?id=pde2008_
P000240> doi:10.1057/9780230226203.1361.
The effects of coalition formation, information distortion, and lobbying as shown
in the development of U.S. ethanol policies are addressed in Ronald N. Johnson
and Gary D. Libecap (2001), "Information Distortion and Competitive Remedies
in Government Transfer Policies: The Case of Ethanol," *Economics of Governance*
2(2): 101–134.

[45] A.C. Pigou (1912), *Wealth and Welfare*, London: Macmillan, 247–248. For a thorough
discussion regarding Pigou's understanding of political action, see Steven G. Medema
(2009), *The Hesitant Hand: Taming Self-Interest in the History of Economic Ideas*.
Princeton, NJ: Princeton University Press, Chapter 3.

governmental body in implementing policy and saying that the political solution depends on

> the intellectual competence of the persons who constitute it, the efficacy of the organisation through which their decisions are executed, their personal integrity in the face of bribery and blackmail, their freedom from domination by the privileged class, [and] their ability to resist the pressure of powerful interests or of uninstructed opinion.[46]

Optimal regulation and taxation will always be conditioned by political pressures because "[e]very public official is a potential opportunity for some form of self-interest arrayed against the common interest."[47] Since Pigou's writing, public choice theorists have expanded our understanding of the complications of political action to address the losses of open access.[48] As we have noted, general voters and taxpayers are rationally ignorant, meaning that they are not well informed on most issues because the costs of regulation are diffuse and the benefits concentrated. On the other hand, when the costs are concentrated, as with entry regulations, those bearing the costs will be "rationally informed." And to the extent that regulations, taxes, or subsidies accrue benefits to special interest groups, they will form coalitions to receive those benefits. Not surprisingly, this can lead to agency capture and rent-seeking.[49] Further, agency officials who implement the regulatory, taxation, or subsidy policies have their own bureaucratic agendas and are often linked closely to the industry or a particular constituency that may advance their agency's interests, rather than the interests of the resource to be protected.[50] Indeed, Stavins (2007, 30–31) argues that

---

[46] Pigou (1932, 125).
[47] Pigou (1912, 248).
[48] Buchanan and Tullock (1962).
[49] George Stigler (1971), "The Theory of Economic Regulation," *Bell Journal of Economics and Management Science* 2: 3–21; J.J. Laffont and J. Tirole (1991), "The Politics of Government Decision Making. A Theory of Regulatory Capture," *Quarterly Journal of Economics* 106(4): 1089–1127; Peltzman (1976), "Toward a More General Theory of Regulation," *Journal of Law and Economics* 19(2): 211–240; Sam Peltzman (1998), *Political Participation and Government Regulation*, Chicago: University of Chicago Press; Anne O. Krueger (1974), "The Political Economy of the Rent-Seeking Society," *American Economic Review* 64(3): 291–303; Gordon Tullock (1967), "The Welfare Costs of Tariffs, Monopolies, and Theft," *Western Economic Journal* 5(3): 224–232.
[50] Ronald N. Johnson and Gary D. Libecap (1994), *The Federal Civil Service and the Problem of Bureaucracy: The Economics and Politics of Institutional Change*, Chicago: University of Chicago Press and NBER, 96–125.

the reason why command-and-control instruments have dominated, despite their costs, is that the main parties involved – certain regulated firms, environmental advocacy groups, organized labor, politicians, and bureaucratic officials – have favored it.[51]

When there are numerous constituencies, politicians must balance conflicting interests in a manner described by Peltzman (1976) and Becker (1983) so as to maximize political support for taking action.[52] As a consequence, politicians select regulatory or tax policies that reduce overall political opposition and raise expected net gains for key constituents. All of this suggests that policies to reduce the losses of open access and free ridership will be much less straight forward than the process illustrated in Figure 2.2 suggests.[53] Moreover, the political economy factors indicate that there is no clear-cut choice between government and private provision of public goods. Markets are attractive because of their ability to enlist private incentives at lower cost of improving environmental quality.

THE REALITY OF REGULATION

Snowmobiles

The challenges inherent in environmental regulation are illustrated even by a case where the resource is owned by the government. This example involves the use of snowmobiles in Yellowstone National Park. Although the science regarding the effect of snow mobiles on

---

[51] Robert N. Stavins (2007, 30–32). The support by various parties for different environmental policies is also discussed in Nathaniel O. Keohane, Richard L. Revesz, and Robert N. Stavins (1998), "The Choice of Regulatory Instruments in Environmental Policy," *Harvard Environmental Law Review* 22: 313–345.

[52] Sam Peltzman (1976); Gary S. Becker (1983), "A Theory of Competition among Pressure Groups for Political Influence," *Quarterly Journal of Economics* 98(3): 371–400.

[53] Frances R. Homans and James E. Wilen (1997), "A Model of Regulated Open Access Resource Use," *Journal of Environmental Economics and Management* 32: 1–27, model regulation endogenously argues that in the case of the fishery, regulation can actually lead to greater rent dissipation than open access because any regulatory-induced rents are also open-access resources, subject to further competition. In a pure open-access setting, these rents would not have emerged, but are the results of restrictions on entry and limits on harvest that lead to stock improvements and additional rents.

the park's resources is not settled, the conflict has been between snow mobile users who want to use Yellowstone as a winter playground and environmentalists who are concerned that the machines pollute the air and disrupt wildlife. Because Yellowstone is a government resource, the dispute could only be solved through political lobbying and litigation. Environmental groups were more effective and convinced policy makers to limit the number of snowmobiles allowed to enter the park each day. But who would these people be? Would entry be granted on a first-come, first-served basis? Would it be by price? Would it be by permit or license? If so, to whom should the permits or licenses be granted? People traveling from afar might be willing to pay more than the local population, but this would mean the latter would lose. Firms on the border of the park renting snowmobiles would have no guarantee that their machines would be the ones granted entry if allocation were on a first-come, first-served basis. The debate, unfortunately, continues to rage, illustrating all three of the problems – information costs, distributional effects, and special interest lobbying – associated with government regulation.[54]

Additional examples illustrate the complexities and costs involved in government regulation. In light of these factors, it will not always be the case that regulation is the efficient default for providing environmental benefits. Property rights and markets can be a more effective alternative in many settings.

Fisheries

As noted in the introduction, wild ocean fisheries are a classic open-access resource. The implications of this have been understood for a long time both by fishers and by pioneering scholars, including Scott Gordon, Anthony Scott, and Vernon Smith.[55] There are some successes in constraining fishing effort and rebuilding stocks, but these are because of a more rights-based management, rather than uniform

---

[54] For a discussion of the ongoing snowmobile controversy, see http://www.national parkstraveler.com/2009/07/interior-secretary-scales-back-snowmobile-use-yellowstone-national-park-calls-more-public-co.

[55] Gordon (1954), Scott (1955) and Vernon L. Smith (1969), "On Models of Commercial Fishing," *The Journal of Political Economy*, 77(2): 181–198.

Figure 2.4. Competing Uses in Yellowstone National Park.
Source: Google Images: Bison and Snowmobiles, http://www.homeaway.com/
vacation-rental/p130280.

regulations in the Pigouvian tradition.[56] Nevertheless, exploitation
rates continue to rise in many fisheries and stocks continue to decline.[57]
Hannesson (2004), Arnason (2002), and Shotton (2000) outline a common pattern in fisheries of open-access losses and delayed unsuccessful
regulation.[58]

---

[56] See Donald R. Leal (2005), "Fencing the Fishery: A Primer on Rights Based Fishing,"
in Donald R. Leal, Ed., *Evolving Property Rights in Marine Fisheries*, Lanham, MD:
Rowman and Littlefield; Rögnvaldur Hannesson (2004), *The Privatization of the
Oceans*, Cambridge, MIT Press; Nicolas L. Gutierrez, Ray Hilborn, and Omar Defeo
(2011), "Leadership, Social Capital and Incentives Promote Successful Fisheries,"
Nature 470: 386–389; and Costello, Gaines, and Lynham (2008).

[57] Ransom A. Myers and Boris Worm (2003), "Rapid Worldwide Depletion of Predatory Fish Communities," *Nature* 423: 280–283; Jennifer A. Devine, Krista D. Baker,
and Richard L. Haedrich (2006), "Fisheries: Deep-Sea Fishes Qualify as Endangered," *Nature* 439, 29; Boris Worm, et al. (2009), "Rebuilding Global Fisheries,"
Science 325, 578–585.

[58] Hannesson (2004, 56). See also Ragnar Arnason (2002), "A Review of Interna-
tional Experiences with ITQ," *Annex to Future Options for UK Fishing Management,
Report to the Department for the Environment, Food and Rural Affairs, CEMARE*,
University of Portsmouth, UK and Ross Shotton, 2000, "Current Property Rights
Systems in Fisheries Management," in Ross Shotton, ed. *Use of Property Rights
in Fisheries Management, Proceedings of the FishRights99 Conference*, Fremantle
Western Australia, Rome: FAO, Fisheries Technical Paper 404/1, 45–50.

A positive start to restricting access to fisheries was the extension of territorial limits to 200 miles. Given that many stocks migrate beyond these exclusive economic zones, or EEZs, there was nothing biologically or environmentally significant about the 200-mile distance in the 1970s. Nonetheless, EEZs allowed coastal governments to gain some control over access to fisheries. Among these were the British Columbia salmon fishery, the North East Atlantic, Icelandic, and North Sea Herring fisheries, and the Norwegian cod fishery.[59] Initial controls were in the form of uniform restrictions on fishing seasons, vessel sizes, and equipment types.[60] Standardized rules minimized information requirements and avoided the distributional effects of restrictions that would differentially affect certain fishers. With non-citizens excluded or given only narrow access privileges, there were some short-term gains to the countries that implemented these regulations.

In general, however, uniform regulations under the EEZs have not been very successful in reducing harvest rates and increasing stocks because they do not and cannot control every margin along which fishers can adjust. With limits on non-citizen fishing, national fleets expanded to fill the void, but with new fishing pressure, stocks declined. Growing concerns led to tighter season constraints, vessel licensing, and new equipment controls, such as minimum net sizes to release adolescent fish.[61]

The experience of the British Columbia halibut fishery is telling. When regulation began in 1980, total capacity was set at 435 vessels, and new vessels rapidly entered to meet the target, with the number rising by 31 percent in nine years. Increased fishing pressure, however, caused stocks to fall, inducing regulators to gradually reduce the season from 65 days to 6 days by 1990. The shortened season led to further private investment in larger and more powerful vessels and a competitive fishing derby to harvest as many fish as possible in the limited time available. Harvests had to be processed and frozen, and more valuable fresh halibut were not available for market after the season

---

[59] Hannesson (2004, 69–71, 103, 116–117).
[60] Hannesson (2004, 38, 107, 116).
[61] Hannesson (2004, 61–62).

closed.[62] Similar problems with uniform regulation occurred in other fisheries. For example, in the 1970s, the Alaska halibut and sablefish season was over 100 days annually, but by 1995 it had dropped to 2 or 3 days.[63] The Canadian sablefish season shrank from 245 days in 1981 to 14 days in 1989; the fishery was closed in 1995 and reopened with tighter restrictions in 1996.[64] There can only be one general conclusion from such fishery regulations: They have not been successful in reducing catch, increasing stocks, raising harvest values, or lowering costs.

Air Quality

The atmosphere is another example of an open-access resource. Emissions arise from manufacturing plants, utilities, vehicle exhaust, and a myriad of other sources that are part of a modern economy. At the same time, as incomes rise, citizens want cleaner air for health or aesthetic reasons. Hence, use of the air as a waste-disposal medium conflicts with demands for clean air. With no well-defined and enforced property rights to the atmosphere, because it is fugitive and virtually impossible to bound at any reasonable cost, there is a potential for emissions to be greater than optimal. So long as releases are limited and the airborne stock is small relative to the assimilative capacity of the atmosphere, there is little adverse impact. As emissions and incomes grow, however, the health and amenity effects of open access to the atmosphere become more serious. If the emitted particles are relatively large so that they fall out of the atmosphere quickly or if emissions interact with local sunlight and geographical factors, as with urban smog, air pollution has localized effects and can be better dealt with at the local level. On the other hand, in cases in which emissions travel larger distances, as with SO_2, or if they mix with the upper

---

[62] R.Q. Grafton, D. Squires, and K.J. Fox (2001), "Private Property and Economic Efficiency: A Study of a Common-Pool Resource, *Journal of Law and Economics*, 43(2): 679–713, 685. See Table I for vessel numbers and fishing seasons. See also K.E. Casey, C.M. Dewees, B.R. Turris, J.E. Wilen (1995), "The Effects of Individual Vessel Quotas in the British Columbia Halibut Fishery," *Marine Resource Economics* 10: 211–30.

[63] Hannesson (2004, 141).

[64] Hannesson (2004, 107).

atmosphere, as with chlorofluorocarbons (CFCs) and CO_2, the effects are more broadly cast and require collective action over a larger geographic area. In most of these cases, however, command-and-control emissions regulation has been slow in adoption and costly because of reliance upon uniform technology and performance standards that do not allow for flexible responses or the ability to have most pollution abatement taken on by those units that can do so at least cost.

Local Air Quality Regulation – California Smog
Consider the problem of urban smog in southern California.[65] Scientific research as early as 1950 revealed that there was a photochemical reaction that converted pollutants from refineries and motor vehicles into smog. In the 1960s the state eventually began issuing air quality alerts. Despite the persistence of smog in the Los Angeles Basin, however, it took approximately thirty-five years before regulations were enacted to directly attack the major source of the problem – auto exhaust.[66] Even when the California Pure Air Act of 1968 authorized air pollution control districts, the primary regulatory response was on technological adjustments to reduce emissions as a condition for licensing new and some used vehicles and to establish uniform emissions standards for stationary sources.[67] Most mobile pollution sources, however, remained relatively unregulated.

Eventually, the Federal Government became involved with passage of the Clean Air Act of 1963. This was followed by the Motor Vehicle Control Act of 1965 and the Air Quality Act of 1967, which required states to set air quality standards consistent with the Clean Air Act. California complied by passing the Pure Air Act of 1968, setting higher emissions standards and creating the Air Resources Board with regulatory jurisdiction over mobile and stationary sources.[68] The Federal Clean Air Act Amendments of 1970 established uniform air quality standards across the country and identified non-attainment areas where more restrictive controls were to be implemented.[69] Although

[65] See Jame E. Krier and Edmund Ursin (1977). *Pollution and Policy: A Case Essay on California and Federal Experience with Motor Vehicle Air Pollution, 1940–1975.* Berkeley: University of California Press.
[66] Krier and Ursin (1977, 6).
[67] Krier and Ursin (1977, 8, 277–279).
[68] Krier and Ursin (1977, 9–10).
[69] Krier and Ursin (1977, 2–3).

pollution levels have been reduced generally, the costs of doing so have been high.[70]

Regional Air Quality Regulation – Acid Rain
One of the best documented examples of the effect of mixing politics and regulation are found in The Clean Air Act Amendments of 1977. Ackerman and Hassler (1981) capture the result in the title of their book, *Clean Coal/Dirty Air: or How the Clean Air Act Became a Multibillion-Dollar Bail-Out for High-Sulfur Coal Producers.*[71] They document that regulations under those amendments did little to reduce sulfur emissions, but purposely encouraged continued use of dirtier eastern coal over the alternative of cleaner, low-sulfur western coal. Eastern coal producers and mining unions feared competition from less-polluting sources. Hence, they formed an alliance with environmental groups to lobby Congress, the White House, and the EPA to enact legislation requiring flue gas scrubbers for all new plants, rather than having them meet specific emission standards, regardless of the means. This reduced the incentive to buy and burn western coal with higher transportation costs to eastern power plants. Indeed, using low-sulfur coal to reduce emissions, rather than adopting the new technology, was prohibited!

Meanwhile, existing power plants were exempted from installing scrubbing technology, which could cost upwards of $10 million for each plant and require large numbers of skilled engineers to operate them. This dramatically raised compliance costs for new sources and potentially increased SO_2 emissions if the new technology failed to work correctly. Moreover, the EPA could not monitor all sources. Not surprisingly, few newer clean plants were built and older dirty plants were kept on line longer than they might otherwise have been. Hence, air quality improved little because dirtier eastern coal was burned.

Important aspects of the clean air objective were lost in political maneuvering. Ackerman and Hassler argue that new executive agencies, such as the EPA, are much more vulnerable to political lobbying

---

[70] Krier and Ursin (1977, 258, 296–307).
[71] Bruce Ackerman and William T. Hassler (1981), *Clean Coal/Dirty Air: or How the Clean Air Act Became a Multibillion-Dollar Bail-Out for High-Sulfur Coal Producers*, New Haven: Yale University Press. See the excellent review of this book by Robert T. Crandall (1981) in the *Bell Journal of Economics* 12(2): 677–682.

than are the older New Deal agencies, which were more protected from such pressures. Subsequent dissatisfaction with the costs of these regulations led to positive changes in federal air quality regulation, but costs of controlling pollution continue to climb. On the positive side, some emission trading programs were implemented including "bubbles," which allowed exchanges of emission permits among different sources in a single plant, netting which allowed plant expansion if overall emissions did not increase, banking which allowed firms to carry forward unused emission credits, and offsets which allowed new plants to purchase credits for reduced emissions from existing plants.[72] Nonetheless, by 1990, U.S. pollution control costs had reached $125 billion annually, nearly a 300 percent increase in real terms from 1972 levels.[73] Because traditional regulation gave advantages to old plants and technology, there were few incentives to develop new technologies to reduce emissions at lower cost. Newer units were forced to adopt the technology specified by the regulator, rather than to develop and use cost-effective techniques for reducing emissions.[74] This outcome should come as no surprise. Pigou warned that "[e]very public official is a potential opportunity for some form of self-interest arrayed against the common interest" played out under the Clean Air Act.[75]

ENDANGERED SPECIES

Open access to wildlife also can lead to over-exploitation and ultimately to extinction, as was nearly the case with North American bison and was the case with the passenger pigeon. This is especially a problem for wildlife species that migrate over territories larger than the

---

[72] These limited trades are estimated to have resulted in savings of $1–$12 billion in pollution control costs (Dewees, 1998, 600).

[73] Stavins (2007, 19–47, 34).

[74] Jody Freeman and Charles D. Kolstad, 2007, "Prescriptive Environmental Regulations versus Market-Based Incentives," in Jody Freeman and Charles D. Kolstad, eds., *Moving to Markets in Environmental Regulation: Lessons from Twenty Years of Experience*, New York: Oxford University Press, 3–16, 5. See also Peter B. Pashigian (1985), "Environmental Regulation: Whose Self-Interests are Being Protected?" *Economic Inquiry* 23(4): 551–584.

[75] Pigou (1912, 248). For an empirical analysis of the Clean Air Act's effect on air quality, see Indur M. Goklany (1999), *Clearing the Air: The Real Story of the War on Air Pollution*. Washington D.C.: The Cato Institute.

size of typical land holdings and have relatively low market values.[76] As we will discuss in subsequent chapters, a property rights solution is not out of the question with some wildlife species, but nonetheless, regulation under the Endangered Species Act (ESA) has been the norm.[77]

There was considerable lobbying among interest groups leading to the adoption of the law in 1973, and since then more lobbying and litigation has taken place over the listing or delisting of species. Indeed, one of the most contentious cases has revolved around the 2009 delisting of the grey wolf from the endangered species list. The key issues of contention are disagreements over the science – is the species still vulnerable? – and the uneven distribution of the costs imposed by the law on landowners.

Under section 9 of the ESA, individuals are not allowed to "take" listed endangered species, meaning "to harass, harm, pursue, hunt, shoot, wound, kill, trap, capture, or collect, or to attempt to engage in any such conduct." This section of the act has been interpreted by the courts to include modifying habitat in a way that could reduce the potential survival of a listed species. Even if such habitat protection reduces property values, there are limited opportunities for compensation under the legislation. Thus, ESA listing can create some perverse incentives.[78]

Consider the example of the red-cockaded woodpecker in the southeastern U.S. Because of a possible uncompensated loss in land value because of woodpecker habitat protection, landowners concerned that their land might harbor the bird can reduce the likelihood

---

[76] Dean Lueck (1989), "The Economic Nature of Wildlife Law," *Journal of Legal Studies* 18(2): 291–324. See also Dean Lueck (2002), "The Extermination and Conservation of the American Bison," *Journal of Legal Studies* 31(June): S609–S652; M. Scott Taylor (2011), "Buffalo Hunt: International Trade and the Virtual Extinction of the North American Bison," *American Economic Review 101* (December 2011): 3162–3195; Scott Farrow (1995), "Extinction and Market Forces: Two Case Studies" *Ecological Economics* 13: 115–123.

[77] For a discussion, see Amy Whritenour Ando (2003), "Do Interest Groups Compete? An Application to Endangered Species," *Public Choice* 114(1–2): 137–159 and Amy Whritenour Ando (1999), "Waiting to be Protected under the Endangered Species Act: The Political Economy of Regulatory Delay," *Journal of Law and Economics* 42(1): 29–60.

[78] Richard L. Stroup (1995), "The Endangered Species Act: Making Innocent Species the Enemy, *PERC Policy Series*: April.

Table 2.1. *Predicted Probabilities of Harvest by Age of Timber Stand and Density of Red-Cockaded Woodpecker Populations within a Five-, Ten-, and Fifteen-Mile Radius*

Density of RCW Colonies	5-mile Density (RCW-5)	10-mile Density (RCW-10)	15-mile Density (RCW-15)
30-year-old timber stand:			
No RCWs	.2840	.2780	.2777
Low RCW density	.2852	.2802	.2300
High RCW density	.3024	.3275	.3376
50-year-old timber stand:			
No RCWs	.4474	.4409	.4407
Low RCW density	.4488	.4435	.4434
High RCW density	.4686	.4973	.5086
70-year-old timber stand:			
No RCWs	.6204	.6146	.6146
Low RCW density	.6218	.6171	.6172
High RCW density	.6406	.6676	.6779

Note: – Low density: RCW-5 = 1; RCW-10 = 3; RCW-15 = 7. High density: RCW-5 = 15; RCW-10 = 66; RCW-15 = 171. Uses specifications in Table 2 for age of stand, timber value, and timber stand variables.

Source: Dean Lueck and Jeffrey A. Michael (2003), "Preemptive Habitat Destruction under the Endangered Species Act," *Journal of Law and Economics*, 46(1): 27–60, Table 3, page 46.

that species will move in by cutting trees before they are old enough to provide nesting cavities. Lueck and Michel (2003) examine how pervasive such actions are. Controlling for other factors that might affect the age of harvest, such as the price of logs, they estimate the effect on logging of proximity to known colonies of woodpeckers. Their hypothesis is that proximity to known colonies would lead to a greater likelihood of regulation under the ESA and therefore to an increased probability of harvest on private lands if red-cockaded woodpeckers were nesting nearby.[79] Table 2.1 shows that regardless of the age of timber stands, *ceteris paribus*, the predicted probability of harvest increases with greater densities of the woodpecker across five, ten, and fifteen mile radiuses from the timber stand. For example, the probability of harvest for fifty-year-old timber stands

---

[79] Dean Lueck and Jeffrey A. Michael (2003), "Preemptive Habitat Destruction under the Endangered Species Act," *Journal of Law and Economics*, 46(1): 27–60.

with no woodpecker colonies within fifteen miles of a private timber stand is about 44 percent. The probability of harvest for the forest with a low-density woodpecker population within fifteen miles is also around 44 percent, but with a high-density, it jumps to over 50 percent. Lueck and Michel conclude that their "finding validates the concerns of some environmentalists who have noted that red-cockaded woodpecker populations have been declining on private land during the 28 years the red-cockaded woodpecker has been regulated by the ESA."[80]

As with most command-and-control regulation, it is one thing to set a limit on behavior and another to enforce it in a way that achieves the desired environmental result. Where habitat is more difficult to destroy, there is less information about the location of an endangered species, or when landowners are prepared to absorb the costs involved, preemptive destruction may be less likely. Nevertheless, this example reveals the perverse outcomes of regulation that fails to incorporate the incentives of those most critical in achieving an environmental or natural resource outcome. Despite many efforts at reform, the ESA has not been substantially modified since its enactment because of intense lobby pressure by environmental and wildlife groups concerned about the added costs of compensation. It seems likely, however, that forcing particular private parties to involuntarily pay for the provision of broad public goods may involve high costs of its own in terms of lost habitat or greater enforcement costs for protecting habitat.

CONCLUSION

Economic analysis of open-access resources provides a simple and clear way of understanding the costs of overuse of scarce natural resources and underproduction of valuable environmental amenities. If private costs are less than social costs, the former occurs, and if private benefits are lower than social benefits, the latter occurs. In either case, social welfare is lower than it could be if access were limited.

Getting from here to there, however, is easier said than done. Economist A. C. Pigou was a leader in promoting the potential for

---

[80] Lueck and Michael (2003, 52).

regulating entry into the commons as a way of achieving optimal use. He also taught us to think about the potential for taxing resource use as a way of raising private costs toward social costs or subsidizing amenity production as a way of raising private benefits toward social benefits.

Even Pigou, however, was not necessarily sanguine about the prospects for regulation, taxation, or subsidization to maximize social welfare, given the pressures of political economy. Regulating access or changing private returns both require that policy makers have knowledge of the optimal level of resource use and have the political support to implement the appropriate policy. The former requires both a scientific understanding of resource stocks and flows as well as information about the value of the resource to the people competing for its use. The latter requires a political constituency, which will depend on a myriad of factors discussed in detail in Chapter 5. Suffice it to say here that, although limiting access can expand the size of the entire pie, who gets the pieces is important in politics. Those who lose access will bear some of the cost and are unlikely to be compensated from the gains. Those who retain or get access may capture some the gains, but this will depend on how the access rights are assigned. If they are auctioned off, the resource rents will go to the government.[81] Alternatively, if rents are given away, political rent-seeking may dissipate some or all of the rents created by limiting access.[82] In summary, the potential gains from regulation, taxation, or subsidization must be compared to potential gains from alternative mechanisms for limiting open access.

---

[81] Not only will an auction distribute the rents to the government, it has the potential for reducing dynamic efficiency. See Anderson, Arnason, and Libecap (2011).

[82] Terry L. Anderson and Peter J. Hill (1983), "Privatizing the Commons: An Improvement?" *Southern Economic Journal* 50(2): 438–450.

3

Property Rights for the Common Pool

Having considered the prospects and pitfalls of government provision of environmental goods and services in Chapter 2, we now turn to the same for markets. In this chapter we carefully examine the arguments of Ronald Coase as they relate to property rights and bargaining costs in the context of environmental markets.[1] Coase is noted for building his analysis on the assumption of zero transaction costs and for concluding that under that condition, resources will be efficiently allocated. We recognize the usefulness of this approach for understanding the relationship between property rights and social costs. Our emphasis in this chapter, however, is on the potential for markets to lower transaction costs relative to those encountered in governmental regulation and to thereby provide environmental goods and services more efficiently.

To be sure, transaction costs might impede market solutions when there are ill-defined and ill-enforced property rights that cannot be easily changed, large numbers of bargaining parties, free riders, limited or asymmetric information about the environmental problem, or non-competitive markets.[2] We do not discount the importance of

---

[1] Ronald Coase (1960), "The Problem of Social Cost," *Journal of Law and Economics* 3: 1–44. Unusual for the depth of coverage of Coase is Charles D. Kolstad (2011), *Environmental Economics*, 2nd Edition, New York: Oxford University Press, 262–274.

[2] For instance, Nathaniel O. Keohane and Sheila M. Olmstead (2007), *Markets and the Environment*, Washington D.C.: Island Press, 65–83, 127–128 emphasize that these transaction costs limit the options for a rights-based or Coasian bargaining solution, except in limited cases. Similarly see Jean-Marie Baland and Jean-Philippe Platteau (1996), *Halting Degradation of Natural Resources: Is there a Role for Rural Communities?* New York: Oxford University Press, 52–56.

market transaction costs, but rather compare them with the transaction costs inherent in government regulation.[3] One advantage of markets, even in the presence of such costs, is that they can be more flexible than government regulations in the face of changing resource values and technology. It is in the interest of market participants to respond effectively and quickly, particularly as the markets are more competitive. Government officials are not direct residual claimants in these situations and have more constituents and political interests to consider in determining how to react to new conditions. This explains why, for example, many government policies and agencies remain long after the conditions that led to their creation have disappeared.

To improve resource allocation, property rights must be well-defined and enforced, whether common or individual. If property rights are well defined and enforced and can be exchanged at low cost, markets provide a solution to what Coase called "The Problem of Social Cost."[4] Market transactions generate information through prices that does not occur as a result of regulation and provide an incentive for private resource owners to respond to such changes. Rather than positioning individuals and firms against the state, as is often the case with enforcing regulations, imposing taxes, or directly controlling resource use, property rights make the agents themselves part of the solution. Moreover, regulated parties typically do not have clear decision-making authority in responding to new environmental

---

[3] As we have done in Chapter 2, we combine most government interventions – regulation, tax, subsidies, and related technology and performance standards together as Coase did in describing them as the "Pigouvian Tradition." See Coase (1960, 39).

[4] The literature on the cost of government intervention is far smaller than the literature on government policy options and refinements of them. A discussion of the transaction costs of government intervention and their direct link to bargaining costs for private solutions to open access is found in Gary D. Libecap and Steven N. Wiggins (1985), "The Influence of Private Contractual Failure on Regulation: The Case of Oil Field Unitization," *The Journal of Political Economy*, 93(4): 690–714. Rögnvaldur Hannesson (2004), *The Privatization of the Oceans*, Cambridge, MA: MIT Press, 173 discusses the role of constituent group politics in molding regulation in their behalf and blocking regulatory reform. Frances R. Homans and James E. Wilen (1997), " A Model of Regulated Open Access Resource Use," *Journal of Environmental Economics and Management* 32: 1–27, make regulation endogenous and show how rent dissipation can be higher under regulated open access than pure open access. This is another form of cost not generally considered.

demands, but rather have to go through the administrative process, where many constituents have a role in the outcome.[5]

This chapter focuses on the costs and benefits of creating property rights and on the importance of exchange for making the opportunity costs of competing resource uses (including those for the environment) transparent. It explores when and how environmental market solutions can be more effective than government regulation; examines governmentally-imposed transaction costs that might stand in the way of market solutions; and identifies how transaction costs might be lowered to increase the effectiveness of environmental markets.

When environmental problems are seen through a property rights lens, it becomes clear that such problems arise from incomplete property rights or high exchange costs or both. Therefore environmental problems arise from *missing markets* rather than from *market failure*. Regardless of the resource in question – water, fish, air, or land – property rights determine whether and by whom costs and benefits are considered in resource-allocation decisions. When property rights are not fully defined, some costs or benefits will not be accounted for, leading to overuse (costs exceed benefits) or under-provision (benefits exceed costs).

THE PROPERTY RIGHTS FRAMEWORK

If property rights are not fully described, enforced, and transferable, individuals will not consider the full opportunity cost of resource use. They will consider only their private costs and benefits of using a resource. If the resource is open to use by anyone, the tragedy of the commons dissipates the resource's value.[6] Property rights – informal

---

[5] We recognize that not all environmental goods, such as amenities, can be easily traded in markets and address some solutions throughout the volume. At the same time, governments also will have little information about the optimal amount of an environmental good to provide or mandate.

[6] Hardin has been criticized for calling for coercive intervention and for the imposition of private property rights from the top down and for neglecting the potential for local cooperative solutions. For example, see Thomas Dietz, Elinor Ostrom and Paul Stern (2003), "The Struggle to Govern the Commons," *Science* 302(5652): 1907–1912 and David Feeney, Fikret Berkes, Bonnie J. McCay, and James M. Acheson (1990), "The Tragedy of the Commons: Twenty-Two Years Later," *Human Ecology* 18(1): 1–19. Their key point is that local, informal property rules and norms can be successful in

or formal – mitigate this loss in a number of ways. They assign the costs and benefits of decisions, make the opportunity cost of alternative uses transparent, constrain competition over the resource, and, importantly, allow for exchange, both to reallocate the resource within and across time. Property rights also identify the parties with the greatest interest in modifying the institutional structure in response to dynamic external changes.

Traditional welfare economics compares benefits and costs of resource use and concludes that markets fail to maximize the net of the two if private costs (benefits) are less than social costs (benefits).[7] Therefore the conventional conclusion is that market failure as a result of positive transaction costs is pervasive. Government regulation, taxes, subsides, provision of environmental goods, or some combination of all these instruments is a necessary correction. As we have stressed, there are also transaction costs with government intervention so that it is not obvious a priori whether the market or the political process is more likely to improve resource allocation.[8] More critically, the conventional approach diverts attention from the questions of why property rights do not exist and whether government instruments would still be preferable if rights could be established.[9] The attention

avoiding the "tragedy" and that there is a large body of empirical evidence in support of this notion. Our arguments hold regardless of whether the property rights structure is informal or formal, group or private. Undoubtedly, scaling up from local common-pool resource problems to broader cases requires different institutional forms than purely informal local arrangements.

[7] See Arthur Cecil Pigou (1932), *The Economics of Welfare*, 4th Edition, London: Macmillan; William J. Baumol (1972), "On Taxation and the Control of Externalities," *American Economic Review* 62(3): 307–322; and F.M. Bator (1958), "The Anatomy of Market Failure," *Quarterly Journal of Economics* 72: 351–379.

[8] For a more modern description of Pigouvian taxes in Charles D. Kolstad (2011) *Environmental Economics, 2nd Edition*, New York: Oxford University Press, 243–47. Ronald N. Johnson and Gary D. Libecap (2001), "Information Distortion and Competitive Remedies in Government Transfer Policies: The Case of Ethanol," *Economics of Governance* 2(2): 101–134 describe how interest group politics and the interests of politicians helped to push ethanol forward as a biofuel despite its relative disadvantages in providing environmental benefits and energy independence.

[9] A case in point is the article by Paul Krugman (2010), "Green Economics: How We Can Afford to Tackle Climate Change," *New York Times Magazine*, April 22: 32–41, 46, 49, wherein he points to market failure with regard to greenhouse gas emissions and argues for rapid government intervention to address the issue through cap-and-trade legislation and carbon tariffs to promote and enforce international cooperation. There may be merit to these arguments, but there is no discussion of

here is on what institutions can lower the costs of defining and enforcing informal and formal property rights and on how markets based
on property rights can lead to exchange as a means of mitigating the
losses of open access.[10]

We depart from traditional analysis by focusing on what determines
whether property rights exist; when they do not, whether it is worth
better defining, enforcing, and trading them; and how doing so may be
more effective than government regulation. Environmental resources
often lack clear property rights because they are highly mobile, diffuse, and costly to bound or because legal restrictions prevent their
formation. For either reason, the absence of property rights creates
open access and rent dissipation as use by one party imposes costs on
all others.[11]

Determining who is imposing a cost on whom, however, depends on
which party has the rights to use the resource. This allocation is critical
if a negotiated solution is to be forthcoming. As Coase illustrated, if
the laundry owner has a right to dry laundry and can enjoin the factory
from emitting air pollution, the laundry owner imposes a cost on the
factory owner. Reciprocally, if the factory owner has the right to dump
waste into the atmosphere, those actions impose a cost on the laundry
owner. Use of the resource by either party generates social costs, but
determining the direction of causality requires knowing who has what
rights.

If rights can be designated, exchange can proceed between the
parties, provided the costs are low enough. Without assigned rights,

the transaction costs of politics driven by constituent group politics and political and
bureaucratic incentives. These certainly will delay, modify, or otherwise distort the
process, especially for carbon tariffs. Our contention is that as much attention should
be given to political economy issues associated with "government failure," as are
given to "market failure." Recognition of the transaction costs of government action
will lead to examination of a larger range of policies that includes more local and
private market solutions.

[10] We acknowledge that recognition of common property and definition and enforcement of formal property rights involves government intervention, and there will be
politics involved in that process as well. The key difference, however, is that once the
rights are recognized, agents can devise solutions through markets. Robert Stavins
(1995), "Transaction Costs and Tradable Permits," *Journal of Environmental Economics and Management* 29: 133–148 discusses the costs of defining and exchanging
air pollution allowances.

[11] Keohane and Olmstead (2007, 143) refer to the lack of exclusivity as the "crux of
commons problems."

anyone is a potential claimant to the value of the resource, making bargaining impossible.[12] When ownership is defined, the number of claimants is limited and identities are made clear so that market exchange is feasible.

Coase showed (as we will discuss later) that the open-access solution is independent of the rights assignment if, and in some cases this is a big "if," transaction costs are sufficiently low to allow exchange.[13] Seen through this lens, the "polluter pays" principle is not necessarily consistent with actual property rights, efficiency, or the objective of remedying the environmental problem.[14]

COASE AND THE COMMONS

Coase's seminal article on "The Problem of Social Cost" presents four crucial points, on which we elaborate, that help us understand the tragedy of the commons in a property rights context:

- Scarcity attracts competition to capture resource value.
- Competitors impose costs on one another.
- Property rights determine whether and by whom costs are considered in production.
- Clearly-defined property rights encourage bargaining to resolve the problem of competing uses.

---

[12] As we noted in the previous chapter, this is the central argument made by Steven N.S. Cheung (1970), "The Structure of a Contract and the Theory of a Non-Exclusive Resource," *Journal of Law and Economics* 13(1): 49–70.

[13] Kolstad (2011, 263–266) provides a detailed discussion of the reciprocal nature of the problem and the outcome under different assignments of property rights using a Coase-like parable of a refiner and a car company. He continues, however, with a broader discussion of how high transaction costs may make Coasian bargaining impractical, rather than comparing the costs of lowering those costs with the alternative of more central government action.

[14] Morality or fairness norms in a society may be the basis for assigning property rights and hence, the direction of causality. The Polluter Pays Principle is derived from fairness beliefs, but it may be less costly and faster if the "victims" pay the polluter to halt emissions in some cases where the polluter has high reduction costs. Subsidies funded by taxpayers for less-polluting solar and wind-based energy also violate the notion of the polluter pays, but these are certainly popular with certain constituencies and often have broad political support as well. For a brief discussion of the principle, see http://en.wikipedia.org/wiki/Polluter_pays_principle.

Figure 3.1. Ronald Coase.
Source: ronald-coase1.jpg. http://www.thebigquestions.com/2009/12/29/happy-99th-birthday-ronald-coase/.

Competition for the Common Pool

So long as resources are abundant relative to the demand for them, open access is not an economic problem. For example, cattlemen bringing their cows to the northern Great Plains found an extraordinary abundance of grazing land: "There was room enough for all, and when a cattleman rode up some likely valley or across some well-grassed divide and found cattle thereon, he looked elsewhere for range."[15]

As supplies tightened, however, one party's access reduces the value available to others and disputes followed. In the case of the western range, as more and more cattlemen, sheepherders, and homesteaders arrived on the Great Plains in the late nineteenth and early twentieth centuries, their farming and ranching activities conflicted with one another. Cattle wandered onto crops, sheep competed with cattle for grass, and farmers competed with one another for irrigation water. Without clear property rights, the tragedy of the commons

---

[15] Ernest Staples Osgood (1929), *The Day of the Cattleman*, Minneapolis: University of Minnesota press, 182–183.

Figure 3.2. On the Western Cattle Range.
Source: http://www.old-picture.com/old-west/Cowboy.htm.

played out in range wars, competitive overgrazing, and eventually considerable economic waste through low rangeland productivity.

Government policy, however, prevented the clear assignment of range rights by rejecting the claims of ranchers in favor of homesteaders, whose farms in turn failed when they were found to be too small to survive the droughts that characterized the region. As homesteads were abandoned, the land reverted to open range.[16] By the 1930s, the resulting competition led to overgrazing, erosion, and infestation by non-native, non-palatable plant species:

There is perhaps no darker chapter nor greater tragedy in the history of land occupancy . . . than the story of the western range. . . . Unexpectedly and almost overnight it became the potential source of great wealth from livestock raising.

---

[16] Gary D. Libecap (1981), *Locking Up the Range: Federal Land Controls and Grazing* Cambridge, MA: Ballinger Publishing; Zeynep K. Hansen and Gary D. Libecap (2004), "The Allocation of Property Rights to Land: US Land Policy and Farm Failure in the Northern Great Plains," *Explorations in Economic History* 41: 103–129; and Gary D. Libecap (2007), "The Assignment of Property Rights on the Western Frontier: Lessons for Contemporary Environmental and Resource Policy," *Journal of Economic History* 67(2): 257–291.

And thereon lies the key to the story. . . . the major finding of this report . . . at once the most obvious and obscure is range depletion so nearly universal.[17]

Once competition inflicts enough costs, the parties have an incentive to find ways of limiting entry either by assigning property rights, communal or private, or by lobbying government for regulation of access. The role of benefits and costs in determining the emergence of property rights was a major contribution of Harold Demsetz (1967) regarding their evolution.[18] Because property rights are costly to create, it is only when increasing scarcity raises the benefits of establishment that they are worth creating.[19]

Reciprocal Costs

Coase argued that property rights assign benefits and costs and promote bargaining, but his emphasis on the reciprocal nature of costs, is underappreciated. To see the relevance of reciprocal costs to open-access problems, consider one of Coase's parables, the conflict between the doctor whose practice depends on quiet and the confectioner whose candy production generates noise.[20] If these two activities are

---

[17] U.S.D.A. (1936), *The Western Range*, 74th Congress, 2nd Session, Senate Document 199, 3. See also Terry L. Anderson and Peter J. Hill (2004), *The Not So Wild, Wild West: Property Rights on the Frontier*, Palo Alto: Stanford University Press.

[18] Harold Demsetz (1967), "Toward a Theory of Property Rights," *American Economic Review* 57(2): 347–359. This paper became the foundation for much of the interface between law and economics. See the special issue of *The Journal of Legal Studies* June 2002, 31 (2, Pt. 2) for relevant papers. James M. Buchanan and Wm. Craig Stubblebine (1962), "Externality," *Economica* New Series 29(116): 371–384 provide a discussion of Pareto-relevant externalities; and Lance E. Davis and Douglass C. North (1971), *Institutional Change and American Economic Growth*, New York: Cambridge University Press, Chapters 1–4 describe the emergence of property and other institutions when it is cost effective for them to be adopted. See also, Gary D. Libecap (1989), *Contracting for Property Rights*, New York: Cambridge University Press, 10–28 for a discussion of the bargaining or contracting to define and enforce property rights.

[19] See Terry L. Anderson and P.J. Hill (1983), "Privatizing the Commons: An Improvement?" *Southern Economic Journal* 50(2): 438–450 and Terry L. Anderson and P.J. Hill (1990), "The Race for Property Rights," *The Journal of Law and Economics* 33(1): 177–197 for an examination of how the race for property rights can dissipate rents.

[20] Coase (1960, 9–10).

located adjacent to one another, there will be conflict for use of the airspace as a medium for transmission of sound waves. The question is whether the doctor has a right to produce medical services in a quiet environment or whether the confectioner has a right to produce candy and in the process generate sound and vibration.[21] Coase's point was that costs to one party are a benefit to the other and vice versa.

To return to another of Coase's parables introduced earlier, a factory's smoke conflicts with a laundry's production of clean clothes. If the factory owner has a right to use air for waste disposal and the laundry owner wants to use air for drying laundry, any effort by the laundry owner to force emissions reductions imposes a cost on the factory owner. Alternatively, if the laundry has a right to dry clothes in clean air and soot falls on the laundry, the factory owner is inflicting a cost on the laundry owner. The important point is that costs are reciprocal. Property rights determine who will bear those costs and set up the basis for contractual exchange.

Because costs are reciprocal, the assignment of rights has distributional consequences, which in turn raises the costs of determining who has what property rights. For example, does an irrigator have the right to withdraw water from a stream, thus reducing habitat for fish or do fishers have the right to stream flows for fish, thus reducing the water available for irrigation? If the former, fishers will have to pay irrigators, and if the latter, irrigators will have to pay fishers. Neither party will want to pay the other, and the associated politics of allocation make it more difficult to assign rights that can lead to market solutions.

Coase's focus on reciprocity helps us understand why he does not use the term "externality" in explaining the problem of social cost. In particular, externality implies a direction of causality on the basis of who has the right. If fishers have a right to fish habitat, then irrigators are imposing an externality on fishers by overusing water for irrigation. However, if irrigators have the right to withdraw water from the stream, then fishers are imposing an externality on irrigators by overusing water for fish. To assert an externality presupposes that a property right exists and implies the direction of causality. Coase does

---

[21] Note that we purposefully avoid using the term "noise" for it generally implies that using the air to transmit sound waves is a bad. It is a bad for the doctor, but it is simply a byproduct of production for the confectioner.

not assume the existence of property rights, but rather requires that we ask who has what rights and if they are present, to determine why they are not enforced. For this reason, Coase could be called a causal agnostic, meaning he did not assume a direction of causation.

Seen in this way, presuming property rights by declaring that there is an externality, clouds Coase's central point that the problem of social cost is a property rights and bargaining problem. Without property rights, we know that not all costs will be considered, but we cannot say who is imposing a cost on whom. Furthermore, declaring that person A's use of a resource creates an externality for person B complicates creating environmental markets by assuming that person B has a right to be free of the costs of A's use. If such a right existed, Coase asks why B is not requiring compensation from A for A's imposition of a cost on B. Why is there no market transaction? If the answer is that B does not have such a right, then the question is why B is not paying A to cease creating the cost? In summary, if there is a missing market because property rights are not defined, then there is a possibility for a market solution if they can be established.

Apply this line of reasoning to the contemporary conflict over whether federal land should be used for livestock grazing. Early in the history of the West, anyone could graze the public domain, but as grass became scarce, grazing was limited to those livestock owners with grazing permits.[22] Initially the question was who could graze, rather than whether there should be grazing. Now, however, the competition is between grazers, who want to capture the value of the forage, and environmentalists, who want to capture the value of recreation or other environmental amenities. Assuming that livestock owners have a legitimate right to graze on federal land, there is an environmental market solution to this competition over land. Environmentalists can purchase and retire the permits held by livestock owners. However, if the demanders of environmental amenities do not accept that livestock owners have the right to graze, they may claim that grazing should be eliminated because it is imposing a social cost. These opposing positions beg the question: are grazers inflicting a cost on environmentalists or are environmentalists inflicting a cost on grazers? Claiming that grazing causes externalities suggests that environmentalists have the

---

[22] The history of federal range land use is described in Libecap (1981).

Environmental Markets

right, but the persistence of the conflict itself suggests that the rights are not clear. Again, missing markets result from unclear property rights. Defining the rights opens the door for environmental markets to evolve and less contentious solutions to emerge.[23]

Property Rights Internalize Costs and Benefits

Property rights hold competing users accountable for the opportunity cost of resource use because the owner must consider what others would be willing to pay for the resource.[24] Whether owners actually receive offers depends on the transaction costs of exchange. Whether they accept or reject the offers depends on the relative value of alternative uses.[25] To see how property rights can affect resource use by creating opportunities for exchange, return to the example of the doctor and the confectioner. The question, as viewed through a Coasian lens, is whether the property rights are defined and enforced. If the doctor has a right to quiet, the confectioner will have to pay the doctor for the cost of reduced quiet and thus face the opportunity cost of making noise. On the other hand, if the confectioner has the right to make noise, the doctor will have to pay for quiet and thus face the opportunity costs of stopping the noise.

When transaction costs are low, the optimal mix of candy and medical service production depends on whether property rights are complete, not to whom they are assigned. With property rights, the competing parties will take full account of all the costs and benefits, and the

[23] We recognize that grazing livestock could lead to other problems, such as stream bank destruction. Here we focus on a simple case in which the grazing of livestock on federal lands disrupts their amenity and recreational value. For a discussion of how attacks on the fairness or justness of these rights can lead to overgrazing, see Jeffrey T. LaFrance and Myles J. Watts (1995), "Public Grazing in the West and 'Rangeland Reform '94,'" *American Journal of Agricultural Economics* 77(3): 447–461.

[24] For a discussion of the opportunities for exchange once the costs of defining and enforcing property rights are considered, see Harold Demsetz (1964), "The Exchange and Enforcement of Property Rights," *The Journal of Law and Economics*, 7: 11–26.

[25] Again, refer to Stavins (1995) for a discussion of the transaction costs of defining and exchanging tradable emission permits, and then the issue becomes how to lower those transaction costs. Also, as we will see, government can reduce uncertainty and promote the use of rights-based systems if it recognizes them as formal property rights. Failure to do so potentially undermines their effectiveness.

Table 3.1. *A Coasian Exchange*

Number of Cattle	Net Value of Additional Cows	Net Value of Wheat Consumed by Additional Cows
1	$50	$35
2	$48	$45
3	$45	$55
4	$41	$65

outcome will depend on the relative values of the two enterprises. If not, competition and conflict among the parties will dissipate resource rents. Avoiding these losses creates the motivation to develop property rights.

Consider a simple numerical example shown in Table 3.1, where two parcels of side-by-side land are used for wheat and cattle production and where straying cattle consume the wheat. In deciding how many cattle to place on the land, the rancher compares marginal benefits and costs. If all costs and values are considered, the optimal number of cows is two. Any fewer and the net value of an additional cow is greater than the cost of wheat consumed; any more cattle and the net value is less. Referring back to Chapter 2, we might achieve this outcome by regulating the number of cattle or by placing a tax on cattle equal to the value of wheat consumed. But consider the bargaining alternative.

Begin by assuming that the cost of fencing is prohibitive and that the cattle rancher must pay for any wheat damaged. How many cows would the profit-maximizing rancher have? If the fourth cow adds only $41 in value but does $65 in damage, it makes no sense for the rancher to have the fourth cow, and similarly for the third. Hence, the optimal number of cows is two. Any more cattle and marginal costs exceed marginal value and profits are foregone.

Now suppose that cattle are free to roam wherever they wish. Will this result in too many cattle consuming too much wheat, as in the tragedy of the commons? Additional cattle eat wheat at an increasing cost to the farmer, but if those costs are not born by the rancher, it appears more cows would be added so long as they have positive net value, and wheat would be consumed without regard to the cost of the consumption.[26] To stop straying cattle, the farmer must fence. If the cost of fencing is prohibitive, the farmer will offer up to $65 to have the fourth cow removed from the herd, $55 for the third, and so on. The farmer will be willing to pay the cattleman to reduce his herd so long as the value of wheat saved is greater than the value of cattle foregone. Either way, the same number of cows, two, will be optimal.[27]

Coase observed that forgone offers are opportunity costs internalized by the parties. If the fourth cow is only worth $41, and the rancher refuses an offer of $65, $24 in profit would be lost. Refusing an offer of $55 to remove the third cow would result in another $10 in forgone profit. Therefore the profit-maximizing rancher would accept offers from the farmer to reduce herd size to two, the optimal number when all costs are considered. Of course, whether the farmer will pay the full value of the forgone cost of wheat or something just above the net value of the additional cow will depend on the bargaining abilities of the two parties.[28] Nonetheless, whether the rancher pays the farmer for lost wheat or the farmer pays the rancher for fewer cattle, herd size and wheat output will be the same. The direction of payment, however, will depend on who has what property rights, but production will be optimized either way.

This result requires two important conditions: (1) that the rights are well-defined and enforced and (2) that the costs of bargaining are low enough to allow the parties to reach agreement. Some cases are more complex than others, and this affects the transaction costs of defining property rights and engaging in trade. If the transaction costs are too high, the potential for bargaining to resolve conflicting uses of environmental and natural resources is reduced. As we have seen,

---

[26] Given the trend shown by these numbers, many more than four cattle would be added.

[27] See Robert C. Ellickson (1986), "Of Coase and Cattle: Dispute Resolution Among Neighbors in Shasta County," *Stanford Law Review* 38: 623–687 for a discussion of negotiations among farmers and ranchers over stocking levels when transaction costs are positive.

[28] When a party with a unique resource is negotiating with a single buyer, both have bargaining power, or in economic terms, there is a bilateral monopoly. In such circumstances, negotiation costs can be high enough to preclude a transaction. Bargaining power and outcomes are discussed in Gary D. Libecap (2009), "*Chinatown Revisited*: Owens Valley and Los Angeles – Bargaining Costs and Fairness Perceptions of the First Major Water Rights Exchange," *Journal of Law Economics and Organization*, 25(2): 311–338.

however, the most effective reaction may be to seek ways of lowering the transaction costs of exchange, which may involve government recognition of property rights, the provision of information, allowing for brokers, enforcement of contracts, or all four. This response may result in a lower-cost solution than resorting to government regulation of the number of cattle or of requiring fencing.

Another example – bees and pollination services – illustrates a case of high bargaining costs when rights are not well defined. In California's San Joaquin Valley, bees usually play a positive role in horticulture, especially in almond production. In a simple case, there is a clear record of bargaining and market exchange, sometimes with almond and other orchard owners paying apiarists for pollination services and sometimes with apiarists paying orchard owners for the right to collect pollen and produce honey.[29] Suppose, however, that we introduce complexity with a third party, citrus growers, whose crops can be damaged by pollination from bees. We now no longer have a simple two-party exchange where transaction costs are low.

Bees have a negative value in the case of seedless varieties of tangerines and mandarin oranges. These varieties remain seedless unless they are cross-pollinated, a real possibility if bees get involved.[30] Unfortunately, bees are not discerning and pollinate whatever flowers they happen to land on. When those flowers are for seedless citrus crops, bee pollination can result in fruit with seeds and significantly reduce the value of the crop. To complicate matters, when the seedless citrus growers spray for other pests, the spray kills bees, harming apiarists. In this case, we have three parties, apiarists and almond growers who benefit from having bees and seedless citrus growers who are harmed by them.

Are the apiarists and almond growers imposing a cost on seedless citrus growers who have a right to be free from bee pollination services? Are citrus growers who spray the bees imposing a cost on

---

[29] Steven N S Cheung (1973), "*The Fable of the Bees*: An Economic Investigation," *The Journal of Law and Economics*, 16(1): 11–33. See also Mary K. Muth, Randal R. Rucker, Walter N. Thurman, and Ching-Ta Chuang (2003), "The Fable of the Bees Revisited: Causes and Consequences of the U.S. Honey Program," *The Journal of Law and Economics* 46(2): 479–516.

[30] "Tangerine Growers Tell Beekeepers to Buzz Off," *Los Angeles Times*, January 20, 2009.

apiarists who have a right to release their bees to produce honey and almond growers who want their crops pollinated? The example demonstrates that traditional Pigouvian analysis based on a divergence between social and private costs misses the reciprocal nature of costs as emphasized above. Costs to one party – fewer bees – are a benefit to the other – citrus crops saved. Viewed in the other direction, benefits to one party – more bees – are a cost to the other – less seedless citrus fruit. Which way the costs go depends on who has what rights.

Even if property rights are not formally specified, the parties involved have an incentive to find ways of clarifying the property rights and bargaining for a solution. Depending on the net economic values involved in honey production and pollination services, the parties could negotiate the timing and placement of beehives.[31] Alternatively, they might litigate the conflict in court or seek legislative solutions to clarify property rights.[32]

Tradable Property Rights Resolve Conflicting Uses

Perhaps no other lesson is associated more with Coase than the idea of bargaining to resolve conflicting demands for resources. As Coase stated:

> If factors of production are thought of as rights, it becomes easier to understand that the right to do something which has a harmful effect ... is also a factor of production.... The cost of exercising a right (of using a factor of production) is always the loss which is suffered elsewhere in consequence of the exercise of that right ... the inability to cross land, to park a car, to build a house, to enjoy a view, to have peace and quiet or to breathe clean air.[33]

Viewed in this manner, the environment is no different from other factors of production – labor, factories, software – although the costs

---

[31] See Robert Cooter and Daniel Rubinfeld (1989), "An Economic Analysis of Legal Disputes and their Resolution," *Journal of Legal Studies* 27: 1067–1097.

[32] California Assembly Bill 771, October 8, 2007, directed the state Secretary of Agriculture to find best management practices for both sides in the controversy. If no agreement were reached by June 1, 2008, the Secretary was to adopt regulations no later than February 1, 2009.

[33] Coase (1960, 44). This point is recognized with regard to cap-and-trade systems by A. Denny Ellerman and Barbara K. Buchner (2007), "The European Union Emissions Trading Scheme: Origins, Allocation, and Early Results," *Review of Environmental Economics and Policy*, 1(1): 66–87.

of defining rights could be higher.[34] If property rights are designated, trading will move resources to higher-valued uses.[35] Alternatively, when property rights do not exist or are not transferable, it is very difficult to direct an environmental asset to new uses; conflicts over different applications arise, values are reduced, and incentives for investment and conservation in the asset are lowered. Efficiency and resource conservation are less likely to ensue when property rights and exchange are constrained.

To illustrate the gains from transferability, consider water in the American West, where rights are relatively well established under the long-standing prior appropriation doctrine.[36] Under this doctrine, water rights are created by diverting water, initially for mining and irrigation, and, if stream flows are insufficient to meet all diversion rights, priority is given to those with the earliest claims. Diversion is a requirement for establishing a right because it is a simple way of proving ownership and beneficial use. Hence, prior appropriation requires rights holders to "use it or lose it."

As the value of water left instream for environmental purposes – effluent dilution, fish habitat, recreation, aesthetics – has increased, however, the diversion requirement has been in conflict with these potentially higher-valued uses. To trade water from irrigation to enhancing stream flows required changing water law to expand what constitutes beneficial water use so that diversion was not required. The intricacies of water rights and water markets are discussed in more detail in Chapter 5, but for now consider the potential for such an environmental market. Since 1994, the Oregon Water Trust (OWT), now the Freshwater Trust, has negotiated with irrigators to release water

---

[34] Coase (1960, 15, 19).

[35] Some environmental organizations can be at the forefront of market activities. See those of the Nature Conservancy http://www.nature.org/ourinitiatives/index.htm and the Environmental Defense Fund http://www.edf.org/.

[36] David H. Getches (1997), *Water Law in a Nut Shell*, 3rd Edition, St. Paul: West Publishing, 74–175 for a discussion of prior appropriation water rights, which assign rights to a fixed amount of water on the basis of priority of claim. The problem of instream flows also is discussed by Terry L. Anderson and Ronald N. Johnson (1986), "The Problem of Instream Flow," *Economic Inquiry* 24(4): 535–554. Given the broad regulatory framework for water and its status as a "use" right, western water rights potentially have *less* protection and are more fragile than most other property rights See Joseph L. Sax (1990), "The Constitution, Property Rights and the Future of Water Law," *University of Colorado Law Review* 61: 257–282; 260.

for instream flows through sales or leases of agricultural water to protect spawning habitat for salmon and steelhead.[37] The organization
first had to lobby the Oregon Legislature to revamp water regulations
so that water rights could be leased or sold to state agencies or conservation groups for stream flow maintenance. Previously, any water
left in a stream and not designated for later diversion was subject to
appropriation by another diverter because, according to the law, it was
not in beneficial use.

Once the law was changed to allow water to be left instream without losing the water right, OWT began negotiations with farmers and
ranchers. In 2006 it paid a third-generation ranch family to stop diverting 6.5 million gallons per-day and to let it flow into the middle-fork of
the John Day River.[38] In another transaction, OWT negotiated with
115 ranchers and farmers to provide adequate stream flows for salmon
spawning in eastern Oregon's Wallowa Mountains. For these environmental markets to work, water rights had to be refined and made
transferable. When this became so, environmental demanders could
negotiate with farmers and ranchers to balance competing demands
for water whereby all parties are made better off.[39]

Other cases are more complicated, and potentially-useful market
opportunities have been overlooked as illustrated by conflicts in the
Sacramento River Delta.[40] The delta is a major estuary where waters

---

[37] http://www.thefreshwatertrust.org/.

[38] See Brandon Scarborough and H.L. Lund (2007), *Saving Our Streams: Harnessing
      Water Markets, A Practical Guide.* Bozeman, MT: The Property and Environment
      Research Center, for details of these and other market transactions to transfer water
      from agricultural to environmental uses.

[39] Janet C. Neuman (2004), "The Good, the Bad, and the Ugly: The First Ten Years of
      the Oregon Water Trust," *Nebraska Law Review* 432–484.

[40] This is not the only high-profile conflict over water in central California. Another
      example in which water rights are not defined or are very uncertain involves the
      requirement to increase flows from Friant Dam to rewater portions of the San Joaquin
      made dry by the dam, which became operational in 1944. Doing so would reduce
      water supplies to agricultural and urban areas without sufficient compensation, at
      least according to those parties that would lose water. For a discussion, see Natu-
      ral Resources Defense Council, *et al.* v. Kirk Rodgers, as Regional Director of the
      United States Bureau of Reclamation, *et al.* (2006), United States District Court,
      Eastern District of California. CIV NO. S-88-LKK/GGH and T. Stroshane (2004),
      "San Joaquin River Decision: Ecological Hope, Economic Fear." *Spillway: Califor-
      nia Water, Land and People.* http://www.spillwaynews.net/BackIssues/v3n4/Spilv3n4
      .pdf.

from northern California and from the San Joaquin River to the south come together to form San Francisco Bay. Much of the delta water, however, no longer flows to the bay because it is collected and pumped through the intakes of California State Water Project and Federal Central Valley Project canals for transport to urban and agricultural uses in Central and Southern California. These water diversions reduce water in the delta, and the reductions are blamed for threatening the survival of smelt and other pelagic species, such as Chinook salmon, steelhead, and green sturgeon.

The property rights to much of the Sacramento Delta water have not been defined and many perceived rights are not formally recognized, in large part because the Endangered Species Act (ESA), which mandates the protection of critical habitats, can trump various other water diversions. In 2008 and 2009 the U.S. Fish and Wildlife Service and the National Marine Fisheries Service, the agencies responsible for administering the ESA, increased water flows to the delta by reducing diversions to the south. Later in 2009, additional restrictions on diversions were ordered by a federal court ruling.[41] Agricultural and urban interests unsuccessfully mobilized to counter the injunction, but the restrictions remained in place inflicting economic damage on agricultural operations and employment in the San Joaquin valley and forcing urban areas to seek water from other sources, often at high economic and environmental cost.[42] These restrictions occurred despite the fact that the science is not settled on the underlying factors affecting the delta's fish populations and on whether increased water quantities will significantly reverse their declines.[43]

---

[41] For a discussion of the Delta controversy and options for resolution, see Jay Lund, Ellen Hanak, William Fleenor, Richard Howitt, Jeffrey Mount, and Peter Moyle (2007), *Envisioning Futures for the Sacramento-San Joaquin Delta*, San Francisco: Public Policy Institute of California and Dean Misczynski (2009), *Fixing the Delta: How Will We Pay For It?*, San Francisco: Public Policy Institute of California.

[42] Interestingly, the ability to use water markets in the San Joaquin valley to react to lower water supplies helped to reduce the costs of the water loss between the east and west sides of the valley. See Michael, Richard Howitt, Josué Medellín-Azuara, and Duncan MacEwan (2010) "A Retrospective Estimate of the Economic Impacts of Reduced Water Supplies to the San Joaquin Valley in 2009," Department of Agricultural and Resource Economics, University of California at Davis, September 28.

[43] In an effort to resolve some of the scientific questions about how much water was necessary and species response, the National Research Council issued a report (2011)

In the wrangling over delta water, there has been little discussion of the potential for water markets to help resolve the conflict. A market solution whereby water could be leased or purchased for protecting delta habitat, perhaps using options markets or forward lease contracts, could help resolve the issue in a more straightforward, timely, and predictable manner with much less contention and cost.[44] Such arrangements, for example, are used by the San Diego County Water Authority (SDCWA) and the Palo Verde Irrigation District in Southern California, where district farmers have agreed to fallow land and release water to the SDCWA and other agencies when urban water is in short supply.[45] Farmers and urban water supply agencies can plan for reduced water diversions because they negotiate and pay for any changes. Further, these trades reveal the opportunity costs of alternative water uses and force water rights holders to consider whether it is worth leasing or selling their water.

THE COSTS OF DEFINING, ENFORCING, AND TRADING PROPERTY RIGHTS

To this point we have emphasized the potential for greater reliance on property rights and market exchange to address the problem of social cost. We now turn more explicitly to transaction costs – the costs of defining, enforcing, and trading property rights. These costs are important because if they are too high, an issue we address here

---

A Review of the Use of Science and Adaptive Management in California's Draft Bay Delta Conservation Plan http://www.nap.edu/catalog/13148.html. Both environmental and agricultural interests have disputed the report. With so much at stake, the growing demand for water, and the uncertainties involved in species' response, this report is unlikely to be the final word on the issue. See also N.E. Monsen, J.E. Cloern, and J.R. Burau (2007), "Effects of Flow Diversions on Water and Habitat Quality: Examples from California's Highly Manipulated Sacramento-San Joaquin Delta." *San Francisco Estuary and Watershed Science* 5(3). http://repositories.cdlib.org/jmie/sfews/vol5/iss3/art2 and C.A. Myrick and J.J. Cech (2004), "Temperature Effects on Juvenile Anadromous Salmonids in California's Central Valley: What Don't We Know?" *Reviews in Fish Biology and Fisheries* 14: 113–123.

[44] John C Hull (2006), *Options, Futures and Other Derivatives*, 6th Edition, Upper Saddle River, New Jersey: Prentice Hall.

[45] See Gary D. Libecap (2011), "Institutional Path Dependence in Climate Adaptation: Coman's "Some Unsettled Problems of Irrigation," *American Economic Review* 101(February): 64–80, 75–76.

and in the following chapters, bargaining and trading through markets to resolve conflicts over the use of natural and environmental resources may not be possible. As Ronald Coase put it, "the reason why some activities are not the subject of contracts is exactly the same as the reason why some contracts are commonly unsatisfactory – it would cost too much to put the matter right."[46] This statement is not unlike Pigou saying that the matter cannot be put right "owing to the technical difficulty of enforcing compensation for incidental disservices."[47]

Even for resources for which it is feasible to establish property rights and use markets, environmental markets may be restricted or rejected because of distributional concerns and political and bureaucratic incentives. Markets inherently reduce the role of politicians and bureaucrats in resource allocation and use decisions, and hence, both may oppose or restrict their use.[48] Property rights and markets limit the ability of politicians to reward favored constituents and the ability of bureaucrats to exercise discretion and expertise regarding resource use.[49] Further, a private property rights regime might be rejected if it does not blend with existing common-property arrangements, a setting often encountered in less-developed countries.[50] If property rights and environmental markets are to reduce uncertainty and provide long-term incentives for mitigating the losses caused by open

---

[46] Coase (1960, 39).

[47] Pigou (1932, 185).

[48] See the discussion by Stavins on why command-and-control regulation has dominated in addressing environmental and natural resource problems in Robert N. Stavins (2007), "Market-Based Environmental Policies: What Can We Learn from U.S. Experience (and Related Research)?" in Jody Freeman and Charles D. Kolstad, eds., *Moving to Markets in Environmental Regulation*, New York: Oxford University Press, 30–31.

[49] For a discussion of bureaucratic incentives, see Johnson and Libecap on the "Implications of a Protected Bureaucracy," in Ronald N. Johnson and Gary D. Libecap (1994), *The Federal Civil Service and the Problem of Bureaucracy: The Economics and Politics of Institutional Change*, Chicago: University of Chicago Press and NBER, 154–176.

[50] See Avinash K. Dixit (2004), *Lawlessness and Economics: Alternative Modes of Governance*, Princeton: Princeton University Press, 138–143 who discusses the problems of a predatory state and the security of property rights. Daniel Fitzpatrick (2006), "Evolution and Chaos in Property Rights Systems: The Third World Tragedy of Contested Access," *The Yale Law Journal* 115: 996–1048.

access, they must have protection from takings.[51] Such protections, however, reduce regulatory discretion by raising the costs of policy changes that undermine existing property rights. Politicians, agency officials, and various environmental advocacy groups understandably resist such property rights guarantees.

Requiring payment if property is taken has efficiency advantages. Compensation for takings generates valuable information about the opportunity costs of proposed policies. If the costs of providing public goods fall on property owners, they will have an incentive to resist resource reallocation and may take evasive actions to avoid the regulation. For example, landowners faced with regulation under the Endangered Species Act have an incentive to ensure that their property is not habitat for a target species by altering the property to make it less habitable.[52] On the other hand, if the government must pay for property taken, there will be clear budget tradeoffs. This situation will force public officials to more carefully weigh the costs and benefits of public good provision and result in more efficient resource use.

Considering the resource and political costs of creating formal property rights, we should not expect them to be implemented in all cases where losses result from open access. Here we lay out some of the key factors that determine the transaction costs of defining and trading property rights.[53]

Resource Value

Until Harold Demsetz's 1967 article, "Toward a Theory of Property Rights," economists did not have a clear understanding that property rights (informal or formal) are created when their value exceeds the definition and enforcement costs.[54] More valuable assets warrant this

---

[51] As provided by the takings and due process clauses of the 5th and 14th Amendments to the U.S. Constitution.

[52] Dean Lueck and Jeffrey A. Michael (2003), "Preemptive Habitat Destruction Under the Endangered Species Act," *Journal of Law and Economics*, 46(1): 27–60.

[53] The nature of transaction costs is discussed in Carl Dahlman (1979). "The Problem of Externality." *Journal of Law and Economics*, 22: 141–62 and Oliver E. Williamson (1979), "Transaction Cost Economics: the Governance of Contractual Relations," *The Journal of Law and Economics*, 22(2): 233–261. Measurement costs are discussed in Yoram Barzel (1982), "Measurement Cost and the Organization of Markets," *The Journal of Law and Economic*, 25(1): 27–48.

[54] Demsetz (1967, 350).

institutional investment because they offer greater rents and because competition would dissipate those rents. The process of institutional change is interactive because just as more valuable resources merit more definite property rights, resources with more secure property rights have higher values.[55]

Although Demsetz did not specify the mechanism by which property rights would develop, he used the example of the Montagnes Indians of Labrador and Quebec to illustrate the close connection between the development of private rights in land and the development of the commercial fur trade.[56] Before trading beaver pelts with Europeans, native hunting was primarily for food and for a few furs for domestic use. With little pressure on the beaver resource, rents were low, making it uneconomical to create property rights to hunting territories. The fur trade, however, increased the value of furs and the effort put into hunting and trapping. Hunters began to impose costs on one another as they competed to capture beaver in the commons. This brought pressure to develop private hunting territories that granted exclusive rights to families. Within these territories animal resources were conserved, territories defended, and trespassers punished. The high value of the fur trade and the relatively small land area that the beaver inhabited within a territory raised the returns and lowered the costs of allocating rights among tribal members.[57]

---

[55] Lee J. Alston, Gary D. Libecap, and Robert Schneider (1996), "The Determinants and Impact of Property Rights: Land Titles on the Brazilian Frontier," *Journal of Law, Economics, and Organization* 12(1): 25–61 directly address the interaction between value and property rights security. For other empirical evidence of the relationship between resource value and property rights precision see Gary D. Libecap (1978), "Economic Variables and the Development of the Law: The Case of Western Mineral Rights," *Journal of Economic History* 38(2): 338–362 discussing the incentives of the territorial and state government in Nevada to recognize local mineral rights arrangements as the value of silver ore discoveries increased; Corbett Grainger and Christopher Costello (2011), "The Value of Secure Property Rights: Evidence from Global Fisheries," NBER Working Paper 17019, Cambridge: NBER, where they examine the impact of insecure fishery quota rights on quota values across countries; and Gary D. Libecap and Dean Lueck (2011), "The Demarcation of Land and the Role of Coordinating Property Institutions," *Journal of Political Economy*, 119(3): 426–467, where they examine the impact of clarity and uniformity in the definition of property rights to land on land values.

[56] Demsetz (1967, 351–353).

[57] See Terry L. Anderson and Fred S. McChesney (1994), "Raid or Trade? An Economic Model of Indian-White Relations," *The Journal of Law and Economics* 37(1): 39–74 for a discussion of how value entered the calculus of immigrants to bargain with or take land from American Indians.

Figure 3.3. Miners Panning for Gold in the Dakota Territory.
Source: http://www.old-picture.com/old-west/Panning-Miners-Gold-Gold.htm.

Similarly, consider the example of the evolution of North American mineral rights. Land values rose sharply with the discovery of gold and silver deposits in parts of the American West in the nineteenth century. These discoveries dramatically changed the nature of property rights to land where there were no previous existing claimants who had a recognized authority to assert ownership.[58] Charles H. Shinn, who studied western mining camps, described the process as follows:

> A few hours' labor convinced the discoverers that the royal metal was there in paying quantities.... Soon the news spread; and within a week there were fifteen or twenty men at work in the...bed or creek. At first the camp had no organization or government, and every man's conduct conformed to his own ideas or fight and justice. Each miner had chosen a 'spot to work in,' and no question of encroachment could possibly arise.... About the close of the first week after the establishment of the camp, the near approach of two miners' operations caused a dispute about the size of the claims. One of the miners considered his rights infringed upon; and a few days later...his

[58] Gary D. Libecap (2007), "The Assignment of Property Rights on the Western Frontier: Lessons for Contemporary Environmental and Resource Policy," *The Journal of Economic History* 67(2): 257–291; 267. Any claims by native peoples were not recognized.

friends circulated an informal oral request . . . asking for a miners' meeting in the evening. They all felt that sooner or later definite laws must be adopted for the government of the camp or disorder would prevail.[59]

Efforts to forestall the losses of open access, which might have occurred had thousands of miners rushed to each location and fought over the property, led to the foundation of more than 600 local mining camp governments in the western United States. These camps were the locus of collective action necessary to distribute informal individual mineral claims. As the value of claims and the investment necessary to work them increased, the informal rules of individual mining camps were no longer sufficient. Capital-intensive deep-vein mining shafts, mills for refining the ore, aqueducts to bring water from the mountains to distant ore deposits, and roads and railroads to move the ore to market required secure property rights to attract investors. Conflict over who owned the richest areas held back development. Hence, rules were codified through territorial and state governments throughout the western United States so that they would apply beyond the reach of individual camps.

The Nevada experience illustrates the process of increasing property rights specificity as asset values rose. Nevada was home of the legendary Comstock Silver Lode, which, by 1889, produced more than 12 percent of all the gold and silver ever mined in the United States. Early in the life of the Comstock Lode, each new ore discovery in the mineral-rich rock band brought conflicts over ownership. Clarifying ownership was one of the chief aims of the Nevada legislature and courts. The importance of expanding the territory's nascent judicial system to adjudicate disputes was enunciated by the *San Francisco Alta California*: "There are very few claims of any value not in the utmost confusion of title and mystery of description. If there shall ever be established here a judicial system, there is a beautiful prospect of litigation; if there be no courts, then there is too much reason to fear force and violence."[60] The territorial legislature acknowledged that

we are called upon to make laws of a peculiar character, to protect and perpetuate interests that differ essentially from those of most of the other

---

[59] Charles H. Shinn (1885), *Mining Camps: A Study in American Frontier Government*, New York: Charles Scribner's Sons, 169.

[60] Libecap (1978, 343) quoting from the March 7, 1860 *San Francisco Alta California*.

territories.... The principal resources of this territory exist in its marvelously rich mines, which for their proper development and advancement require judicious thought and enactments by which titles to them can be secured and permanency given to that class of property.[61]

Between the discovery of the Comstock Lode in 1859 and its exhaustion in 1895, the legislature passed 123 statutes and courts ruled on 55 cases involving conflicting claims. Most of the new laws and court opinions dealt with defining and enforcing mineral rights. They focused on (1) defining requirements for physical claim boundaries; (2) describing actions that mineral claimants were to take to protect their holdings from trespassers; (3) outlining procedures for recording a mineral rights claim; (4) listing provisions for the transfer of ownership; (5) specifying actions that were to be taken to maintain ownership (such as occupancy and development);(6) defining requirements for forming mining companies; (7) outlining the duties of judges and other enforcement officials; and (8) provisions for punishment for claim jumping.[62]

To provide further legal clarification, the mining laws of Nevada and other western territories and states were incorporated into federal law in the Mining Laws of 1866 and 1872. The 1872 law (30 U.S.C. 22–54) remains in operation today, and the security it provided to the industry helped to foster the development of American hard rock mining as the world's leader.[63]

Value, of course, depends not only on exogenous shocks, such as an increase in the demand for a resource, as with beaver pelts, or the discovery of new resources, as with gold and silver ore, but also on endogenous actions by owners to enhance resource value. With reasonable security, owners have an incentive to invest in and exploit

---

[61] Libecap (1978, 345) quoting from the *Journal of the Council of the First Legislative Assembly of the Territory of Nevada* (San Francisco, 1862, 8).

[62] Libecap (1978, 349–350).

[63] Libecap (1978), (1989, 30), and (2007). See also John Umbeck (1977), "A Theory of Contract Choice and the California Gold Rush,' *The Journal of Law and Economics* 20: 421–437. The broader development of U.S. hard rock mining and the avoidance of a "resource curse" are described Paul A. David and Gavin Wright. "Increasing Returns and the Genesis of American Resource Abundance." *Industrial and Corporate Change* 6, no. 2 (1997): 203–245. The 1872 law is controversial today as the remnants of past abandoned mines contaminate surrounding soil and streams. This clearly is an area where the property rights have not been completely defined, allowing for pollution, and there are efforts to revise the law without weakening its ability to provide the security necessary to support further development.

a resource stock. If the rights are complete, this process can occur without inflicting uncompensated environmental damages.[64]

Physical Resource Characteristics

The definition and enforcement of property rights requires determining the boundaries and composition of the asset in order to clarify what is owned and what is not. Boundaries define where the asset begins and ends. This reduces trespassing, limits conflicting claims, and promotes trade by clarifying the owners with whom exchange can take place. Market transaction costs are lower when parties can defend their property rights, can define and measure what is traded, can identify parties with whom bargaining must occur, and can verify the terms of the contract.

Stationary, Observable Resources
It is easier to define and measure boundaries for stationary, observable resources. For example, a classic and common method of defining property is with fences made of wood, rocks, or hedge rows. These markers visibly define property boundaries.

Technological change can lower bounding costs, as with the invention of barbed wire or with the development of Global Positioning Satellites (GPS) and corresponding Global Information Systems (GISs) capable of providing coordinates for land parcels and even for ocean grids.[65] In some fisheries where entry has been restricted, owners of boats with access are required to carry GPS emitters to indicate their location. This information can then be used to determine if the vessel is in prescribed fishing territory. It also makes possible spot checks of harvest to insure that captains are adhering to quota or other harvest and equipment limits.

---

[64] Terry L. Anderson, Ragnar Arnason, and Gary D. Libecap (2011), "Efficiency Advantages of Grandfathering in Rights-Based Fisheries Management," *Annual Review of Resource Economics* 3: 159–179, emphasize the rents created by entrepreneurs finding and developing natural resources, such as fisheries.

[65] Terry L. Anderson and P.J. Hill (1975), "The Evolution of Property Rights: A Study of the American West," *The Journal of Law and Economics* 28(1): 163–180 and Richard Hornbeck (2010), "Barbed Wire: Property Rights and Agricultural Development," *Quarterly Journal of Economics* 125(2): 767–810 for estimates of the productivity gains from more definite property rights to land through barbed wire.

Figure 3.4. Bounding of Stationary Resources, such as Land.
Source: IgoUgo, http://photos.igougo.com/pictures-photos-p202999-
Patchwork_Quilt_of_Green_fields_and_rock_Fences.html.

It comes as no surprise that property rights are more complete
and environmental markets most advanced for natural resources that
are immobile and observable. Accordingly, groups such as the Nature
Conservancy commonly purchase or lease properties that have important amenities and other environmental values. These are examples of
environmental markets in operation.

Mobile, Unobservable Resources
The costs of boundary definition and enforcement are higher for
mobile or unobservable resources, such as groundwater, deep-vein
minerals, air, and fish and wildlife. In some cases the costs are so prohibitive relative to benefits that no rights are assigned and the tragedy
of the commons unfolds. The abundant passenger pigeon, which
went from being perhaps the world's most abundant bird species to
extinction within 300 years, is an example.[66] A close call was the near

[66] T.R. Halliday (1980), "The Extinction of the Passenger Pigeon Ectopistes Migrato-
rius and Its Relevance to Contemporary Conservation," *Biological Conservation* 17:

Figure 3.5. Barbed Wire Fence.
Source: http://upload.wikimedia.org/wikipedia/commons/8/81/Barbedwire3.jpg.

extinction of the North American bison, whose numbers were estimated to be around 20 million in 1800 but only 1,000 by 1890.[67]

One method of reducing costs for bounding such resources is to define property rights in terms of observable parameters. In the United States, for example, ownership of deep-vein hard rock minerals is assigned to the surface property owner where the vein breaks the surface – its outcropping – regardless of where it travels underground.[68] Similarly, access to groundwater and oil and gas deposits are granted

157–162. Scott Farrow (1995), "Extinction and Market Forces: Two Case Studies," *Ecological Economics* 13: 115–123. For a broader discussion of the problem of property rights to wildlife see Dean Lueck (1989), "The Economic Nature of Wildlife Law," *The Journal of Legal Studies* 18(2): 291–324.

[67] Dean Lueck (2002), "The Extermination and Conservation of the American Bison," *Journal of Legal Studies*, 31(S2): S609–S650; M. Scott Taylor (2011), "Buffalo Hunt: International Trade and the Virtual Extinction of the North American Bison," *American Economic Review* 101(December): 3162–3195.

[68] Libecap (1978, 345).

Figure 3.6. The Nature Conservancy's Babacomari Ranch in Arizona.
Source: http://www.nature.org/ourinitiatives/regions/northamerica/united
states/arizona/babacomari-ranch-slideshow.xml.

to surface land owners who obtain ownership by pumping.[69] Further,
surface water rights are defined by proximity to water under the riparian doctrine, which gives land owners adjacent to a stream the right to
an undiminished quantity and quality of water, or by the measurable

---

[69] Gary D. Libecap and James L. Smith (2002), "The Economic Evolution of Petroleum
Property Rights in the United States," *The Journal of Legal Studies* 31(2, pt. 2): S589–
608. There is variation across the states in terms of groundwater rights. See Jedidiah
Brewer, Robert Glennon, Alan Ker, and Gary D. Libecap (2007), "Transferring
Water in the American West: 1987–2005," *Michigan Journal of Law Reform* 50(4):
1021–1053, 27–28; and Henry Smith (2008), "Governing Water: The Semicommons
of Fluid Property Rights," *Arizona Law Review* 50(2): 445–478. Because multiple
surface owners may extract from the same oil and gas reservoir or groundwater
source, dissipation is possible. For example, see Susanna Eden, Robert Glennon,
Alan Ker, Gary Libecap, Sharon Megdal, and Taylor Shipman (2008), "Agricultural
Water to Municipal Use: The Legal and Institutional Context for Voluntary Transactions in Arizona," *The Water Report* 58: 9–20, 14. In California, the process of
defining more definite rights to groundwater can involve court intervention to measure and assign water rights through adjudication. The process can be contentious
and take a long time. See Association of Groundwater Agencies (2009), "Adjudi-
cated Basins and Watermasters in California." (2004), http://www.agwa.org/adjud-
basins.html, September 11.

diversion of water under the prior appropriation doctrine, which establishes rights to fixed quantities of water on a first-in-time, first-in-right basis.[70]

In a practice similar to riparian water rights, international agreements grant coastal countries property rights to adjacent waters and seabeds up to 200 miles from their shore lines as exclusive economic zones (EEZs).[71] Within the EEZ, the country has jurisdiction over any fish and other aquatic species that live within or travel through it. The EEZs remove these portions of the high seas from pure open access and create a kind of common property subject to each country's regulatory and property rights regimes. These regimes, however, often have not done well at solving the open-access problem. Not only must country politicians face the political problem of deciding which fishers have access, but when highly migratory, transboundary species are involved, political incentives change because many of the benefits of successful constraints accrue to citizens of neighboring countries. Naturally, highly-migratory species typically suffer much more from overharvest than do more stationary ones.[72]

When resources are non-rivalrous or nearly so and virtually impossible to bound, as is the case for highly-migratory fish stocks, the global atmosphere, oceans, and rivers crossing political boundaries, environmental markets with property rights and bargaining are an improbable solution for the problem of social cost. Even if rights can be defined to resources that straddle jurisdictions, it is difficult to enforce them without a higher level of government. For example, if contaminants are dumped into a river in one country and then flow across the border into

---

[70] Riparian rights are described in Getches (1997, 4–6); prior appropriation claims to flows in Anderson and Johnson (1986) in Brewer, Glennon, Ker and Libecap (2007, 1026), and Ronald N. Johnson, Micha Gisser, and Michael Werner (1981), "The Definition of a Surface Water Right and Transferability," *Journal of Law and Economics* 24(2): 273–288.

[71] For a discussion, see Rögnvaldur Hannesson (2004), *The Privatization of the Oceans* Cambridge, Mass: MIT University Press, 51–54.

[72] Stephanie F. McWhinnie (2009), "The Tragedy of the Commons in International Fisheries: An Empirical Examination," *Journal of Environmental Economics and Management* 57: 321–333; 328–329; Jennifer A. Devine, Krista D. Baker, Richard L. Haedrich (2006), "Deep-Sea Fishes Qualify as Endangered: A Shift from Shelf Fisheries to the Deep Sea is Exhausting Late-Maturing Species that Recover Only Slowly," *Nature* 439, 5 January: 29; Ransom A. Myers and Boris Worm (2003), "Rapid Worldwide Depletion of Predatory Fish Communities, *Nature* 423 15 May: 280–283.

another country, causing downstream damage, what recourse does the latter have for enforcing claims against citizens of the former?[73] The global atmosphere offers the greatest challenges because emissions in one country can flow well beyond its boundaries. It is not possible to fence out global air pollution and difficult to enforce claims for damages in one country caused by emissions from another. In Chapter 7 we explore this problem in greater detail.

The Cost of Trading

In addition to the costs of defining and enforcing property rights, there are the costs of negotiating the terms of exchange. Broadly speaking, exchange requires locating the relevant parties; communicating information about the asset to be traded and the terms of trade (offer and ask prices); inspecting, verifying, and measuring the asset; negotiating a sale price over mutually-accepted asset attributes; and drafting and enforcing the contract. The transaction cost literature emphasizes that each of these activities can complicate the timing, extent, and nature of exchange.[74]

Bargaining costs increase significantly when it is difficult to observe the resource. This problem is particularly true with an underground resource such as groundwater or oil. During the hay days of U.S. oil discovery and production in the early twentieth century, oil companies sought to buy out other parties on a reservoir in order to avoid a competitive race to extract the oil. However, this solution was rarely used because it was difficult for parties to agree on the relative value of individual leases. Later in the productive history of oil and gas fields, however, it was easier to agree on lease values. This outcome was possible because secondary extraction required injection of water and other fluids into the subsurface rock structure to release

---

[73] For a discussion of cross-state effects with regard to interstate implementation of the provisions of the Clean Water Act, see Hilary Sigman (2005), "Transboundary Spillovers and Decentralization of Environmental Policies," *Journal of Environmental Economics and Management* 50: 82–101.

[74] Coase (1960, 15–19); Barzel (1982); Dahlman (1979, 148); Demsetz (1964, 1967); and Williamson (1979) and (2005), "The Economics of Governance," *American Economic Review* 95(2): 1–18. For an empirical discussion of the high transaction costs of trade, see Libecap (2009).

trapped oil without which the field would have little or no productive value.[75]

The problem is illustrated by British Petroleum's efforts to acquire ARCO and other competitive producers on the Prudhoe Bay oil field in Alaska. The Prudhoe Bay deposit was discovered in 1966. With multiple parties owning small parts of the field, there was continuing disagreement on the value of the oil and gas and on the appropriate extraction techniques. As a result, the competing firms resorted to different extraction paths and competitive investments to differentially produce oil or gas. After 33 years, when the costs rose and the field aged, more coordinated secondary recovery injection was required, and the major parties finally agreed on a consolidation plan in 1999.[76]

Land transactions provide clear examples of how exchange costs can vary. In situations where land uses are compatible with one another and may even be compliments, one party may own the land and contract with the other users at low cost. For example, a farmer whose wheat fields provide pheasant habitat may bargain with pheasant hunters to capture the value of the habitat. Similarly, land trusts need not own land if easements (a type of contractual arrangement) can specify what the land trust wants without having to monitor how the land is used for other purposes. For example, the Montana Land Reliance (MLR), a land trust whose mission is "to partner with landowners to provide permanent protection for private lands that are significant for agricultural production, forest resources, fish and wildlife habitat, and open space," in 2012 had easements on more than 800,000 acres of land. Those easements require that the land remain in the uses protected for its mission, making it easy for the MLR to monitor. This arrangement explains why land trusts producing environmental amenities often use easements rather outright ownership to achieve their goals.[77]

---

[75] See Libecap and Smith (2002, S591-S593).

[76] Gary D. Libecap and James L. Smith (2001), "Regulatory Remedies to the Common Pool: The Limits to Oil Field Unitization," *Energy Journal* 22(1): 1–26, and Libecap and Smith (2002, S603–S606).

[77] http://www.mtlandreliance.org/mission.htm. Dominic P. Parker (2004), "Land Trusts and the Choice to Conserve Land with Full Ownership or Conservation Easements, *Natural Resources Journal* 44(2): 483–518.

Nonetheless, when environmental land uses conflict with other applications and monitoring costs rise, the immediate transaction costs of purchasing property may be less than subsequent monitoring costs. For example, the Nature Conservancy obtained land near Glacier National Park to provide grizzly bear habitat that is especially critical in the spring. If a rancher owned the land and grazed livestock, there would be the potential that bears would prey on them. Hence, the rancher would have little incentive to tolerate or encourage bears by providing habitat. To avoid this conflict, the Nature Conservancy purchased the land, and leases it for grazing, but only during those times when grizzly bears are unlikely to be in the area.[78]

GOVERNMENT AS A TRANSACTION COST REDUCER

Perhaps the most widely accepted role of the state is that it can help to define and enforce property rights. Using its power of coercion, it can determine the formal mechanism for specifying who has what rights, and it can use its police powers to enforce them. For these reasons, the state can potentially lower transaction costs.

Defining and Enforcing Property Rights

By enforcing property rights, government can encourage investment, encourage exchange, and align incentives to move resources to higher-valued uses. Not only do property rights help eliminate resource waste inherent in the tragedy of the commons, they promote stability and enterprise evident in cross-country studies of economic performance.[79]

---

[78] For another discussion, see Terry L. Anderson (2004), "Viewing Land Conservation through Coase-Colored Glasses," *Natural Resources Journal* 44(2): 361–381.

[79] Stephen Knack and Philip Keefer (1995), "Institutions and Economic Performance: Cross-Country Tests Using Alternative Institutional Measures," *Economics and Politics* 7: 207–227; Robert J. Barro (1998), *Determinants of Economic Growth: A Cross-Country Empirical Study*, Cambridge, MA: MIT Press; Rafael La Porta, Florencio Lopez-De-Silanes, Andrei Shleifer, and Robert Vishny (2002), "Investor Protection and Corporate Valuation," *Journal of Finance* 62: 1147–1165; Daron Acemoglu, Simon Johnson, and James A. Robinson (2002), "Reversal of Fortune: Geography and Institutions in the Making of the Modern World Income Distribution," *Quarterly Journal of Economics* 117(4): 1231–1194; Daron Acemoglu and Simon Johnson (2005), "Unbundling Institutions," *Journal of Political Economy* 113(5): 949–995.

Formal definition and enforcement of property rights by governments often evolves from less formal, decentralized processes. For example, early brand books that defined property rights to cattle were published by private cattlemen's associations. These local forms of registration were not sufficient when the geographic size of markets expanded. Hence, when territorial and state governments were formed, brand registration and inspection was assumed by government agencies. Similarly, water rights that evolved in localized mining camps and irrigation districts in the nineteenth century worked well for local transactions, but as broader geographic water demands appeared, states took a more active role in codifying and enforcing water rights. For example, as recently as 1974, the newly ratified Montana State Constitution established a specific water court to adjudicate all water rights in the state, reflecting the growing demand on the limited resource. The process has been long and complicated, but when it is finished, it will lower the transaction costs of utilizing water markets.

Uniform Measurement of Property Rights

The state can lower transaction costs by harmonizing the way in which property rights are defined and cataloged in uniform units – hectares, acres, grams, pounds, liters, squares, cubic inches, and so forth. For example, many state water agencies in the western United States record water rights denominated in units such as cubic feet per second (cfs) or acre feet (the quantity of water necessary to cover one acre of land one-foot deep or approximately 325,000 gallons). These are more precise measurements than those that evolved in mining camps where water was measured in miners' inches, measured as the amount of water that would flow through a one-inch hole in a board placed in a diversion ditch.[80]

The rectangular survey system provides another example of demarcating rights that improved on individualized irregular plot shapes known as metes and bounds. The rectangular system was mandated by the federal government under the Land Law of 1785 for all federal lands to promote rapid private settlement and expansion of land markets, when the government had few other sources of revenue.

[80] See http://www.western-water.com/A_Look_at_Miners_Inches.htm.

Controlling for other factors, such as topography, the rectangular system substantially increased land values, reduced title conflicts, and expanded market size.[81] The differences in the two demarcation systems are revealed in the following comparison of property descriptions under metes and bounds and under the rectangular survey:

Metes and Bounds: Beginning at a white oak in the fork of four mile run called the long branch & running No 88° Wt three hundred thirty eight poles to the Line of Capt. Pearson, then with the line of Person No 34° Et One hundred Eighty-eight poles to a Gum....

Rectangular Survey: ¼ South-West, ¼ Section North-West, Section 8, Township 22 North, Range 4 West, Fifth Principal Meridian.[82]

Not surprisingly, the rectangular system promoted markets and trade because property was demarcated in a standardized manner that predefined boundaries, minimized local knowledge requirements, provided for addressing and location, and created parcel uniformity for exchange. Even so, the rectangular system is costly to implement and is used only when potential land values and flat terrain (lowering survey costs) merit it.

Creating Property Rights for Environmental Markets

In cases where the costs of bounding a resource are so high that defining property rights to the resource itself is impractical, it may be feasible to create a use right to the resource. The atmosphere, highly-migratory fish stocks, and regional open space are examples of assets that are costly to measure and bound. As such, they are often left as open

---

[81] Gary D. Libecap and Dean Lueck (2011), "The Demarcation of Land and the Role of Coordinating Property Institutions," *Journal of Political Economy* 119(3): 426–467 describe how the use of the rectangular survey and demarcation of land into squares lowered transaction costs of enforcement and trade. See also Gary D. Libecap, Dean Lueck, and Trevor O'Grady (2011), "Large Scale Institutional Changes: Land Demarcation within the British Empire," *Journal of Law and Economics* 54(4), Markets, Firms, and Property Rights: A Celebration of the Research of Ronald Coase: S295–S327 for a discussion of the determinants of the spread of the rectangular survey system across the British Empire.

[82] C.W. Stetson (1935, 90), *Four Mile Run Land Grants*, Washington: D.C.: Mimeoform Press and Andro Linklater (2002, 180–181), *Measuring America*, London: Harper Collins as quoted in Libecap and Lueck (2011, 426).

access, subject to command-and-control regulation, or both. Subject to the costs of defining, measuring, monitoring, and allocating the rights, use rights can limit who has access to a resource and thus prevent rent dissipation. By capping the amount of emissions released into the atmosphere, the total allowable fish that can be harvested, or minimum amount of open space that must be left in a natural state, governments create scarcity value.

If the rights are then tradable, a market can evolve, thereby generating incentives to find efficient ways of using the limited resource. The performance of these mechanisms, as with all property rights, depends on security, duration, and ability to exchange. If any of these attributes are abridged, the efficacy of the rights-based solution is reduced. We return to this issue later in the volume.

Reducing Hold-Out Potential

The state also can lower transaction costs of agreement on property rights by defining the rules for bargaining. Again, referring to the case of oil and gas reservoirs, the most complete arrangement to avoid competitive open-access losses, other than buy-out, is unitization. With unitization a single firm is selected as the unit operator to develop the reservoir with other, would-be competing firm owners, sharing in the net returns according to a pre-negotiated sharing formula. To be most effective, all parties must participate to eliminate the open-access problem. With unanimity, however, there is potential for one owner to holdout in an effort to capture a larger share of the rents that are created. Recognizing that this can stifle unitization, state legislatures intervened at the behest of oil firms fearful of continuing losses to reduce the percentage of parties that had to agree to a unit with adoption of so-called coercive unitization statutes. In the case of Oklahoma, for instance, the legislature lowered the voting rule from 100 to 63 percent of operators, weighted by acreage.[83] Where these laws are in place, unitization is more widespread.

---

[83] For a discussion of the contracting problems involved, see Steven N. Wiggins and Gary D. Libecap (1985), "Oil Field Unitization: Contractual Failure in the Presence of Imperfect Information," *American Economic Review* 75(3): 368–385 and Libecap and Wiggins (1985).

Protecting Third Parties

If resources have multiple claimants, trading property rights by one can affect the rights of another. This problem is clearly illustrated in water transfers that change the timing, nature, and location of use. But the problem is a general one for many environmental resources. This is most obvious for water where the resource is used and reused as it flows to the sea. If a water right being used by one irrigator is sold to another, there are two possible sources of third-party impairment. First, the new use may consume more water per-unit-diverted – say the irrigated crop is switched from wheat to tomatoes – and therefore return less to the stream. In a fully appropriated water system, a reduction in the amount of water returned reduces downstream flows depended on by other users. Second, the transfer may result in a new diversion point, perhaps upstream, and similarly could impact other users downstream whose water supplies might be altered.[84]

The potential for third-party impairment is more complicated when there are property rights to instream flows. Any change in the place of diversion or in consumption from a diversion is likely to affect stream flows, and the connection is difficult to measure. Add to this that instream flows may provide benefits that are non-rivalrous and possibly non-excludable – as with scenic, recreational, and environmental uses – and transaction costs can rise considerably.

The state can reduce the transaction costs through legal processes for determining who might be harmed before any transfers are made. Defining what constitutes a beneficial water use helps clarify what transfers can occur. This limits the potential for third-party impairment, but it also makes it difficult to meet new demands that are not defined as beneficial.[85] Another procedure that reduces third-party impairment is the requirement that planned transfers must be legally announced and subject to contested case hearings that give potentially-impaired third parties an opportunity to object to proposed water

---

[84] Terry L. Anderson and Ronald N. Johnson (1986), "The Problem of Instream Flows," *Economic Inquiry* 24(October) 535–554.

[85] Beneficial use and other requirements for maintaining water rights are discussed in Gary D. Libecap (2012), "Water Rights and Markets in the Semiarid West: Efficiency and Equity Issues," in Daniel H. Cole and Elinor Ostrom, eds., *Property in Land and Other Resources*, Cambridge, MA: Lincoln Institute, 389–411, 401–406.

transfers. Finally, to smooth exchanges, the state limits those who have standing to make impairment claims. Otherwise, holdup becomes a very real potential.

CONCLUSION

Although Coase's insights regarding the problem of social cost are well known to economists generally, they have not been applied systematically to natural resource and environmental conflicts. When they are, it becomes obvious that the tragedy of the commons is a property rights problem. Unlike Pigouvian taxation or command-and-control regulatory solutions, a Coasian approach focuses attention on who has what rights, how those rights evolved, how they might be better defined and enforced, and how the transaction costs of exchanging them might be lowered to encourage greater efficiency and less conflict. The growing number of examples of successful environmental markets based on well-defined, enforced, and transferable property rights suggests that there are opportunities to align incentives to improve environmental quality and natural resource stewardship. The key is to devise and support rights-oriented institutions and to apply them where they may be the low-cost remedy to the environmental problem.

4

Local Property Rights to the Commons

We have emphasized the losses of open access attributable to individual efforts to capture resource rents in the absence of property rights. Although it is rational for individuals to ignore their effect on the overall value of an open-access resource, it can also make sense for individuals to act collectively to constrain their actions to protect and increase rents. The common solution proposed by economists is either private property rights that limit access or governmental regulation.

Another solution that has received more recent attention is a blend of informal property rights and local collective action known as common property resource management or CPRM. Common property resource management limits entry to individuals who are members of the group and excludes outsiders. CPRM generally works best if there are internal governance structures to link individual actions with group goals and if the state recognizes and enforces common property resource organizations and boundaries. Examples of CPRM include local grazing associations, fishing cooperatives, mutual irrigation companies, and groundwater management cooperatives.[1] Common property can reduce over-exploitation relative to open access, but competitive incentives remain within the group to varying degrees, depending on institutional design and group cohesion. Accordingly, it may still be less efficient than sole ownership or, in some cases, than regulation.

---

[1] For a discussion of the politics of common property management as it relates to groundwater in the United States, see Edella Schlager and William Blomquist (2008), *Embracing Watershed Politics*, Boulder: University of Colorado Press.

As with environmental markets based on private property rights, CPRM can allow trade, but it is more often informal, usually among group members and sometimes involving the approval of community leaders. Casual water exchanges among farmers within irrigation districts in the western U.S. are an example of common property trade. Farmers within irrigation districts often do not have clearly-defined individual rights to water when the district holds the water rights. However, they have customary use claims that allow an irrigator to acquire additional water during a growing season from other irrigators on an informal basis.[2]

Because moving from open access to CPRM creates resource rents for group members, it faces some of the same resistance from politicians and bureaucratic officials observed with privatization, an issue we explore more in Chapter 5. However, because the rents are captured at the local level on the basis of historic use, politically-controversial equity issues may be avoided.[3] Moreover, rents from locally-managed resources generally are relatively low and thus, attract less rent-seeking from non-community members who otherwise might place pressure on the state to give them a share of the returns. If, however, CPRM results in higher values, entry is attracted and politicians and other potential claimants, perhaps political elites, may attempt to capture rents. This is more likely to be a problem in less-developed countries where the rule of law is limited and governance systems are weak.[4] The challenge, therefore, is to achieve state recognition without encouraging political

---

[2] Howard Chong and David Sunding (2006), "Water Markets and Trading," *Annual Review of Environmental Resources* 31: 11.1–11.26 and Richard Howitt and Kristiana Hansen (2005), "The Evolving Western Water Markets," *Choices* 20(1): 59–64.

[3] Not always, however, as Elinor Ostrom (1990), *Governing the Commons: The Evolution of Institutions for Collective Action*, Cambridge University Press, 173–176 describes the imposition of standardized rules by the Canadian government on fishing practices in Nova Scotia rather than recognizing local arrangements to address stock depletion. This is the same problem with general government regulation we described in Chapter 2.

[4] Avinash K. Dixit (2004), *Lawlessness and Economics: Alternative Modes of Governance*, Princeton: Princeton University Press, 138–143 discusses the problems of a predatory state and the security of property rights. See also, Daniel Fitzpatrick (2006), "Evolution and Chaos in Property Rights Systems: The Third World Tragedy of Contested Access," *The Yale Law Journal* 115: 996–1048; 1012 and Jean-Marie Baland and Jean-Philippe Platteau (1996), *Halting Degradation of Natural Resources: Is There a Role for Rural Communities?* Rome and New York: FAO and Oxford University Press, 47.

Environmental Markets

rent-seeking.[5] If it can be limited, CPRM may lead to long-standing local common property regimes or to the evolution of more formal property rights as values increase and the benefits of sole ownership and broader exchange rise.

In this chapter we examine the conditions where CPRM has developed. Our understanding of how common property or community-based institutions constrain over-harvest or over-extraction owes much to the work of the late-Nobel laureate, Elinor Ostrom. In case studies and experimental settings, she examined the importance of tightly-knit communities with clear leadership, norms, repeat exchanges, and trust for constraining individual behavior to conserve resources. These institutional arrangements provide an alternative to formal regulation, tax policies or private property rights, but at the same time provide for resource stewardship or in some cases, a basis for environmental markets subsequently to evolve.

THE CONDITIONS FOR SUCCESSFUL COLLECTIVE ACTION

Elinor Ostrom (1990, 1998, 2000, 2011) outlines factors that contribute to cooperation in the management of common pool resources, and for our purposes we have categorized them according to resource attributes and group attributes. These factors easily lend themselves to a transaction cost interpretation as developed by Ronald Coase. They are drawn from case studies and laboratory experiments.[6] The factors include information costs, resource characteristics, and attributes

---

[5] This raises public choice issues as described in Sam Peltzman (1976), "Toward a More General Theory of Regulation," *Journal of Law and Economics* 19(2): 211–240; Gary S. Becker (1983), "A Theory of Competition among Pressure Groups for Political Influence," *Quarterly Journal of Economics* 98(3): 371–400; Anne O. Krueger (1974), "The Political Economy of the Rent-Seeking Society," *American Economic Review* 64(3): 291–303; Gordon Tullock (1967), "The Welfare Costs of Tariffs, Monopolies, and Theft," *Western Economic Journal* 5(3): 224–232. For a discussion of efforts to secure government recognition of local common property regimes, see James M. Acheson (2003), *Capturing the Commons: Devising Institutions to Manage the Main Lobster Industry*, Lebanon, NH: University Press of New England.

[6] Elinor Ostrom (1990); Elinor Ostrom (1998), "Self Governance of Common-Pool Resources," in Peter Newman, ed. *The New Palgrave Dictionary of Economics and The Law*, New York: Macmillan, Vol. 3: 424–432; Elinor Ostrom (2000), "Collective Action and the Evolution of Social Norms," *Journal of Economic Perspectives* 14(3):

Figure 4.1. Elinor Ostrom, Co-Recipient of the 2009 Nobel Prize in Economics.
Source: http://newsinfo.iu.edu/asset/page/normal/7865.html.

of the collective group. Like private property rights, common property resource management regimes recognize the effects of individual actors on resource rents, the role of norms and repeat dealing in enforcing limits on access to the commons, the importance of group size and geographic scale on the costs of defining and bounding access to resources, and the importance of local knowledge and information.

Resource Attributes

Many of the same factors that make private property rights more viable – stationary resources, ease of measuring and monitoring resource use, and low cost of defining boundaries – also make common property resource management more effective. When the resource is comparatively small, visible, and immobile, boundaries are more easily designated by local collective action. Compliance by group members can be observed and entry by non-community members can be monitored.

When group members are closely tied to the resource and can readily detect its response to conservation efforts and capture the

137–158; and Elinor Ostrom (2011), "Beyond Markets and States: Polycentric Governance of Complex Economic Systems," *American Economic Review* 100(3): 641–672. A useful summary of her analysis is provided by Baland and Platteau (1996, 286–90).

associated increased rents, agreement on restrictions on production or harvest is more likely.[7] Under these conditions, participants can devise rules for access, use, and management and enforce them. Such observation is most likely with renewable resources where stocks respond to new protective schemes, but it is also relevant for non-renewable resources if individual actions directly affect extraction costs or change the time-pattern of production to a more valued one or if reduced exploitation raises the price of the resource.

Whether a group will implement CPRM and whether group members will abide by its limits depend importantly on how long it takes for reduced pressure on the resource to manifest itself with increased returns. When the resource response time is comparatively short, individuals are more likely to see a direct connection between their actions and greater value. If, on the other hand, reaction times are very long, group member will not see a link between their efforts and improvements in the resource, and will be more likely to defect from CPRM.

CPRM is also more likely to be successful if group members understand the dynamics of the natural system being managed. More dynamic systems with complex interactions between human and natural factors make it more difficult to predict and observe the benefits of limited entry on the resource and therefore make agreements on group management strategies harder to achieve.

As we have noted, entry can be stimulated by the success of the group in raising values. If group members recognize this potential and it cannot be prevented, their incentives for conservation and rent-increasing actions are reduced. For example, in the case of the Navajo Reservation, Johnson and Libecap (1980) found that sheep herders, even those occupying so-called customary grazing areas, are aware of the potential of their neighbors to encroach on their range should there be attractive grazing opportunities.[8] With this in mind, Navajo herders typically overgraze their areas in order to capture the value of the grass stands and reduce the incentive for others to trespass, even if, in the long term, the range is degraded.

---

[7] In the cooperative settings examined by Ostrom and others, this is a pure rate of time preference. In contrast, a discount rate arising in common property situations could look large because of poor institutions or a lack of cooperation.

[8] Ronald N. Johnson and Gary D. Libecap (1980), "Legislating Commons: The Navajo Tribal Council and the Navajo Range," *Economic Enquiry* 18(1): 69–92.

Group Attributes

Small groups naturally are better able to adopt common property management practices than are larger groups.[9] Unless there are important economies-of-scale in management and monitoring, smaller groups should outperform larger ones. They are more likely to be homogeneous, able to rapidly negotiate agreements, observe compliance, communicate resource conditions and any needed management adjustments, and engage in reciprocal exchange on other margins that encourage adherence to group practices to avoid open-access losses. Often such groups have recognized leaders who organize and channel membership behavior with agreed-upon rewards and graduated sanctions for violation.[10] These are obviously special characteristics, but where they exist, especially in traditional, artisanal production in certain inshore fisheries, indigenous timber and pasture use, and small-scale irrigated farming, they are very effective in averting the tragedy of the commons.

Compliance is reinforced if group members can draw on a history of similar cases where cooperation has been successful. Community norms and customs reflect these experiences and facilitate durable arrangements so long as resource values and group size and composition remain stable. Like creating effective producer cartels, maintaining effective CPRM is easier when production processes are homogeneous and observable. In the case of cartels made up of a few firms with comparable costs, individual firms have the same profit-maximizing pricing and output levels that coincide with the group objectives for monopoly output and pricing. When these conditions

---

[9] The classic discussion of the problems of group size is found in Mancur Olson (1965), *The Logic of Collective Action: Public Goods and the Theory of Groups,* Cambridge: Harvard University Press. He argued that the provision of public goods in large groups required the delivery of private rewards to those who participated. Others have argued that group size may be less of a constraint, see Arun Agrawal and Sangeev Goyal (2001), "Group Size and Collective Action: Third Party Monitoring in Common Pool Resources," *Comparative Political Studies* 34(1): 63–93 and Baland and Platteau (1996, 301, 316, 335). These are generally homogenous groups.

[10] For a discussion of the role of leadership in local resource management, see Nicolás L. Gutiérrez, Ray Hilborn, and Omar Defeo (2011), "Leadership, Social Capital and Incentives Promote Successful Fisheries," *Nature* February 17, 470: 386–389.

are violated, cartels tend to fail.[11] Despite the importance of homogeneity for group coordination, some parties with specialized capital, skills, and knowledge can do well even under open-access settings. In such cases convincing them to join the CPRM regime and abide by the rules may require allowing them to retain their disproportionate share of the rents. This requirement can violate group equity norms and may undermine CPRM.[12]

Low discount rates extend the time horizon over which the benefits from CPRM can be realized and hence make compliance more likely when immediate returns are small. Aligning management costs with individual benefits also increases the incentive for compliance, and such alignment is easier if group members have similar production costs. These conditions smooth negotiations among members regarding adoption of governance norms. Trust among members also ensures adherence to group practices. Familiarity provides information on the basis of repeat dealings and other community institutions such as religious centers, clubs, and clans, can enhance enforcement.[13] Finally, prior group experience in other management settings allows for adaptation to resource management issues by identifying leaders, selecting

---

[11] For a summary of cartel bargaining and outcomes, see Barbara Alexander and Gary D. Libecap, 2000, "The Effect of Cost Heterogeneity in the Success and Failure of the New Deal's Agricultural and Industrial Programs," in *Explorations in Economic History* 37, 370–400. See also D.K. Osborne, 1976, "Cartel Problems," *American Economic Review* 66(5): 835–844 and Bjark Fog 1956, "How are Cartel Prices Determined?" *Journal of Industrial Economics* 5: 16–23.

[12] Ronald N. Johnson and Gary D. Libecap (1982), "Contracting Problems and Regulation: The Case of the Fishery," *American Economic Review* 72(5): 1005–1022; Corbett Grainger and Christopher Costello (2012), "Resource Rents, Inframarginal Rents, and the Transition to Property Rights in a Common Pool Resource," working paper, Department of Agricultural and Resource Economics, University of Wisconsin, Madison. This notion underscores the often observed resistance of "high liners" in fisheries from supporting more formal governance regimes. Robert T. Deacon, Dominic P. Parker, and Christopher Costello (2013), "Reforming Fisheries: Lesson from a Self-Selected Cooperative," *Journal of Law and Economics* 56(1): 83–125.

[13] For a discussion, see Aver Grief (1993), "Contract Enforceability and Economic Institutions in Early Trade: The Maghribi Traders' Coalition," *American Economic Review* 83(3): 525–548. For more discussion of enforcement and collaboration, see Sheilagh Ogilvie (2011), *Institutions and European Trade: Merchant Guilds 1000–1800*, Cambridge: Cambridge University Press and Avner Greif, Paul Milgrom, and Barry R. Weingast (1994), "Coordination, Commitment, and Enforcement: The Case of the Merchant Guild," *The Journal of Political Economy* 102(4): 745–776.

practices that were effective, and choosing useful monitoring arrangements.

There are numerous studies of common property regimes used to address common pool resource problems. Many of these involve field case analyses in less-developed countries where formal property rights to land and other resources often are not established and where governments are ineffectual, at least in addressing local open-access problems. Hence, common property is the primary institutional means of avoiding the losses.[14]

Those arrangements that are effective exhibit many of the key characteristics for successful collective action. In her 1990 book, Elinor Ostrom describes how the damages predicted in prisoners' dilemma games, in which a lack of cooperation makes all parties (and the resource) worse off, have been avoided in particular settings. She outlines a framework of self-governance and then illustrates where it has been useful in the management of pastures and forests in parts of Switzerland and Japan, in the organization of irrigation institutions in regions of Spain and the Philippines, and in the governance of certain groundwater basins in Southern California.[15]

Generally, effective examples exhibit trust among members of fairly small, homogenous groups where the parties depend on the

---

[14] B. Adhikari, and J. C. Lovett (2006), "Institutions and Collective Action: Does Heterogeneity Matter in Community-Based Resource Management?" *Journal of Development Studies*, 42(3), 426–445; P. Frost, B. Campbell, M. Luckert, M. Mutamba, A. Mandondo, and W. Kozanayi (2007), "In Search of Improved Rural Livelihoods in Semi-Arid Regions through Local Management of Natural Resources: Lessons from Case Studies in Zimbabwe," *World Development* 35(11): 1961–1974; J. Johnson (2000), "Determinants of Collective Action on the Local Commons: A Model with Evidence from Mexico," *Journal of Development Economics* 62(1): 181–208; Emilio F. Moran and Elinor Ostrom, eds. (2005), *Seeing the Forest and the Trees* Cambridge: MIT Press; Joanna Burger, Elinor Ostrom, Richard B. Norgaard, David Policansky, and Bernard D. Goldstein eds. (2001), *Protecting the Commons: A Framework for Resource Management in the Americas*, Washington D.C.: Island Press; Elinor Ostrom (1992), *Crafting Institutions for Self-Governing Irrigation Systems*, San Francisco: ICS Press.

[15] Ostrom (1990, 29–55). See 182–214 for a discussion of the framework and 58–101 for a discussion of successful cases.

resource – local irrigation wells and ditches, rangeland, timber stands, and fisheries. Trust serves to reduce uncertainty and enforcement costs because the parties are expected to adhere to agreements (usually implicit) about resource use, even in unusual situations. The parties typically are in close proximity to one another, are involved in day-to-day interaction, have graduated punishment mechanisms, including loss of social esteem when in violation of social rules and norms, and are able to draw on past cooperation as guidance for addressing new conditions.[16]

Effective common property regimes do not always emerge, however. Ostrom describes inshore Canadian (Nova Scotia), Sri Lankan, and Turkish fisheries, Sri Lankan irrigation projects, and Southern Californian groundwater basins where open-access losses continue. These arise because the parties have not been able to agree on individual use rights and governance mechanisms, do not have clear resource boundaries, have not received formal government recognition to endorse self-governance and to prevent entry by outsiders, or all of the above. Even though CPRM has a mixed record of success, just as do private

---

[16] E. Dennis, J. Ilyasov, E. Van Dusen, S. Treshkin, M. Lee, and P. Eyzaguirre, P. (2007), "Local Institutions and Plant Genetic Conservation: Exchange of Plant Genetic Resources in Rural Uzbekistan and Some Theoretical Implications," *World Development* 35(9): 1564–1578; R. M. Aggarwal (2000), "Possibilities and Limitations to Cooperation in Small Groups: The Case of Group-Owned Wells in Southern India," *World Development* 28(8): 1481–1497; H. Tai (2007), "Development through Conservation: An Institutional Analysis of Indigenous Community-Based Conservation in Taiwan," *World Development* 35(7): 1186–1203. J.M. Chermak and K. Krause (2002), "Individual Response, Information, and Intergenerational Common Pool Problems," *Journal of Environmental Economics and Management* 43(1): 47–70; J. Platteau, J. and E. Seki, E. (2007), "Heterogeneity, Social Esteem and Feasibility of Collective Action," *Journal of Development Economics* 83(2): 302–325. J. Platteau and T. Strzalecki (2004), "Collective Action, Heterogeneous Loyalties and Path Dependence: Micro-Evidence from Senegal," *Journal of African Economies* 13(3): 417–445; B. Ray and R.N. Bhattacharya (2011), "Transaction Costs, Collective Action and Survival of Heterogeneous Co-management Institutions: Case Study of Forest Management Organisations in West Bengal, India," *Journal of Development Studies* 47(2): 253–273; L. M. Ruttan (2008), "Economic Heterogeneity and the Commons: Effects on Collective Action and Collective Goods Provisioning," *World Development* 36(5): 969–985; G. Varughese and E. Ostrom, E. (2001), "The Contested Role of Heterogeneity in Collective Action: Some Evidence from Community Forestry in Nepal," *World Development*, 29(5): 747–765; and T. Vedeld (2000), "Village Politics: Heterogeneity, Leadership and Collective Action," *Journal of Development Studies* 36(5): 105–134.

property and environmental markets, and government regulation, it is part of the array of institutional options to mitigate open-access losses. To the many examples documented by Ostrom, we add two historical cases from the United States and two contemporary examples from fisheries. The first historical case illustrates how CPRM can evolve into private property, and the second how CPRM unraveled in the face of a hostile government response, driven by distributional demands for land by new entrants. The first fishery example shows how special property rights can effectively reduce rent dissipation when resources are somewhat mobile, and the second example reveals the difficulty in maintaining a successful cooperative in the face of legal challenges.

Mining Camps

Early American land policy developed around agriculture with the Northwest Ordinance of 1785, the various Preemption acts, other federal statutes that progressively lowered land prices, and most importantly, the Homestead Act of 1862, which granted private property rights to small plots of land. From the Atlantic seaboard to the ninety-eighth meridian (see Figure 4.2), this policy worked well to establish rights and avoid losses of competitive use.[17] Through about 1880, around the time that the frontier moved beyond that limit, millions of acres of federal land had been distributed to private claimants.

The Far West, beyond the ninety-eighth meridian, was at once remote from established federal land policy and at the same time inhospitable to it. There also were different resources, especially mineral and rangeland, that were desired. Accordingly, claimants devised their own arrangements. Institutions to assign rights to mineral lands after the California Gold Rush of 1848 were a key example. Initially, they were common property under local mining camp governments.[18]

---

[17] Gary D. Libecap (2007), "The Assignment of Property Rights on the Western Frontier: Lessons for Contemporary Environmental and Natural Resource Policy," *The Journal of Economic History* 67(2): 257–291.

[18] Important studies include John Umbeck (1977), "A Theory of Contact Choice and the California Gold Rush," *Journal of Law and Economics* 20(2): 421–437; John Umbeck (1977), "The California Gold Rush: A Study of Emerging Property Rights," *Explorations in Economic History* 14: 197–226; John Umbeck (1981): "Might Makes Right: A Theory of the Formation and Initial Distribution of Property Rights," *Economic Inquiry* 19(1): 38–59. James I. Stewart (2006), "Migration to the Agricultural

Figure 4.2. The Far Western United States.
Source: Gary D. Libecap (2007), "The Assignment of Property Rights on the Western Frontier: Lessons for Contemporary Environmental and Natural Resource Policy," *The Journal of Economic History* 67(2): 257–291, 266.

Prospectors who rushed into regions suspected of having rich gold or silver ore deposits had no official government sanction to claim mineral land, as it was not addressed in federal land law, and early on there was no civilian government to provide a legal framework for assigning property rights. Mining camp governments were the result. Between 1848 and 1890 or so, well over 600 mining camps were founded in California, Nevada, Montana, Idaho, Colorado, the Dakotas, Arizona, and Alaska.

Frontier and Wealth Accumulation, 1860–1870," *Explorations in Economic History* 43: 547–577; Gary D. Libecap (1978), "Economic Variables and the Development of the Law: The Case of Western Mineral Rights," *Journal of Economic History* 38(2): 338–362; Gary D. Libecap (1979), "Government Support of Private Claims to Public Minerals: Western Mineral Rights," *Business History Review* 53(3): 362–385; Karen Clay and Gavin Wright (2005), "Order without Law? Property Rights During the California Gold Rush," *Explorations in Economic History* 42: 155–183; William Hallagan (1978), "Share Contracting for California Gold," *Explorations in Economic History* 15: 196–210; and Richard O. Zerbe and C. Leigh Anderson (2001), "Culture and Fairness in the Development of Institutions in the California Gold Fields," *Journal of Economic History* 61(1): 114–143.

Mining camp rules were drafted quickly because the number of individuals in each area was small, and they had relatively homogeneous backgrounds and expectations. Between 75 and 90 percent of the miners were of American or European origin, had above-average levels of schooling, limited prospecting skills, and initially none had information advantages regarding the location of ore. In the few recorded cases where there was an absence of cooperation (such as the Sonoran mining camp in California), the population was mixed, with large numbers of Mexican and American miners who had very different conceptions of cooperation, justice, and the law. In all cases, there were high expected gains of avoiding disruptive conflict over mineral ground. Rules were drafted whenever twenty or thirty prospectors congregated in a new mining district.

First-possession to a single, specific location of mineral land was the standard allocation rule. The first prospector to arrive at a location thought to have deposits of valuable ore was granted private claiming rights. Each party had, at least in principle, an equal chance at first choice of a spot. Accordingly, first-possession encouraged socially valuable search and exploration. Those who discovered a new district typically were granted two mineral claims, whereas all others were allowed a single claim. Each mining claim had to be marked and worked according to local mining camp rules. For example, one district in 1852 required miners to work their claims at least one day out of three during the mining season, and another in 1853 specified that a miner was to dig a ditch on his claim "one foot wide and one foot deep" within three days of locating a claim. Abandoned claims could be occupied by others. In the meantime, other prospectors were prohibited from entry until the claim was deemed to be abandoned. Indeed, given the uncertainty of the location of ore, prospectors expected to locate and move numerous times before striking it rich, so that they needed a flexible way of obtaining and relinquishing the right to search for ore in any particular place. As uncertainty was reduced through new ore discoveries, accommodating search became less important than supporting investment and production so that enforcement of valuable claims against trespass became more critical.

Mining camp rules provided for procedures for arbitration of disputes and for punishing violators of the rules. Most mining codes specified that property conflicts be resolved in courts before juries of a dozen or more miners. Although there was variation both across the mining camps and across time, mining codes always placed a limit on claim size that varied according to the type and expected value of the claim. Importantly however, these claim sizes were determined by local factors, not outside government requirements. Smaller claims were allowed in potentially richer stream beds where gold was thought to concentrate and water for extraction was nearby, whereas larger claims were allowed on drier hill sides that offered lower prospects. Enforcement costs were higher for the more valuable stream claims necessitating smaller individual holdings than for the less-attractive hillside claims.

In the early period of a mining district's development, all placer (surface) and quartz (deep vein) ore claims tended to be small, for example, fifty to one hundred feet wide, traveling to the center of a stream for placer claims and two hundred foot slices along the exposed vein for quartz claims. But mining camp rules were flexible so that as ore played out, claim sizes were extended. Whereas placer claims were bounded in terms of surface area, quartz claims were assigned to the ore veins themselves and were separate from surface ownership. Extra lateral rights were granted whereby the vein owner was allowed to follow the deposit wherever it traveled beneath the surface. In general there were no restrictions on the private sale of mineral claims. Some mining districts limited trading of claims, possibly because of the costs of marking, enforcing, and exchanging in the early stages of development. As conditions settled, however, sale became routine, first to allow entry to those without any land in the district and then to consolidate claims for more capital-intensive production.

Camp rules initially were informal and gradually were given more structure as mining values rose, the number of claimants and congestion increased, and the technology of mining and the nature of the ore and extraction changed. In this process, common property gradually developed into private property, recognized by both state and federal governments. Among the examples of western U.S. natural resource property rights, local mining camps and subsequent mineral ownership developed in the most straightforward and successful manner.

Figure 4.3. Nineteenth Century Roundup on the Western Great Plains. *Source:* 1891 photograph by John C. H. Grabill, photographer, http://www .old-picture.com/old-west/Roundup-Cattle.htm.

Livestock Associations

As with prospectors searching for a means of avoiding competitive open access over mineral land, ranchers who moved into the upper Great Plains in the 1870s and 1880s to take advantage of rich pastures had no existing government sanctions for their claims. And, as with mineral rights, local common property developed. There was no specific provision in federal land policy for ranchers to obtain formal property rights to all of the land that they required. Because of the broken terrain and limited precipitation, livestock carrying capacities of the western range were low. With twenty-five acres or more required to sustain a single cow for a year, upwards of 10,000 acres were commonly required to support enough animals to achieve economies-of-scale in grazing.[19]

These allotments were well beyond anything formally possible under the Homestead Act, which granted property rights to small plots

---

[19] See Gary D. Libecap (2007): 271–275; Terry Anderson and P.J. Hill (1975), "The Evolution of Property Rights: A Study of the American West," *Journal of Law and Economics* 18(1): 177–198; and Terry L. Anderson and P.J. Hill (2004), *The Not So Wild, Wild West: Property Rights on the Frontier*, Palo Alto: Stanford University Press.

of 160 acres for farming. Accordingly, to avoid the losses of competitive overgrazing and to reduce conflict over land, ranchers organized livestock associations to divide the land and to jointly manage communal herds:

A custom has grown up and become thoroughly established among people of this community that once a stock man has developed water on and taken possession of the range by fully stocking the same that he will not be molested by other stockmen in his possession and enjoyment of such range.[20]

Taylor Dennen's examination of livestock associations shows how they constrained entry and use of rangeland and that they were effective in controlling open-access losses.[21] Association rules included restrictions on the number of animals that could be placed in common herds, limits on who could participate (only local ranchers with patented homesteads and locally recognized rangeland claims), delineation of individual, informal landholdings, registration of cattle brands, and specification of the labor each rancher was to contribute for managing the herd. Common herds were maintained to monitor the drift of livestock and to direct them to fresh grass stands, to control breeding within the herd, to cooperate in the branding of young animals, and to block entry by outsiders. There were annual cooperative roundups for branding and for collecting yearlings for sale. Livestock organizations reduced cattle mortality during severe winters by limiting grazing and thereby conserving winter pastures. Association membership was highly valued when it was transferred with ranch property upon sale.

These livestock associations remained effective common property institutions until additional herders came with sheep, not needing the cooperation of the associations, and new, small homesteaders came after 1880 with the endorsement of the federal government. The ensuing competition over land and the lack of legal support resulted in the gradual breakdown of livestock association rules. The quasi-legal practices of ranchers were attacked and their fences removed by the federal government. As the ability of the associations to control entry

---

[20] Statement by William Jones, rancher, Eddy County New Mexico, 10 April 1917, quoted in Gary D. Libecap (1981), *Locking up the Range: Federal Land Controls and Grazing*, Cambridge, MA: Ballinger, 16.

[21] R. Taylor Dennen (1976), "Cattlemen's Associations and Property Rights in Land in the American West," *Explorations in Economic History* 13: 423–436.

declined, the incentives of members to violate internal rules increased, and the groups, along with their informal land allocations began to break down.[22] In the absence of fencing, the only way ranchers could maintain their informal claims to land was to reduce the incentive to enter it by overgrazing: "The only protection a stockman has is to keep his range eaten to the ground and the only assurance that he will be able to secure the forage crop any one year is to graze it off before someone else does."[23]

Overgrazing to mark and protect rangeland claims was costly. It made cattle herds more vulnerable to drought because grass stands were driven to low levels with little reserve when precipitation was scanty. The costs of overgrazing to define and enforce land claims against other potential users were reflected in lower calf crops, higher death losses, smaller cattle weights, and diminished animal values. The lack of otherwise enforceable property rights to the range contributed to its deterioration, as emphasized by the Department of Agriculture in its 1936 study of the condition of the western range resource that we noted in Chapter 3.[24]

Japanese TURFs

Because most fish migrate and even more sedentary species require considerable area for spawning and development, fish stocks are best managed when there are spatial property rights. Because multiple species often share the same ocean area, these rights are most effective in managing resource stocks when various fish stocks and habitat are included, often as common property. The advantages of sole ownership of fisheries were described by Anthony Scott (1955), and the advantages of territorial use rights for fishing or TURFs were outlined by Francis Christy (1982). TURFs are most broadly used in Japan, but they also are found in Chile, Mexico, and elsewhere.[25]

---

[22] Ernest Staples Osgood (1929), *The Day of the Cattleman*, Minneapolis: University of Minnesota Press, 186 and Libecap (1981, 31–37).

[23] USDA researchers, W. C. Barnes and James T. Jardine, quoted in Libecap (1981, 24).

[24] Libecap (1981, 23–8); See USDA, 1936, *The Western Range*, 74th Congress, 2nd series, *Senate Document 199*.

[25] Anthony Scott (1955), "The Fishery: The Objectives of Sole Ownership," *Journal of Political Economy* 63(2): 116–24; Francis T. Christy, Jr. (1982), *Territorial Use*

In Japan TURFs are based on Fishery Management Organizations (FMOs) that can include both coastal and offshore fisheries and these FMOs in turn are made up of more narrowly-based Fishery Cooperative Associations (FCAs) of fishers. Entry into each FCA involved in a TURF is restricted and there may be multiple FCAs in each TURF. FCAs and FMO jurisdictions are geopolitical rather than biological, so they are not perfect for stock management, but this condition reflects their origins in fishing communities in Japan and the close knit nature of those villages provides the trust, reciprocity, and monitoring necessary for successful group or common property management as described by Ostrom.

Despite the potential mismatch between migration patterns and TURF jurisdiction, these common property organizations have a number of factors that make them more successful in protecting the stock and generating rents than is the case under open access or centralized government regulation. First, TURFs provide group ownership for the members of each FCA. Where multiple FCAs must agree on management, FMOs coordinate decisions. The sense of ownership changes the dynamic from one of a race-to-fish under open access, or one of reaction against centrally-devised, government restrictions, to one of shared possession of the resource.[26] Second, only members can fish within the TURF. Third, they do so under locally-imposed rules regarding number of fishing vessels, amount and type of gear used, seasons, monitoring, penalties for rule violation, fishing grounds, and marine restricted areas, which protect juvenile stock. Many FCAs within TURFs have revenue-pooling agreements so that members who are not allowed to fish or who have their fishing restricted more than others still benefit from any positive response of the stock to management. The FCAs also maintain records on harvest and jointly engage in marketing output and input purchases.

Rights in Marine Fisheries: Definitions and Conditions, Rome: FAO fisheries Technical Paper 227. See also H. Uchida and James E. Wilen (2004), "Japanese Coastal Fisheries Management and Institutional Designs: A Descriptive Analysis," in Y. Matsuda and T. Yamamoto, eds., *Proceedings of the Twelfth Biennial Conference of the International Institute for Fishery Economics and Trade*, Corvallis, Oregon: International Institute for Fishery Economics and Trade. The examples described here are from R. Townsend, Ross Shotton, and H. Uchida (2008), *Case Studies in Fisheries Self-Governance*, Rome: FAO Fisheries Technical Paper 504.

[26] H. Uchida and M. Makino, 2008, "Japanese Coastal Fishery Co-Management: An Overview," in Townsend, Shotton, and Uchida (2008, 221–228).

Of the five Japanese TURFs described in Townsend, Shotton, and Uchida (2008), fishery management of the walleye pollock (Suketoudara) stock appears to be the least successful.[27] The pollock migrate large distances and cross multiple FCAs so that beneficial actions by one for the shared stock are captured by others that are less restrictive in management. Nevertheless, the TURF is an improvement over open access and central regulation. One FCA in the Nishi section is particularly successful as a result of its use of cooperative rotation of vessels to equalize access and avoid congestion when pollock congregate in its jurisdiction, revenue pooling, limits on the number of hooks used with each vessel, and group marketing.

The Sakuraebi (small shrimp) TURF in central Japan may be the most successful. The shrimp are very valuable, have few substitutes, are extremely sedentary, remaining within the bay administered by the two FCAs associated with the TURF, are an annual crop so that stock management is easier than for more long-lived species, and congregate in specific areas to be harvested.[28] Prior to establishment of the FCAs under central regulation of season and licensing, the fishery resembled a derby, with a rush to the area where the shrimp were located. Within the FCAs, access is regulated, proceeds are pooled, vessels are directed as to where and when they can fish to synchronize harvest across the year in order to maximize revenues, and the FCA markets the shrimp. This TURF most resembles the sole ownership conditions outlined by Scott (1955).[29]

THE CHIGNIK ALASKA FISHERY COOPERATIVE

We now turn to our last example of common property with a case that was successful in addressing open-access losses but, as with livestock

---

[27] H. Uchida and M. Watanobe, "Walleye Pollack (Suketoudara) Fishery Management in the Hiyama Region of Hokkaido, Japan," in Townsend, Shotton, and Uchida (2008, 163–174).

[28] Although in this case, a short-lived species seems to promote management. It could go the other way, as short-lived species may be more prone to environmental shocks (el Nino).

[29] The other TURFs discussed in the Townsend, Shotton, and Uchida (2008) volume include S. Suenago, "Sandfish Resource Co-Management in Akita Prefecture, Japan," (191–200); M. Tomiyama, T. Komatsu, and M.Makino, "Sandeel Fisheries Governance in Ise Bay, Japan" (201–210); and M. Makino, "Marine Protected Areas for the Snowcrab Bottom Fishery off Kyoto Prefecture, Japan" (211–220).

Figure 4.4. A Sakuraebi Vessel within the Successful Japanese TURF.
Source: H. Uchida and O. Baba (2008) "Fishery Management and the Pooling Arrangement in the Sakuraebi Fishery in Japan" in Townsand, Shotton, and Uchida eds (2008) 175–190, 178.

associations, was not durable. In this case, internal distributional conflicts undermined what were otherwise effective arrangements and led to their rejection by the courts.

Fishery cooperatives that have exclusive access to a particular fishing area and the ability to coordinate among their members are also examples of common property, which have the potential to increase rents over government regulation of licenses, fishing seasons, and total allowable catch. The Chignik Alaska Salmon Cooperative operated between 2002 and 2004. Prior to the cooperative, approximately 100 independent purse seine license holders competed for a share of the fishery-wide allowable catch. The Alaska Board of Fisheries, as the state regulatory body, granted the cooperative a share of the total allowable catch with the remainder left for competitive harvest under state regulation. The co-op and the remaining independents were assigned different fishing times and each sector's season was closed when its share of the total harvest was reached. In this way, the co-op and its members were effectively granted sole use rights to the fishery for a period of time. Each new co-op member signed a one-year contract granting the co-op the right to manage fishing effort (when, where, how much, and whether or not the vessel would be used).

The cooperative reduced member fishing by limiting the active number of permits and vessels. The proportion of permits actively fished within the cooperative ranged from only 25 percent to 28 percent and, as a result, the overall portion fished in the Chignik fishery fell from 94 percent in 2001 to 41 percent in 2002. Independent fishers did not reduce effort and the proportion of their permits fished ranged from 92 percent to 100 percent between 2002 and 2004. Additionally, the cooperative allowed only more skilled fishers with lower costs to fish, and this action increased overall rents in the cooperative, which were pooled among all members. Cooperative fishers also coordinated on the location of fishing in order to reduce costs. Because the co-op season was not competitive, its members could wait until the salmon migrated close to shore or congregated in rivers during low tide, rather than having to intercept them further out in the sea before other fishers caught them. Further, the co-op spread harvest during its season so that more valuable fresh fish could be caught and shipped, rather than racing to catch and freeze them before they were caught by competitors.

As a result, the co-op's season before its share of the total allowable catch was met was lengthened by thirty-two days, a 48 percent increase from non-co-op years. Members also cooperated to hold fish in net pens to keep them fresh until they could be processed and thereby manage daily harvest to meet exact targets. Independent harvesters had no ability for this type of valuable collective action. Finally, co-op members shared information and inputs in harvest, something which is also infeasible in an open access or regulated setting where fishers compete until the total allowable catch is exhausted.

All in all, the co-op increased the value of a fishing permit in the Chignik fishery by $48,814, or over 26 percent, of the mean value of permits between 1998 and 2008, excluding co-op years. Its success was rewarded by the Alaska Board of Fisheries, which increased its overall share of the total allowable catch. This action disadvantaged independents and they filed a lawsuit challenging the legality of co-op. It was disbanded by the court in 2005.[30] Hence, this example of a valuable common property regime was sidetracked by distributional conflicts and external judicial rulings. With the loss of the co-op the fishery was once again placed at more risk.

---

[30] Deacon, Parker, and Costello (2013).

CONCLUSION

In this chapter we have described how local arrangements emerge through common property to mitigate open-access losses. Common property, as with the most effective private property regimes, develops as a bottom-up institution whereby actual users with a history of resource exploitation and information devise arrangements to limit competition and enhance resource rents. As we have discussed, common property is durable under special conditions. Where these are met, it has impressive records of success, and in this manner justifies the critics of Garrett Hardin who had overlooked the strengths of this institution in his call for coercive government regulation or private property rights.

Even so, common property arrangements are vulnerable to exogenous shocks, especially those that increase resource values or lower extraction or use costs, because these invite entry, bringing parties that are not part of the original community contract or defection. Common property regimes are susceptible to neglect or override by governments in response to influential constituencies. Common property may be more exposed than private property to such intervention and expropriation because individual ownership and responsibilities are more diluted. Individual owners bear the full costs of regulatory overreach, but with common property, these costs are spread among all group members. Accordingly, organizational structure is critical for protecting communal interests, and the effectiveness of this structure in turn depends on the same factors that influence successful collective action. Although common property relies more on homogeneity, private property and markets can accommodate heterogeneity and external shocks. Indeed, this is one of the key advantages of markets.

5

The Politics of Property Rights

When property rights to valuable environmental and natural resources exist, there are many potential benefits. It is possible to restrict competitive entry to avoid the losses of open access, to encourage long-term investment in the resource (including conservation), to promote exchange, which can channel the resource to higher-valued uses, and to avoid wasteful and potentially divisive conflict that occurs when valuable resources are open to all. Property rights – common and private – are useful as alternatives to government regulation for many environmental and natural resource problems. They may be the low-cost option, relative to regulation or tax policies, and they may better align users' incentives with conservation or other mitigation goals.[1]

Even with these advantages, property rights often are resorted to late in resource use after many of the rents have been dissipated from excessive exploitation. For example, in 1973, fishery economist Francis Christy called for the use of individual transferable quotas (ITQs) as property rights to the right to fish within an overall total allowable catch (TAC) to avoid overfishing.[2] Serious adoption of ITQs did not occur for some 20 years when they were put into place in Iceland

---

[1] A case in point that we examine in more detail involves comparison of the costs of meeting Clean Air Act objectives via regulation to mitigate the losses of SO_2 emissions in the United States as compared to the use of tradable emission permits. See Nathaniel O. Keohane (2007), "Cost Savings from Allowance Trading in the 1990 Clean Air Act: Estimates from a Choice-Based Model," in Jody Freeman and Charles D. Kolstad, eds., *Moving to Markets in Environmental Regulation*, New York: Cambridge University Press, 194–229.

[2] Rögnvaldur Hannesson, 2004, *The Privatization of the Oceans*, Cambridge: MIT Press, 71.

and New Zealand.[3] Similarly, the notion of tradable emission permits as property rights to reduce air pollution was put forward by Thomas Crocker in 1966 and by J.H. Dales in 1968, but their adoption also took another 30 years.[4] Further, when property rights are adopted, they often are limited. ITQs and emission permits in the United States are not legal property rights subject to takings protection, but use rights, subject to reassignment or termination by the government. Trading in ITQs is restricted to certain parties and the quantity of quotas that can be held. These limitations on property rights reduce the ability of environmental markets to more fully address the losses of the common pool.[5] The question is why? In this chapter, we explore the political economy of property rights.

When property rights are implemented, they require government recognition and enforcement if the resource is valuable enough to attract continued competitive entry and use. Governments endorse informal common property regimes, giving them official definition and support.[6] Governments also recognize private property rights, enforcing them with the police power of the state, resolving disputes through the judicial system, and promoting exchange by enforcing contracts.[7] Once government is part of the process, however, politics becomes critical in understanding when and how property rights emerge. To meaningfully mitigate the losses of open access, property rights require exclusion. Some parties must be denied or restricted in their use of a previously open resource. It has to be so, otherwise overuse continues. Excluded parties may object to the rights allocation and the new distribution of wealth associated with it, especially if the value of the

---

[3] Hannesson (2004, 171).

[4] Thomas D. Crocker(1966), "The Structuring of Atmospheric Pollution Control Systems," in H. Wolozin, ed., *The Economics of Air Pollution*, New York: W.W. Norton, 61–68; J.H. Dales (1968), *Property and Prices*, Toronto: University of Toronto Press.

[5] For a discussion of the legal condition of property rights in U.S. fisheries, see Mark Fina and Tyson Kade (2012), "Legal and Policy Implications of the Perception of Property Rights in Catch Shares," *Washington Journal of Environmental Law and Policy* 2: 283–328.

[6] See Elinor Ostrom (1990), *Governing the Commons*, New York: Cambridge University Press, 101.

[7] The economic history of property rights recognition and the politics involved in western U.S. natural resources is outlined in Gary D. Libecap, 2007, "The Assignment of Property Rights on the Western Frontier: Lessons for Contemporary Environmental and Resource Policy," *Journal of Economic History* 67(2): 257–291.

resource rises with the establishment of rights, which of course is the objective. The resource is now more attractive and they are restricted from it. Questions of equity arise, politics can intervene, and outcomes can emerge that narrow property rights and their ability to confront the tragedy of the commons.

CONFLICT OVER PROPERTY RIGHTS

Before examining some of the conceptual arguments relevant for understanding the political economy of property rights, we provide two examples of how political factors have affected the development and use of property rights to address environmental problems. These examples forcefully show how equity or fairness issues can clash with efficiency or improvements in the quality, quantity, and allocation of the resource stock.

The Mitchell Slough

When the Bitterroot Valley of western Montana was settled in the mid-to-late-nineteenth century, farmers established priority claims (called prior appropriation water rights) by constructing diversion dams, head gates, and canals to deliver water to their crops. This process was necessary in the semi-arid West for bringing water from streams and other sources to more remote areas where it was required for production, such as irrigated agriculture and mining.[8] The Mitchell Slough, constructed in the 1860s as an irrigation ditch, is a classic example in which irrigators created value by diverting water from the Bitterroot River and using it as an input for their apple orchards, hay meadows, and other irrigated crops. As the value of water and land for recreation rose in the late twentieth century relative to its value for irrigation, riparian landowners along the upper reaches of the irrigation ditch saw new possibilities to create value. To do so, they joined together,

---

[8] For examination of the efficiency of early water rights through prior appropriation in the West, see Mark T. Kanazawa (1998), "Efficiency in Western Water Law: The Development of the California Doctrine, 1850–1911," *Journal of Legal Studies* 27: 159–185. See also, Charles W. McCurdy (1976), "Stephen J. Field and Public Land Law Development in California, 1850–1866: A Case Study of Judicial Resource Allocation in Nineteenth-Century America," *Law and Society Review* 10(2): 235–266.

Figure 5.1. Mitchell Slough – Before Reclamation, After Reclamation, and After Court Decision.
Source: Personal photos of authors.

and invested approximately $1 million per mile to reclaim the ditch by turning it into a productive trout fishery.[9] Their investments included creating meanders in the ditch's water flow, developing spawning beds, adding riffles in the stream, and providing bank cover necessary for improved trout habitat. They planned to use the fishery for their purposes.

With access to the reclaimed irrigation canal, now a trout stream, limited by trespass laws, the landowners captured most of the value through personal enjoyment and higher property values. Nonetheless, some value accrued to other anglers because trout that spawned and grew in the Mitchell Slough could migrate freely into the Bitterroot River where open public access is allowed by Montana law.

As the fishery developed, following the investment in habitat, more nonowners sought access to the fishery. They argued that the Mitchell Slough was historically part of the Bitterroot River and therefore, under the Montana Constitution, it was open access by law. The state of Montana places naturally-flowing streams into the public domain, and hence, available to all citizens. The question was whether or not the property owners along Mitchell Slough had the right to block citizen use. If the waterway was manmade as an irrigation ditch, they did; if the waterway was initially part of the river, they did not. This was the issue around which the battle was waged.

The desire of citizens to fish this newly-valuable fishery is understandable. So are the implications of open access. Rather than respecting property rights to the reclaimed irrigation ditch and its trout, in the 1980s a series of court battles began contesting whether riparian

[9] See   http://missoulanews.bigskypress.com/missoula/the-battle-for-mitchell-slough/Content?oid=1135390.

landowners along natural waterways could limit recreational access to water. Politicians joined in, supporting numerous and influential sports and fishing groups that opposed the restriction. The battle continued for almost 20 years. Although a lower court initially sided with the landowners, the Montana Supreme Court reversed the ruling in 2008 on the grounds that the Mitchell Slough was part of the Bitterroot River and therefore accessible under Montana law.[10]

The upshot of the court's ruling was to weaken the property rights of private land and water owners and to authorize entry to the fishery they had created. As additional trout fishers began fishing in the reclaimed waters, the incentives of landowners changed. Facing the loss of fish and privacy, the owners reversed the Mitchell Slough back to an irrigation ditch. They shut off the flow of water from the river through the Mitchell Slough except when necessary for irrigation. Without a continuous flow of water throughout the year, some spawning beds dried up and some pools lacked sufficient oxygen for trout survival. In short, legal open access diminished alternative water values potentially created by more secure property rights. As landowner Ken Siebel put it in a letter to Montana Governor Judy Marz in 2003, "If the ditch is opened to the public, there will be no winners. We would prefer to have the Mitchell revert to its former condition than sacrifice the security of our homes."[11] Because of the small area involved, there was the possibility of a negotiated agreement between landowners and fishers, had property rights been respected. Some additional fishers might have been granted access under conditions stipulated by the landowners, but not all could have been. Otherwise, resource values would have been degraded. Once the rights were rejected, there was no basis for negotiation. No one could be excluded and open access reigned, even though the fish stock was lost.

Mono Lake

The controversy over water rights in Mono Lake in California provides another example of how equity issues and the politics behind

[10] Bitterroot River Protective Association, Inc. v. Bitterroot Conservation District, 2008 MT 377.
[11] Quoted in http://missoulanews.bigskypress.com/missoula/the-battle-for-mitchell-slough/Content?oid=1135390.

Figure 5.2. Mono Lake and the Los Angeles Aqueduct.
Source: Google Images-Mono Lake: http://gocalifornia.about.com/od/top
picturegallery/ig/Mono-Lake-Pictures/. Los Angeles Aqueduct: http://maven
sphotoblog.com/2011/04/15/los-angeles-aqueduct-cascades-facility/.

them can undermine property rights and the possibilities for improved
resource values. Between 1930 and 1940, the Los Angeles Department of Water and Power (LADWP) acquired the water rights from
landowners along the four tributaries, Rush, Lee Vining, Parker, and
Walker creeks, that fed Mono Lake, an alkaline and hypersaline body
of water, 300 miles northeast of the city. The landowners held riparian water rights under California law that gives all landowners whose
property is adjoining to a body of water the right to make reasonable
use of it. If there is not enough water to satisfy all users, allotments
are generally fixed in proportion to frontage on the water source. These
rights cannot be sold or transferred other than with the adjoining land,
and water normally cannot be transferred out of the watershed because
of impairment to downstream riparian rights holders.

In this case, the LADWP bought all of the land in order to mitigate any downstream effects.[12] The agency received permits from the
State Water Resources Control Board to appropriate the water for
urban use through the Los Angeles Aqueduct. At least until the 1960s,
Mono Lake was not highly valued among the general population and
urban water use was seen as the highest and best valued use. Between
1940 and 1970, when a second aqueduct was completed, an average of

[12] Gary D. Libecap (2007), *Owens Valley Revisited: A Reassessment of the West's First
Great Water Transfer*, Palo Alto: Stanford University Press, 133–135 for a discussion
of the acquisition of water rights. Riparian water rights are described in David H.
Getches (1997), *Water Law in a Nutshell*, 3rd Ed., St. Paul: West Publishing.

57,067 acre feet (326,000 gallons per acre foot) was exported to Los Angeles annually. Depending on their uses, an acre foot can support 1 to 2 families per year. When a second aqueduct was completed in 1970, exports to the city jumped to 100,000 acre feet or more through 1975 to meet growing urban demand. By that year, the Mono Basin alone was supplying about 15 percent of Los Angeles's water, supplementing that from the Owens Valley, and the flow of both generated electric power as the water moved through the Los Angeles canal system, driven by gravity flow.[13]

Over time, the tributary stream diversions and related water exports had adverse effects on Mono Lake and its surroundings. Between 1941 and 1981, the lake's level fell about 46 feet and its surface area receded from 90 to 60 square miles.[14] In reaction, beginning in 1979, conservation groups, including the National Audubon Society, Friends of the Earth, the Sierra Club, and the Mono Lake Committee sued to curtail Los Angeles's use of Mono water, ultimately citing the public trust doctrine.[15] In 1983, in *National Audubon Society v. Superior Court* (33 Cal 3d 419), the California Supreme Court charged the State Water Resources Control Board with monitoring water use and re-allocating it in a manner consistent with the public trust.

The 1983 ruling effectively rejected the LADWP's private water rights for urban consumption and made the water a public or open resource. Under the court's interpretation of the public trust doctrine, the regulatory agency was to review water use and reallocate it periodically so as to be consistent with public welfare. How the State Water Resources Control Board would make this determination, however,

[13] See, Libecap (2007, 132–153), for a general discussion of the Mono Basin controversy.
[14] Jedidiah Brewer and Gary D. Libecap (2009), "Property Rights and the Public Trust Doctrine in Environmental Protection and Natural Resource Conservation," *The Australian Journal of Agricultural and Resource Economics* 53: 1–17.
[15] As a legal principle, the public trust doctrine historically had applied narrowly to the right of the public to access navigable waterways without being impeded by private riparian owners. Although there had been controversial, limited extension of the doctrine in the nineteenth century to public ownership of some tidelands and subsurface lakebeds, the notion that the public had superior rights to non-navigable waters, wildlife and other natural resources that were held in trust by the state, as suggested by Professor Sax and others in the late twentieth century, represented a profound expansion of the doctrine. See Joseph Sax (1970), "The Public Trust Doctrine in Natural Resources Law: Effective Judicial Intervention," *Michigan Law Review*: 471–566.

remained an open question. Accordingly, the ruling did not resolve conflicting demands over Mono Lake's water that was valuable to the city of Los Angeles as well as to recreational fishing groups and others concerned about the future of the lake.

In 1993, the LADWP predicted that the long-term costs of replacing Mono water could be $1 billion.[16] This figure did not include the costs of stranded, non-deployable capital in water export and hydro-electric generation. Because so much was at stake in the reallocation of the water without full compensation, the LADWP invested in efforts to advance its respective position in the all-or-nothing battle over rights to the water.[17] At the same time, environmental and sports groups sought permanent, judicial reassignment of the tributary waters to the lake.[18] Litigation continued, and in 1994, water diversions finally were halted by the State Water Resources Control Board until the lake's level could rebound to a target of 6,377 feet.[19] It has been estimated that lake level targets will not be met until 2021.[20]

All told, it took nearly 20 years and millions of dollars in judicial battles among the antagonists to decide the matter, and all the while, Mono's level was dropping. There was the potential for negotiated trade of some water, however, because the parties had very different costs and benefits in the outcome. LADWP rate payers bore direct costs in covering the costs of the lost capital, electricity generation, and new water sources. There also were environmental tradeoffs because alternative water from the Colorado River Basin required pumping for delivery to Los Angeles and subsequent purification, at high energy cost and associated greenhouse gas emissions. Advocates for retention of water in the Mono Basin devoted time and effort, often pro bono. Accordingly, the groups that wanted more water retained for the

---

[16] John Hart (1996), *Storm over Mono: The Mono Lake Battle and the California Water Future*, University of California Press, 162.

[17] In 1991, LADWP estimated that it had spent approximately $12 million for outside lawyers and consultants since 1979. Hart (1996, 176).

[18] It is not obvious that the judicial remedy was in society's interests. The advocacy groups did not have to bear the opportunity costs of the water that was shifted from urban users, nor of the infrastructure for transporting it. In this sense, the water was reintroduced into the common pool.

[19] Hart (1996, 171). There had been various court injunctions prior to that time limiting the export of water from the Mono Basin.

[20] Craig A. Arnold (2004), "Working Out an Environmental Ethic: Anniversary Lessons From Mono Lake," *Wyoming Law Review* 4(1): 1–55.

lake and its tributary streams might have bargained with the LADWP based on its property rights to the water and achieved partial resolution for their objectives far more quickly and at lower overall cost.[21] The conflict, however, became so politicized that neither politicians, nor judges were willing to recognize Los Angeles' water rights. Once property rights were rejected, the basis for bargaining was lost.

Unfortunately, these sorts of battles are all too common, costly, and, in many cases, ineffective in providing environmental quality. With these examples in mind, we now turn to the political economy of property rights allocation.

THE POLITICAL ECONOMY OF PROPERTY RIGHTS

The more secure, durable, and complete are property rights, the more effective they are for eliminating the losses of the common pool. Property rights include the right to investment and use privileges, to the long-term stream of benefits and costs associated with them, to transfer ownership to others, including heirs, and to exclude parties from the resource (otherwise it reverts to open access). As such, the assignment of property rights has clear distributional implications. Even if ownership raises resource values, there are changes in wealth and political and social standing among the population.[22] Disagreements over the division of property rights can be mitigated if it is consistent with historical use, if it appears to be just, or if compensating payments from expected winners to expected losers are made.[23]

Distributional conflicts are the essence of politics and therefore potentially mold formally created rights. For most environmental and

---

[21] We recognize that there are potential bargaining problems in settings such as this, but the path chosen was obviously a contentious and costly one. With the option of selling water has an opportunity cost, the LADWP had incentives to make adjustments. And because the agency is also a political institution, it would have had political motives for reaching some accommodation. One reason for the long and costly battle was that the opponents to the LADWP's withdrawals had multiple motivations that made resolution more difficult. Most opponents primarily disputed the city's water rights. Others also wanted to keep more water in Mono Lake and its tributaries for recreational and amenity purposes.

[22] Gary D. Libecap (1989), *Contracting for Property Rights*, New York: Cambridge University Press, 17–19.

[23] Distributional conflicts also arise in common property settings, but there, conditions exist for mitigation – small numbers, homogeneous populations, similar resource management objectives, trust, and common norms of behavior.

resource issues, there are numerous constituencies involved, making it necessary for politicians to balance competing interests. To maximize overall political support, politicians direct benefits to influential parties, while reducing perceived costs to other citizens.[24] In dealmaking, some of the gains from an idealized property rights setting are lost as property rights are modified or limited. Whether or not the final resolution raises resource values depends on the adjustments made in political negotiations. We will see these tradeoffs in the examples presented in this and the following chapters. As Coase's analysis implies, when transaction costs are positive, property rights are never whole, compensation to aggrieved parties is unlikely to be fully sufficient, monitoring is incomplete, and rent dissipation is never fully constrained. Transaction costs also hold for government regulation and tax policies in the form of lobbying, log rolling, and other political negotiation and government enforcement costs. They may be higher than those for property rights and environmental markets in achieving environmental goals. As a result, in all cases second-best solutions exist and the goal is to achieve the outcome that most advances environmental and natural resource quality and value.

These distributional implications of establishing formal property rights are clearly illustrated in fisheries where there finally has been movement toward adoption of rights-based management.[25] Despite regulatory limits on the number of vessels, seasons, and equipment, stocks in many fisheries have continued to drop.[26] At very low levels of biomass, their commercial and biological viabilities are placed

---

[24] See Sam Peltzman (1976), "Toward a More General Theory of Regulation," *Journal of Law and Economics* 19(2): 211–240; Gary S. Becker (1983), "A Theory of Competition among Pressure Groups for Political Influence," *Quarterly Journal of Economics* 98(3): 371–400.

[25] Donald R. Leal, ed. (2005), *Evolving Property Rights in Marine Fisheries*, Lanham, MD: Rowman and Littlefield. For a discussion of some threats to fishery property rights see Bill Chameides (2011), "Progress in Solving Fisheries Problems Threatened: Could a New House Bill undo the 2006 Fix to Our Fisheries Problem?" *Scientific American* October 3, http://www.scientificamerican.com/article.cfm?id=progress-in-solving-fisheries-probl.

[26] Frances R. Homans and James E. Wilen (1997). "A Model of Regulated Open Access Resource Use," *Journal of Environmental Economics and Management* 32: 1–21 argue that regulation without a clear rights structure can lead to greater rent dissipation than open access.

at risk.[27] When regulation has proven ineffective, individual transferable quotas and other forms of catch shares have been adopted.[28] Nevertheless, not everyone will necessarily win with the creation of property rights, and hence, some will oppose this institutional change. Some fishers (highliners), who have adapted well to open access, may be concerned that more formal property rights will not reflect their special skills, and if there are restrictions on trading rights, these fishers could lose relative to the *status quo* because they cannot acquire sufficient quota their skills merit.[29] Additionally, sports fishers and commercial fishers often compete for fishing property rights.[30] Their interests may be so different that they cannot agree on a property rights distribution to protect the fishery. In the Red Snapper fishery of the Gulf of Mexico, the recreational sector that includes charters consistently exceeds its quota. This practice undermines the commercial IFQ (individual fishing quota) program. As the stock falls, both groups suffer, but agreement on effective management has been elusive. With limited compliance and variable stock conditions, there has been much uncertainty about the effectiveness of any property rights arrangement, reducing its attractiveness.[31]

Moreover, establishing property rights and reducing open-access competition lowers the demand for some inputs as owners cut back on

[27] Two examples are the California sardine fishery and the Newfoundland cod fishery. See John Radovich (1982), "The Collapse of the California Sardine Fishery: What Have We learned?" *California Cooperative Oceanic Fishery Investigative Report* 23: 56–78 and Mark Kurlansky (1997), *Cod: A Biography of the Fish That Changed the World*, New York: Walker.

[28] Christopher Costello, Steven D. Gaines, and John Lynham (2008), "Can Catch Shares Prevent Fisheries Collapse?" *Science* September 19, 321(5896): 1678–1681; Ragnar Arnason (2008), "Iceland's ITQ System Creates New Wealth," *The Electronic Journal of Sustainable Development* 1(2); Richard G. Newell, James N. Sanchirico, and Suzi Kerr (2005), "Fishing Quota Markets," *Journal of Environmental Economics and Management* 49: 437–462.

[29] For an example in the Gulf Coast shrimp fishery, see Ronald N. Johnson and Gary D. Libecap (1982), "Contracting Problems and Regulation: The Case of the Fishery," *American Economic Review* 72(5): 1005–1022.

[30] See John Carpenter (2005), "Halibut Charters Face Prospect of IFQs," *Morning Edition* May 18. http://www.ifqsforfisheries.org/news/news_morningedition.php.

[31] For example, many red snapper fishers in the Gulf of Mexico fishery resisted the adoption of share quotas, in this case, IFQs or individual fishing quotas, until they observed how they worked in another fishery – British Columbia groundfish IFQs. See Hoyt Childers (2009), "Management Regime Shift," *National Fisherman* April, http://www.ifqsforfisheries.org/news/news_nationalfisherman09.php.

their use of capital (vessels and equipment), labor (crews), and processing (preparing frozen or canned fish) as part of the cost savings inherent in ownership. Those input owners and processors for whom demand is reduced resist formal property rights unless they are compensated in some manner. For instance, adoption of a property rights system in 1991 in the British Columbia Halibut fishery allowed for longer fishing seasons, delivery of fresh fish to market for longer periods, and fewer vessels and crews. Accordingly, the demand for labor and vessels fell as did the need for processers who previously had frozen and stored fish caught when seasons were shorter.[32] These parties were made worse off, while the overall fishery began to flourish.[33] It is not surprising that these interests opposed the property rights system. Another and related distributional outcome is that with exchange of tradable fishing property rights the nature and composition of the industry can change, with a shift toward larger vessels based in more remote ports. Local fishing communities are especially sensitive to the consolidation of ownership and the potential for the fleet to move elsewhere.[34] Their political representatives often successfully seek restrictions on transferability.[35]

As a result of these factors, there may be many resource users who desire to keep things as they are and oppose the move to property rights, even with open-access losses, unless there are important concessions. These concessions, such as limits on ownership, trade,

[32] R. Quentin Grafton, Dale Squires, and Kevin J. Fox (2000), "Private Property and Economic Efficiency: A Study of a Common-Pool Resource," *The Journal of Law and Economics* 43(2), 679–713, 685 and Keith E. Casey, Christopher M. Dewees, Bruce R. Turris, and James E. Wilen (1995), "The Effects of Individual Vessel Quotas in the British Columbia Halibut Fishery," *Marine Resource Economics* 10: 211–30.

[33] Another example that we analyze in more detail later involves resistance to the establishment of a fishing cooperative that reduced the number of vessels and fishing pressure and encouraged coordinated fishing effort. Those who did not join the cooperative successfully challenged it in court and it was dismantled along with the benefits provided. Robert T. Deacon, Dominic P. Parker, and Christopher Costello (2013), "Reforming Fisheries: Lessons from a Self-Selected Cooperative," *Journal of Law and Economics* 56(1): 83–125.

[34] Rögnvaldur Hannesson (2005), "The Privatization of the Oceans," in Leal (2005 25–48, 42).

[35] For a forceful discussion of the need to restrict transferability and to protect fishing communities, see Bonnie J. McCay (2011), "Enclosing the Fishery Commons," in Daniel H. Cole and Elinor Ostrom, eds., *Property in Land and Other Resources*, Cambridge, MA.: Lincoln Institute, 219–251.

duration, and security of the property rights granted, inhibit their ability to address open access and the added resource values that can be created through them.[36]

The fact that not everyone will benefit from establishing property rights creates a challenge for politicians who must identify who is likely to be harmed and is influential enough to impose political costs unless their concerns are addressed. To the extent that these parties are well-entrenched, cohesive, and wealthy, or sufficiently numerous and politically active within a jurisdiction, no politician can ignore their demands while considering property rights solutions.[37] If property rights are to be effective, the key challenge for politicians is to avoid serious compromises in the nature of the rights assigned. Regulatory agency officials face the same pressures as they are often involved in the process of establishing and regulating formal property rights. Bureaucrats work in communities, and the costs they face in their daily activities are affected by community support. Further, their agency's budgets and mandates are subject to political bargaining in annual congressional budget reviews.[38] For instance, listing a species as endangered under the Endangered Species Act can have important repercussions for landowners whose property rights are curtailed by regulations designed to protect critical habitat. Ando (1999) has shown

---

[36] Rögnvaldur Hannesson (2004), *The Privatization of the Oceans*, Cambridge, MA: MIT Press, 173. Additionally, see the discussion of efforts to require crab fishers in Alaska to deliver 90 percent of their catch to a select group of processors under a proposed IFQ system in Donald R. Leal and Michael De Alessi (2003), "Processor Quotas Threaten IFQs," *Anchorage Daily News* December 30.

[37] The classic works on interest groups and interest group politics in economics are Mancur Olson (1965), *The Logic of Collective Action* Cambridge, MA: Harvard University Press; James M. Buchanan and Gordon Tullock (1962), *The Calculus of Consent*, Ann Arbor, MI: University of Michigan Press; Becker (1983); Peltzman (1976); and George J. Stigler (1971), "The Theory of Economic Regulation," *Bell Journal of Economics and Management* 2: 3–21. In political science, see Harold D. Lasswell (1936), *Politics: Who Gets What, When, How?* New York: McGraw Hill; Barry Weingast and William Marshall (1988), "The Industrial Organization of Congress; or, Why Legislatures, like Firms, are not Organized as Markets," *Journal of Political Economy* 96 (February): 132–168; Kenneth Shepsle and Barry Weingast (1982), "Institutionalizing Majority Rule," *American Economic Review* 72: 367–371; and Kenneth Shepsle and Barry Weingast (1987), "The Institutional Foundations of Committee Power," *American Political Science Review* 81: 85–104.

[38] For more on this, see Ronald N. Johnson and Gary D. Libecap (1994), *The Federal Civil Service and the Problem of Bureaucracy*, Chicago: University of Chicago Press, 4–10, 154–176.

that public opposition or support can substantially slow or hasten the process of listing candidate species under the Endangered Species Act.[39]

Assuming that politicians and bureaucrats can determine who the winners and losers are when property rights are established, they must find ways to pay off the latter to defuse their opposition. And after they determine who to pay, they must decide the form, duration, and amount of payment. Those who do not receive property rights or are made worse off as a result of a decrease in the demand for their inputs may receive subsidies, buyouts, or favorable tax treatment. Some transfer arrangements are more efficient than others. For example, in fisheries the buyout of excess vessels and licenses from vessel boat owners can mitigate political opposition to improved fishery management while reducing pressure on the stock. Buyouts can be by governments or by conservation organizations.[40]

An interesting example of the use of buyouts to mitigate opposition while reducing fishing effort involves collaboration among fishers, the Nature Conservancy and Environmental Defense in the adoption of three "no-trawl zones" along the central California coast, covering nearly 6,000 square miles (roughly the size of Connecticut) between Morro and Monterey Bays. This region had historically been overfished even under regulation that limited the number of trawling permits.

Following the establishment of the 200-mile exclusive economic zone, the U.S. fishery in the region expanded dramatically, with new vessels and fishers entering the industry. However, as capitalization and employment in the fishery rose, catch-per-unit of effort declined along with a precipitous drop in bottom-dwelling rockfish and groundfish stocks. Not only were fishers overharvesting, trawling was

---

[39] Amy Whritenour Ando (1999), "Waiting to be Protected under the Endangered Species Act: the Political Economy of Regulatory Delay," *The Journal of Law and Economics* 42(1, pt. 1): 29–60. Also see Dean Lueck and Jeffrey A. Michael (2003), "Preemptive Habitat Destruction under the Endangered Species Act," *The Journal of Law and Economics* 46(1):27–60 for a discussion of how the prospect of regulation can elicit changes in resource management designed to ward off controls.

[40] For a discussion of buyback schemes in fisheries, see Rita Curtis, Dale Squires, and Patrick Berthoud (2007), *Fishery Buybacks*, New York: John Wiley and Sons.

damaging the habitat essential for stock regeneration.[41] As a remedy, the Nature Conservancy and Environmental Defense proposed no-trawl zones that would create protected habitat for fish, but at the same time, reduce the size of the fishery – less space for fishing and fewer fishers and vessels. To avoid a contentious battle, fishers and the conservation groups jointly mapped out three areas for biodiversity protection and then the Nature Conservancy agreed to purchase excess trawling permits, banking half of them and leasing the rest to fishers. The lease contracts specified the types of gear and practices that could be used, locations to be fished, and species that could be caught. Not only were fishers compensated in this process, but their sustainable fishing practices could be advertised to retailers to raise product values.[42] This was a win-win property rights and market solution. The implicit property rights of fishers were recognized and bargaining was feasible.

Determining the gains from property rights, however, can be complex. The costs of open access and hence, the gains from its remedy may not be obvious at least until the problem is very severe. This can be especially true if the science regarding a natural resource or environmental problem is not conclusive. For instance, is the decline in fish catch the result of overharvest or external environmental factors, such as changes in water temperature or pollution? Or similarly, what is a reasonable rate of water withdrawal from an aquifer if the natural recharge rate, the size of the underground reservoir, and the permeability of the subsurface medium are not well understood? Non-point water and air pollution also raise questions about assigning discharge or emission rights to a single source.

The challenge of assessing the aggregate costs of an environmental or resource problem (and the benefits of reducing it) grows as the

---

[41] National Research Council, Committee on Ecosystem Effects of Fishing (2002), *Effects of Trawling and Dredging on Seafloor Habitat*, Washington D.C.: National Academy Press.

[42] Cooperation using Markets for Management on the Central California Coast. http://www.nytimes.com/2006/08/08/science/earth/08fish.html Cooperation using Markets for Management on the Central California Coast. http://www.nytimes.com/2011/11/28/science/earth/nature-conservancy-partners-with-california-fishermen.html Cooperation using Markets for Management on the Central California Coast. The Nature Conservancy: http://www.nature.org/ourinitiatives/regions/northamerica/unitedstates/california/howwework/california-coastal-and-marine-program.xml.

spatial range of the resource, number of participants, and variability of political jurisdictions increase. For mobile, global resources it may be impossible to determine specific sources of pollution or depletion or to coordinate across multiple, heterogeneous individuals, groups, agencies, and governments in collecting information about the resource and devising acceptable solutions.[43] Distributional conflicts spread across borders and their resolution requires not only negotiations between politicians and local parties, but among representatives of the countries involved. We address the problems of broader open-access conditions in Chapter 7.

With these complexities, disputes increase political risk and reduce the expected benefits to politicians of taking action. For these reasons, a political response to open access in the assignment of property rights often is not considered until the problem reaches crisis proportions. At a crisis stage, the costs of the open-access or regulatory *status quo* become much clearer, swamping distributional concerns (there are no advantages to any party from maintaining existing conditions, where there may be no future returns) and galvanizing efforts to finally resolve the problem. For example, growing overcapitalization in the New Zealand fishing industry, coupled with a sharp deterioration in the stock of many of its fisheries led to the end of intensive government regulation and the adoption of ITQs in 1986.[44]

MECHANISMS FOR ALLOCATING PROPERTY RIGHTS

With these political economy points in mind, we now turn to the ways in which property rights can be assigned. There are four main allocation rules used: pure political distribution, uniform allocation, auction, and grandfathering or first-possession.

---

[43] For an application of the problem of scope applied to wildlife populations in the U.S., Canada, and the UK, see Dean Lueck (1989), "The Economic Nature of Wildlife Law," *Journal of Legal Studies* 18(2): 291–324.

[44] Robin Connor (2001), "Initial Allocation of Individual Transferable Quota in New Zealand Fisheries," in Ross Shotton, *Case Studies on the Allocation of Transferable Quota Rights in Fisheries*, Rome: Rood and Agriculture Organization, 222–249, 223, 229, 243. See also, Basil M.H. Sharp (2005), "ITQs and Beyond in New Zealand Fisheries," in Donald R. Leal, ed., *Evolving Property Rights in Marine Fisheries*, Lanham, MD: Rowman and Littlefield, 193–211.

Political Distribution

Pure political distribution of ownership claims – be they catch shares in fisheries, rights to dispose of waste into air or water, water rights, or rights to harvest wildlife – gives tremendous discretion to politicians or bureaucrats in the allocation of resource rents. Because this method is so obviously political, it is not common in countries where the rule of law is strong and democratic processes hold politicians more accountable. Where these institutions are weaker, giving politicians and bureaucrats more leeway, rent-seeking over resource ownership is the norm. Indeed, this rent-seeking for ownership can result in the "resource curse." The curse occurs when countries with valuable, fixed natural resources do not experience economic growth on the basis of these resources because the rents from them are dissipated as politicians, bureaucrats, and their constituents compete for their value.[45]

Uniform Allocation

Uniform allocation or equal sharing rules offer some advantages over pure political allocation. Such rules avoid blatant political distribution of resource rents by offering equal access to all potential claimants. Lotteries, for example, give each claimant an equal, random draw in the assignment of rights to the resource.[46] Similarly, rules that equalize the opportunity for participation, as with homestead for distributing federal land in the continental U.S. between 1862 and 1976 and distributing Oklahoma land in 1889, discourage political rent-seeking, although they may encourage a costly race to capture.[47] Another

---

[45] Macartan Humphreys, Jeffrey D. Sachs, and Joseph E. Stiglitz, eds. (2007), *Escaping the Resource Curse*, New York: Columbia University Press. See Dominic P. Parker, Randal R. Rucker, and Peter H. Nickerson (2013), "Property Rights and Natural Resource Curses: Micro Evidence from a Tribal Fishery," working paper, Department of Agricultural and Resource Economics, University of Wisconsin, Madison.

[46] For an interesting example of the use of lotteries to allocate land and analysis of the long-run impacts of winning on subsequent generations, see Hoyt Bleakley and Joseph Ferrie (2012), "Shocking Behavior: The Cherokee Land Lottery of 1832 in Georgia and Outcomes Across Generations," working paper, Booth School of Business, University of Chicago.

[47] The Oklahoma land rush is an example of uniform allocation in that individuals were given equal chances to secure newly opened land for claiming. It also is an example of first possession or prior appropriation in that those who were first to arrive on a site

advantage of uniform allocation is that it avoids the measurement costs of verifying claims on the basis of past use or first-possession assignments discussed below. Uniform allocation rules are also comparatively simple to administer, especially when the access and use rights are short-term, such as with lotteries for annual hunting licenses. If there are no restrictions on subsequent exchange of property rights once assigned and if transaction costs are low, uniform allocation will ultimately place ownership rights in the hands of those people who value them most highly.

Despite these advantages, uniform allocation rules have not been used often to assign property rights for at least three reasons. First, there are few cases where there are no incumbents or stakeholders. Second, if there are no incumbents it may be because the resource is not sufficiently scarce to make it worth the political cost of creating and assigning ownership. Third, if uniform allocations truly offer equal access to all would-be claimants, they have little value to politicians because they have no ability to affect the distribution.

Auction

A third potential allocation mechanism is auction. Auctions are favored by many economists because they generate revenues for the treasury to be used to offset distortive effects of income taxation and because they place property rights directly into the hands of those who value them highest, thereby avoiding the transaction costs of reallocation.[48] In practice, however, auctions have been adopted more rarely than economists who espouse their virtues would expect. This

had first claim to it. Accordingly, the race itself may create losses as people compete to become better racers See Terry L. Anderson and P.J. Hill (1983), "Privatizing the Commons: An Improvement?" *Southern Economic Journal* 50(2): 438–450 and Terry L. Anderson and P.J. Hill (1990), "The Race for Property Rights," *The Journal of Law and Economics* 33(1): 177–197 for discussions of how the race for property rights can also dissipate rents.

[48] Ian W.H. Parry, Robertson C. Williams III, and Lawrence H. Goulder (1999), "When Can Carbon Abatement Polices Increase Welfare? The Fundamental Role of Distorted Factor Markets," *Journal of Environmental Economics and Management* 37: 52–84. The notion of a double dividend through an improvement in the environment and an improvement in economic efficiency from the use of environmental tax revenues to reduce other taxes such as income taxes that distort labor supply

may be because auctions are complex and difficult to organize and because the amount and distribution of revenues created by them are highly dependent on political factors.[49] Auctions are also opposed by incumbents, who may be well-organized and oppose having to pay for ownership of a resource they already use. Where they have been applied, limited auctions are used to provide some mechanisms for new entry or thin markets in cap-and-trade systems.[50]

Grandfathering

The most common allocation mechanism is grandfathering or first-possession.[51] Examples include ITQs in fisheries and SO_2 emission permits under the Clean Air Act Amendments of 1990. Similarly, most proposals for allocating CO_2 emission permits call for prorating them to existing emitters although there has been gradual movement to greater use of auctions.[52]

Grandfathering assigns ownership to incumbents who generally obtained their claim on a first-come, first-served or first-in-time, first-in-right basis. Having a direct stake in access to the resource, first possessors are important constituents in the property rights distribution because they want consideration of previous investments – physical or

and saving decisions is critically examined by Don Fullerton and Gilbert E. Metcalf (1997), "Environmental Taxes and the Double-Dividend Hypothesis: Did You Really Expect Something for Nothing?" NBER Working Paper, w6199.

[49] See the discussion by John McMillan (1994), "Selling Spectrum Rights, *Journal of Economic Perspectives* 8(3): 145–162, regarding the experimentation and costs of designing auctions for the spectrum.

[50] Virginia McConnell and Margaret Walls (2009), "U.S. Experience with Transferable Development Rights," *Review of Environmental Economics and Policy* 3(2): 288–303 discuss one case of auctions for TDRs in Chesterfield, New Jersey. In the Regional Greenhouse Gas Initiative involving 9 New England and Mid Atlantic states, CO_2 emission allowances are auctioned http://rggi.org/.

[51] Dean Lueck (1995), "The Rule of First Possession and the Design of the Law," *The Journal of Law and Economics* 38(2): 393–436; Terry Anderson, Ragnar Arnason, and Gary D. Libecap (2011), "Efficiency Advantages of Grandfathering in Rights Based Fisheries Management," *Annual Review of Resource Economics* 3:159–179.

[52] Paul L. Joskow and Richard Schmalensee (1998), "The Political Economy of Market-Based Environmental Policy: The U.S. Acid Raid Program," *The Journal of Law and Economics* 41(1): 37–83. Dallas Burtraw and David A. Evans (2009), "Tradable Rights to Emit Air Pollution," *Australian Journal of Agricultural and Resource Economics* 53(2): 59–84.

human capital – especially if these investments are in resource-specific, non-mobile assets.

There can be efficiency gains from first-possession, provided that rights are granted to first possessors in accordance with past investments and historical production so as to avoid a race for property rights.[53] Generally, first-possession rules recognize current parties, who have experience in exploiting the resource and hence, are likely to be low-cost, high-valued users because they have outcompeted less efficient parties.[54] Further, by recognizing historical production patterns and capital outlays, first-possession rules can signal security in property rights and encourage future investments. First-possession allocation also can increase resource rents if it draws on existing local knowledge and encourages production of additional information and cooperation once rights are established.[55] Finally, first-possession allocation maintains rents in the industry and thereby lowers the cost of capital and encourages investment in risky new ventures through internal financing that otherwise might not be available through external capital markets.[56]

Despite having the potential to increase resource rents, grandfathering has been criticized on several grounds. Perhaps the most often heard criticism is that grandfathering is not fair because it discriminates against new entrants and gives away the rents that rightfully belong to the public. Another criticism is that it can lead to damaging ownership concentration. Finally, determining the allocation window, or the baseline period, is often very contentious among those who would receive an allocation. More recent users naturally have more limited production records if the distribution is based on more distant periods. These criticisms reflect the distributional implications inherent in political definition and enforcement of any property rights. There is really

---

[53] For a discussion of the potential for rent dissipation in the establishment of property rights, see Anderson and Hill (1990), and David D. Haddock (1986), "First-Possession versus Optimal Timing: Limiting the Dissipation of Economic Value," *Washington University Law Quarterly* 64: 775–792.

[54] Johnson and Libecap (1982), show that heterogeneity among fishers limits rent dissipation even under open access and the rule of capture.

[55] Ronald N. Johnson (1995), "Implications of Taxing Quota Value in an Individual Transferable Quota Fishery," *Marine Resource Economics* 10(4): 327–340.

[56] For a strong argument in favor of grandfathering for dynamic benefits, see Anderson, Arnason, and Libecap (2011).

no way to avoid them, although clearly some allocation mechanisms involve fewer disputes than do others.[57]

CONCLUSION

The political economy of property rights helps explain why property rights are often implemented late in the depletion of a resource, why the rights granted through government are often constrained, and therefore why environmental markets are slow to evolve. To be sure, there are transaction costs associated with the physical measurement, bounding, and trading of property rights as explained in Chapter 3, and government intervention can help lower these costs. Centralized and standardized measurement and recordation as with the rectangular survey, the authorization of a fishery cooperative, or the 200-mile territorial limit into the ocean make definition and enforcement of property rights more feasible.[58]

Politics, however, adds other transaction costs in necessary coalition building, lobbying, and log rolling that influence property rights definition. Property rights created by government may be potentially at more risk paradoxically when they are successful and new rents and wealth emerge. Old distributional criticisms can resurrect when differential outcomes become more apparent between winners and losers. New political pressures can arise to redistribute or constrain property rights. Such redistribution can undermine the effectiveness of property rights and environmental markets. The examples that follow in Chapter 6 illustrate how well property rights can work and what can happen to environmental markets when they are attenuated.

---

[57] Steven Shavell (2007), "On Optimal Legal Change, Past Behavior, and Grandfathering," *Journal of Legal Studies* 37(1): 37–85 argues that grandfathering provides social stability and recognizes past compliance with legal rules.

[58] Gary D. Libecap and Dean Lueck (2011), "The Demarcation of Land and the Role of Coordinating Property Institutions," *Journal of Political Economy* 119(3): 426–467; Deacon et al. (2013) on fishery cooperatives; and Hannesson (2004) on the importance of the exclusive economic zone.

6

From Property Rights to Markets

Whether property rights evolve from the bottom up or are assigned directly by government, they can provide important benefits by supporting environmental markets. Chapters 3 and 4 provided examples of the evolution of informal property rights and their role in providing environmental quality. In this chapter we turn to cases where environmental markets are based on formal property rights codified through a political and legal process. The examples are water rights, conservation credits, emission allowances, and tradable fishery shares. The details illustrate how environmental markets work and the nature of the property rights underwriting them.

In all of the cases, the rights are not based on fee simple titles but instead are use privileges. This distinction is important because privileges are just that, use opportunities that can be modified, reassigned, or revoked more easily by political or judicial action than is the case with formal title. Political action occurs through Congress and regulatory agencies, and judicial review through the courts. Use privileges have no constitutional takings protections, and monetary losses from government interventions are not compensable. Although use privileges give regulatory agencies greater flexibility, they are more uncertain and can have shorter time horizons and weaker incentives for investing in or reallocating the environmental resource than can more secure formal rights. When property rights are vague, environmental markets are weakened, and more environmental benefits must come from command-and-control regulation and tax policies. We examined the problems with those approaches in Chapters 2 and 3. A major lesson of this chapter is that property rights must be protected

~~from~~ ~~regulatory~~ takings if ~~we are to harness markets to improve~~ envi-
~~ronmental~~ quality. We provide examples of successful markets, some
emerging ones, and some that have been weakened by ~~political~~ and
~~bureaucratic intervention~~. This range of experiences reveals what is
possible, what more remains, and what dangers can arise. We begin
with two successful instances regarding water.

WATER TRADING FOR INSTREAM FLOWS

Our first environmental market example involves efforts by the Freshwater Trust (formerly the Oregon Water Trust) to temporarily lease
water from farmers during late summers in order to maintain stream
levels and riparian habitat and to lower water temperatures for protecting fish stocks.[1] There are similar actions in other western states,
but Oregon has gone the furthest.[2] Water trusts are private, nonprofit
organizations that acquire water rights through leases and sales ~~from~~
~~irrigators through~~ market transactions, in order to enhance instream
flows. They are an excellent example of what can be possible for
improving environmental quality through voluntary exchange.

These instream flow markets adhere to the conditions described
by Elinor Ostrom for regional resource management to be successful.
They are local, involving small numbers of buyers and sellers or lessors
and lessees who have similar objectives to protect natural flows and
habitat. Initial transactions can be viewed with suspicion because farmers and ranchers and environmentalist have not always been allies, but
once a relationship is established, trust is built between the parties and
they engage in repeat water exchanges. The parties can observe the
results of their actions through the survival of the fish stock, and in the
case of Oregon, there can be no entry – that is, others cannot legally
divert the water released to the stream. Instream flows are recognized

---

[1] Our discussion is drawn from: Brandon Scarborough and Hertha L. Lund (2007), *Saving Our Streams: Harnessing Water Markets*. Bozeman: PERC; Terry L. Anderson and Brandon Scarborough (2011),"Oregon Water Trust: Saving Our Streams through Markets," Bozeman: PERC; Mary Ann King (2004), "Getting Our Feet Wet: An Introduction to Water Trusts," *Harvard Environmental Law Review* 28: 495–434; and Janet C. Neuman (2005), "The Good, the Bad, and The Ugly: The First Ten Years of the Oregon Water Trust," *Nebraska Law Review* 83(2): 432–484.
[2] King (2004), describes various organizations in Oregon, Washington, Montana, Colorado, and in the Great Basin states.

as a legitimate water use under Oregon law and protected from capture by downstream parties.[3]

The Oregon Water Trust was organized in 1993 as a nonprofit organization that focuses on restoring and preserving stream flows through markets.[4] It began water transactions in 1994 with its first lease and first water right purchase in 1999. Before the Trust could begin, legislation was necessary to change water rights in the state. In all western states, private water rights are maintained through beneficial use – the old notion of "use it or lose it." Water not placed into beneficial use is in the public domain and can be claimed by others. The issue that had to be addressed was whether leaving water instream rather than diverting it for irrigation or other uses could be considered a beneficial use. In 1987 Oregon adopted an instream water rights law that recognizes that water left instream for the "conservation, maintenance and enhancement of aquatic and fish life, wildlife, fish and wildlife habitat and any other ecological values" is consistent with beneficial use.[5] The instream flows legislation protected water rights and maintained existing priority dates that rank water rights for both instream flows and for traditional diversion for irrigation. Had this not been done, water leased for stream level maintenance might have been assigned a much lower priority (on the basis of the date of the transaction, rather than that of the original water right) and hence been vulnerable to diversion by other irrigators with higher-ranked claims.[6] This legislation allowed traditional irrigation water rights holders the right to lease, sell, or donate any conserved water to other parties for environmental purposes, thus creating a financial incentive for improved water use efficiency.

The push for the recognition of instream flow rights and markets came from the deteriorating state of Oregon's rivers and freshwater

---

[3] Neuman (2005, 435–437) describes the local nature of these water markets.

[4] Newman (2005, 443–467) provides an assessment of the successes of and problems encountered by the Oregon Water Trust.

[5] Neuman (2005, 476).

[6] Western water rights are based on prior appropriation and ranked according to the date of the original claim. Higher priority claims have first access to water and lower priority claims have access to any residual. See Gary D. Libecap (2011), "Institutional Path Dependence in Climate Adaptation: Coman's 'Some Unsettled Problems of Irrigation,'" *American Economic Review* 101 (February): 64–80, 69–70 for a discussion of water rights.

fish stocks. The state contains more than 115,000 miles of streams, roughly 26 percent or 30,000 miles of which fail to support aquatic life according to the Environmental Protection Agency (EPA). Moreover, following more than a century of diversions and new appropriations, many rivers and the tributaries that feed them suffer from chronically low flows, some running completely dry in late summer.

Tradable water rights facilitate lease and purchase agreements and therefore provide incentives for improvements in consumptive water use or alterations in timing of diversions that can reconnect stream segments and ensure healthy fish populations. These markets require locating willing sellers and determining prices. To develop markets, the Trust established relationships with farmers, state and federal agencies, local conservation districts, fish and wildlife biologists, tribal biologists, and local and regional conservation groups. This action built confidence, generated information about potential market partic- ipants, and provided new learning about how to exchange water in set- tings that can often be very complicated. Generally, the Trust focuses on smaller streams and tributaries where even a limited amount of additional instream water can have meaningful ecological benefits. The additional water and lower water temperatures provide sufficient flows for successful upstream travel by spawning fish and for improving habitat for juvenile fish.

The organization works to find market values for water, which can be difficult in the absence of any past transactions and limited infor- mation about the value of instream water for fish habitat. A number of factors influence price, including the value in current uses, the priority date of the water right, the physical availability of water, water qual- ity, the length of the water contract for stream flows, and the potential number of other buyers and sellers. The Trust typically uses short-term leases that provide flexibility, are lower cost than purchases, and are viewed with less skepticism among local farmers because the use of water is not permanently changed. Long-term stream protection, how- ever, may require acquisition of water rights, which can be expensive and difficult to negotiate.

With leases (renewable annually, single year, or longer-term), water owners forego use of their water for a specified period, during which time water is left instream. At the end of the lease term, the water right reverts back to its original place and purpose, usually irrigation.

Figure 6.1. Freshwater Trust and Ranchers Protecting a Stream.
Source: http://www.thefreshwatertrust.org/slide_pat-voigt.

Freshwater Trust trades have improved nearly 900 miles of streams, reaching nine of Oregon's 21 river basins and restoring nearly 53,000 acre-feet of water instream. Figure 6.2 shows the stream flow restoration projects between 1994 and 2006, expressed in cubic feet

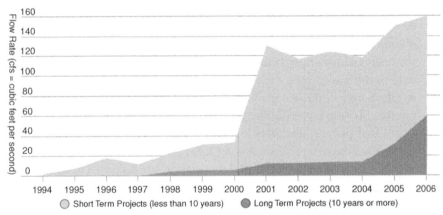

Figure 6.2. Water Transactions for Stream Flow Maintenance, Freshwater Trust.
Source: Reproduced from Terry L. Anderson, Brandon Scarborough, and Lawrence R. Watson (2012), *Tapping Water Markets*, Washington D.C.: Resources for the Future, 102–106.

per second of water protected instream.[7] Long-term contracts have increased markedly in recent years, and this trend is expected to continue as markets expand and right holders gain confidence in their use. Roughly 30 percent of protected flows are from donated rights, with the remaining 70 percent acquired through short-term lease or permanent purchase agreements.

The Freshwater Trust in Oregon illustrates how local environmental markets develop and thrive when basic conditions are met: (1) the parties share in the goal of protecting the resource; (2) there are differences in the marginal value of resource use between production and environmental quality that can be exploited to promote exchange; (3) legal recognition of environmental uses exists; (4) the parties trust one another; (5) other; long-standing resource uses are not placed at risk from the environmental trade; (6) there is a minimum of outside, bureaucratic interference that can add uncertainty and introduce regulatory complexities that did not exist prior to the exchange; and (7) there are mechanisms for buyers and sellers to find one another, bargain, and enforce agreements.

WATER TRADING IN THE COLORADO–BIG THOMPSON PROJECT OF COLORADO

The Colorado-Big Thompson (CBT) Project is a Bureau of Reclamation (BOR) water project that brings supplemental water from the Colorado River Basin on the west slope of the Rocky Mountains to the South Platte River Basin in northeastern Colorado on the east side of the mountains. It supplies about 30 percent of the region's water, and is managed by the Northern Colorado Conservancy District.[8] Figure 6.3 shows the CBT's location.

The Colorado-Big Thompson has by far the most active water market in the western United States in terms of numbers of trades and

---

[7] Cubic feet per second is a measure of rate of flow. One cubic foot of water flowing through a stream for a twenty-four hour period is the equivalent volume of roughly two acre-feet of water. Often lease agreements are expressed in CFS, representing the amount of water that will remain instream during a specified period.

[8] Charles W. Howe and Christopher Goemans (2003), "Water Transfers and their Impacts: Lessons from Three Colorado Water Markets," *Journal of the American Water Resources Association* October: 1055–1065, 1056.

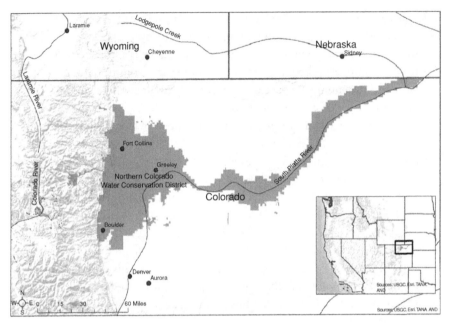

Figure 6.3. The Colorado–Big Thompson Project (Northern Colorado Conservancy District) in Colorado.
Source: U.S. Geological Survey.

sales.[9] For this reason we have more data and can illustrate the nature and timing of exchanges. The Colorado-Big Thompson Project was constructed by the Bureau of Reclamation (BOR) between 1938 and 1957. Water is pumped across the continental divide through tunnels and stored in twelve reservoirs and moved through a series of canals to agricultural, urban, and industrial users.[10] There it feeds 1.6 million acres of land in portions of eight Colorado counties. The CBT annually delivers an average of 270,000 acre feet to its members.[11] The water is allocated through tradable uniform water units, whereby each is a share of the annual amount of water available to the CBT.[12]

[9]   Libecap (2011, 71).
[10] Daniel Tyler (1992), *The Last Water Hole in the West: The Colorado-Big Thompson Project and the Northern Colorado Conservancy District*, Boulder: University of Colorado Press.
[11] http://www.ncwcd.org/ncwcd_about/about_main.asp. Accessed June 8, 2011.
[12] As discussed by Charles W. Howe, Dennis R. Schurmeier, and W. Douglas Shaw, Jr. (1986), "Innovative Approaches to Water Allocation: The Potential for Water Markets," *Water Resources Research*, 22(4): 439–445, 443, each share or unit is 1/310,000 of the water available to the Northern Colorado Conservancy District.

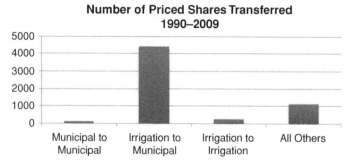

Figure 6.4. Total Water Trades by Category, Colorado–Big Thompson Project.
Source: Authors' calculations based on data in http://www.bren.ucsb.edu/news/water_transfers.htm.

The water in each unit fluctuates annually based on water supply, and all shares are adjusted in the same manner. Because shares are homogenous, transfers across users, especially across sectors, occur with minimal fees and paperwork.[13] These property rights as shares are quite different from traditional prior appropriation rights, which are not uniform. Additionally, the district administers proposed trades rather than the larger and more politically and institutionally complex Bureau of Reclamation that has many more procedural requirements and political constituencies.

Although most of the original water was assigned for agricultural use, the CBT region has a rapidly-growing number of urban users. Increasingly, urban water uses are more highly valued than agricultural applications, and urban purchases of water rights are growing as a share of total market activity. In some cases, city water agencies purchase agricultural water as insurance against drought periods to provide stable urban supplies and, when not needed, lease the water back to agriculture. Figure 6.4 shows the total number of water shares traded for various types of exchanges between 1990 and 2009 in constant 2009 dollars.[14] It is clear from the data that the most active transactions are those from agriculture to urban.

[13] Janis M. Carey and David L. Sunding (2001), "Emerging Markets in Water: A Comparative Analysis of the Central Valley and Colorado-Big Thompson Projects," *Natural Resources Journal* 41 (Spring): 283–328, 305.

[14] The data are drawn from the UCSB Bren School water transfer data set, http://www.bren.ucsb.edu/news/water_transfers.htm. The methodology involved in comparing

Number of Priced Shares Transferred

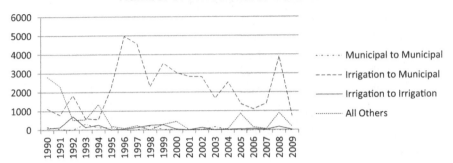

Figure 6.5. Water Trades by Category across Time, Colorado–Big Thompson Project.
Source: Authors' calculations based on data in http://www.bren.ucsb.edu/news/water_transfers.htm.

Figure 6.5 describes the patterns of trades, and again, it is evident that agricultural-to-urban transactions have been the most active over the twenty-year period.

Figure 6.6 describes the pattern of water share prices across time. Prices for all uses are comparable, as they should be when opportunity costs are incorporated, water quality is similar, and transaction costs are low. By contrast, in the Truckee Basin of Nevada, which does not have the institutional advantages of the CBT, water rights and quality are less homogeneous and conveyance facilities more limited. Hence, prices across uses are very different. There, the median price for 1,025 agriculture-to-urban water rights sales that took place between 2002 and 2009 (2008 prices) was $17,685 per acre foot, whereas for thirteen agriculture-to-agriculture water rights sales over the same period the median price was $1,500 per acre foot.[15]

Water will become more valuable in the semi-arid western states, with population growth, increased environmental and recreational demand, along with traditional uses in agriculture, residential, and industrial sectors. Any precipitation pattern shifts due to potential climate change may further constrain supplies. As these forces play out, water markets will become increasingly important. The Colorado-Big

---

sales and shorter-term lease prices is described in Jedidiah R. Brewer, Robert Glennon, Alan Ker, and Gary D. Libecap (2008), "Water Markets in the West: Prices, Trading, and Contractual Flows," *Economic Inquiry* 46(2): 91–112, 99.

[15] Libecap (2011, 65).

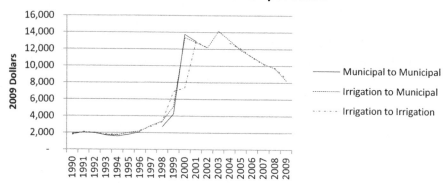

Figure 6.6. Mean Prices/Share by Category, Colorado–Big Thompson Project. *Source:* Authors' calculations based on data in http://www.bren.ucsb.edu/news/water_transfers.htm.

Thompson provides a template for what might be possible when rights are secure and tradable units are uniformly defined. Other water markets in the western United States are less well developed.[16] We now turn to another case, the markets for ecosystem services, where the environmental resource is less well-defined, markets are more limited, but where there are many potential opportunities for growth.

MARKETS FOR ECOSYSTEM SERVICES

Markets for ecosystem services cover a wide range of environmental goods, wetlands preservation, water quality improvement, open space protection, land conservation, continuation of traditional (agricultural) uses, and endangered species habitat enhancement.[17] In each case, for a market to operate, a regulatory cap is placed on the total quantity of the environmental good that must be present in a defined geographic area, and individuals or organizations are given tradable

---

[16] Brewer et al (2008) and Libecap (2011).

[17] A summary of some of the environmental benefits provided in the broad category of ecosystem services is provided in Lynn Scarlett and James Boyd (2011), *Ecosystem Services: Quantification, Policy Applications, and Current Federal Capabilities*, Discussion Paper RFF DP 11–12, Washington D.C.: Resources for the Future. See also Becca Madsen, Nathaniel Carroll, Daniel Kandy, and Genevieve Bennett (2011), *2011 Update: State of Biodiversity Markets*, Washington, D.C.: Forest Trends, 5. Available at: http://www.forest-trends.org/documents/files/doc_2848.pdf.

credits for provision of the good. These credits may be shares of the cap or physical amounts of the environmental good. Any proposed activity that reduces the total must be offset by increasing the environmental good elsewhere in the regulated area.[18] This requirement creates the opportunity for gains from trade between those wanting to use the resource in a way that reduces the quantity of the desired amenity and those who can produce an offsetting amount at a lower cost.

In order for this type of environmental market to develop, a number of conditions must be met: (1) there must be differences in abatement costs so that those obligated to comply with the environmental cap can see advantages in purchasing credits or offsets, rather than providing the amenity themselves; (2) there must be willing buyers and sellers who can locate one another at low cost; (3) there must be available price or value information, which is sometimes difficult when markets have few transactions; (4) trades must be legally recognized and enforced; and (5) there must be a minimum of bureaucratic intervention that otherwise creates uncertainty about the nature and durability of the trade. There is a variety of ecosystem service market types.

CONSERVATION EASEMENTS AND LAND TRUSTS

Land trusts and conservation easements are the two largest voluntary market approaches for ecosystem services in the United States. They provide open space amenities such as scenery, wildlife habitat, and recreational trails on private land. The Nature Conservancy is the largest trust, but more than 1,500 smaller trusts operate in local regions throughout the United States. Nationwide, the number of trusts grew

---

[18] Again, as we have noted previously, setting the cap is a command-and-control activity, subject to constituent group politics and it may or may not be socially optimal. Given that caveat, trading shares in the cap may be the low-cost option for achieving an environmental or resource objective, depending on the relative transaction costs of setting the cap and trading shares in it as compared to regulation. Further, even if there are high transaction costs in setting the cap, the key difference between a cap-and-trade system and command-and-control regulation is that reallocation is feasible, individual incentives are captured to invest in the resource, and trading can lower the overall costs of meeting the regulatory goal. Hence, as a practical matter, markets for ecosystem services offer a more efficient way of achieving regulatory mandates.

from 535 in 1984 to 1,663 in 2005.[19] Land trusts purchase private land and set it aside for amenity provision, although the land may be used for other productive activities, such as ranching, forestry, oil and gas production, or recreation. Land trusts also purchase or receive donations of conservation easements from landowners, which are binding agreements to restrict dense residential or commercial development and to regulate agricultural or forestry practices. Because easements encumber land use, market values can fall 20 to 80 percent and the difference between the regular market value and the encumbered land value represents the value of the easement.

Easements can be donated by landowners to receive chartable tax deductions or to lock the land into long-term uses that current owners desire, such as low-density livestock raising. Between 1984 and 2009, the Nature Conservancy easements grew from 98,000 acres to 2.9 million acres, and between 1984 and 2005, those held by local land trusts grew from 148,000 acres to 6.2 million acres. Property rights are transferred voluntarily from land owners to the trusts through land acquisitions and conservation easements for environmental purposes. Related activities include the federal Conservation Reserve Program, in which farmers are paid by the U.S. Department of Agriculture to keep environmentally-sensitive lands in conservation uses for ten to fifteen years. There may also be payments to reduce soil erosion, protect wetlands, improve water quality, and achieve other benefits or establish permanent conservation easements. In 2004, 14 percent of rural residence farms and 24 percent of commercial farms received some conservation payments.[20]

---

[19] Dominic P. Parker and Walter N. Thurman (forthcoming), "Conservation Easements: Tools for Conserving and Enhancing Ecosystem Services," in Robert T. Deacon, ed., *Encyclopedia of Resource, Energy, and Environmental Economics* (Natural Resources Policy Instruments Section), Amsterdam: Elsevier Publishers, working paper, Department of Agricultural and Resource Economics, University of Wisconsin Madison, 2.

[20] Scarlett and Boyd (2011, 42). James Boyd and Lisa Wainger (2003), *Measuring Ecosystem Service Benefits: The Use of Landscape Analysis to Evaluate Environmental Trades and Compensation*, Discussion Paper 01–63, Washington D.C.: Resources for the Future, provide examples of wetlands mitigation projects and valuation techniques. See also R. Scott Farrow, Martin T. Schultz, Pinar Celikkol, and George L. Van Houtven (2005), "Pollution Trading in Water Quality Limited Areas: Use of Benefits Assessment and Cost-Effective Trading Ratios," *Land Economics* 81(2): 191–205.

WATER QUALITY PERMIT EXCHANGE AND WETLAND
MITIGATION BANKS

Both of these related activities generally follow establishment of total maximum daily load (TMDL) requirements for pollution control within a watershed. This is the cap under which tradable pollution permits or mitigation credits are created. TMDLs are authorized by the Clean Water Act, and they establish maximum daily, seasonal, or annual pollution limits for municipal and industrial wastewater dischargers. They can include both point and nonpoint pollution sources although most regulation focuses on point sources that are easier to identify and control. TMDLs are set and administered by the EPA, the U.S. Army Corps of Engineers, and state water quality control agencies. Once a TMDL is established, regulators tighten discharge restrictions to reduce pollutant loads over time to meet water quality standards. Under the Clean Water Act, states compile lists of water bodies that do not fully support beneficial uses such as aquatic life, fisheries, drinking water, recreation, industry, or agriculture. These water bodies offer the greatest potential for environmental markets.

Pollutant trading programs are tools for meeting water quality goals set out in a TMDL in the most cost-effective manner. Dischargers that have lower abatement costs or unregulated land-based pollutant sources, such as farms, can "over-comply" and gain credits that can be sold directly to dischargers that have higher abatement costs or be placed in a mitigation bank, available for any party to purchase. Because point sources of pollution from industrial plants and municipalities have been regulated for forty years, marginal abatement costs are high relative to nonpoint agricultural sources that have not been regulated. This is where more low-cost opportunities for abatement exist. Although the potential for including nonpoint pollution sources in trading programs is great, there is the risk that participation will invite more intensive regulation. Understandably, many in agriculture are reluctant to take part in such markets.[21] Another risk that limits

---

[21] For a discussion, see Karen Fisher-Vanden and Sheila Olmstead (2013), "Moving Pollution Trading from Air to Water: Potential, Problems, and Prognosis," *Journal of Economic Perspectives* 27(1): 147–172, 149, 164–166. Nonpoint pollution from agriculture has not been directly regulated under federal law.

growth of water quality permit markets and mitigation banking is the prospect that agencies, such as the EPA, will backslide and lower the cap after a party expands wastewater treatment, controls pollution, or restores a wetland to sell credits. Finally, when a point-source discharger seeks to purchase credits to offset a portion of its permitted discharges, all effluent covered in the permit must be reopened for regulatory examination.[22]

Accordingly, the extent of pollution credit exchanges and mitigation banking varies across water basins and regulatory agencies. Some programs allow for trading only among dischargers that are subject to the TMDL cap, whereas others allow for trades to include unregulated parties within the watershed who agree to limit their discharges to gain transferable credits or who are paid by regulated parties to do so. Although nearly three dozen water pollution trading programs have been established in the United States, many have seen no trading at all, and few of them operate on an economically-significant scale. The EPA estimated that expanded water quality trading between point and nonpoint sources could reduce compliance costs associated with TMDL regulation at $1 billion annually between 2000 and 2015.[23]

The most common water pollution trading regimes are: bilateral trades; sole-source offsets where the discharger is granted permission to increase releases at one point if they are offset elsewhere in the same watershed; a clearinghouse where a broker links buyers and sellers of credits; mitigation banks where sellers secure credits by investing in pollution control and wetland restoration, obtain credits from regulatory agencies, and offer the credits to buyers as needed; and exchange markets where multiple buyers and sellers bargain in a recognized forum.[24]

In 2008, the Army Corps of Engineers estimated that conservation and mitigation markets involved trades valued at $1 billion per year.[25] Water quality mitigation banking also can encourage restoration of

[22] Fisher-Vanden and Olmstead (2013, 167).
[23] Fisher-Vanden and Olmstead (2013, 147, 149).
[24] Fisher-Vandan and Olmstead 92013, 151–152) and http://www.ecosystem marketplace.com/pages/dynamic/web.page.php?section=water_market&page_name =tmdl_market.
[25] Scarlett and Boyd (2011, 52).

degraded wetlands.[26] If planned development threatens to exceed a TMDL, discharge credits can be obtained from parties that have rejuvenated sites and placed credits into a bank, or the developer can secure credits through offsetting wetland improvement investments. Wetland mitigation banks got their start when President George H. W. Bush adopted a policy of no-net-loss of wetlands in 1989, followed by the Memorandum of Agreement in 1993 among various federal agencies, which established wetland mitigation banking. Since then, wetland mitigation banking has grown. According to the Institute for Water Resources, by 2000 there were at least 230 private banks with some form of bank instrument and an additional 180 state-run banks. By 2010, there were 798 active wetland and stream mitigation banks, and that number grew substantially from the previous year, as shown in Figure 6.7.

In any of these credit exchanges, there are numerous measurement requirements regarding the physical and chemical characteristics of the water and emissions in it, timing of pollution, and identification of hot spots or short-term pollution spikes that may occur even if overall pollutant loads are reduced. Trading ratios also must be established to determine how many credits must be used to offset discharges. All of these raise transaction costs and help explain why markets for ecosystem services are yet to achieve their full potential. One option for expansion is to expand the spatial scope of each market and the number of possible traders by combining multiple TMDLs across watersheds. Another option is to adjust the way in which nonpoint source mitigation is measured for credits. Currently, regulators require significantly more abatement from nonpoint sources for every credit used by point-source dischargers. Although measuring nonpoint pollution reduction is more difficult, this practice increases the cost of nonpoint-to-point source exchanges.[27]

---

[26] Linda Fernandez and Larry Karp (1998), "Restoring Wetlands through Wetlands Mitigation Banks," *Environmental and Resource Economics* 12: 323–344 and Matthew H. Bonds and Jeffrey J. Pompe (2003), "Calculating Wetland Mitigation Banking Credits: Adjusting for Wetland Function and Location," *Natural Resources Journal* 43: 961–977.

[27] Fisher-Vanden and Olmstead (2013, 165). Marc Ribaudo, Robert Johansson, and Carol Jones (2006), "Environmental Credit Trading: Can Farming Benefit," *Amber Waves* 4(1) discusses measurement problems, regulatory concerns, as well as the

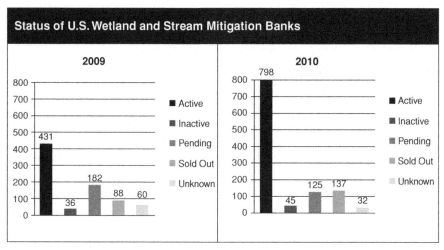

Note: The decrease in the category "unknown" is due to data "spring cleaning", in which many bank records that could not be updated or verified since 2005 were removed from our database.

Figure 6.7. Wetland Mitigation Banks.
Source: Becca Madsen, Nathaniel Carroll, Daniel Kandy, and Genevieve Bennett, (2011), *2011 Update: State of Biodiversity Markets*, Washington, DC: Forest Trends, figure on page 5. Available at: http://www.forest-trends.org/documents/files/doc_2848.pdf.

CONSERVATION BANKING

Conservation banking is used to meet the objectives of the Endangered Species Act (ESA), as administered by the U.S. Fish and Wildlife Service (USFWS) and NOAA. Generally, a critical habitat area is designed by the regulatory agency, and this serves as the cap. Within that area, private landowners, municipalities, and other parties develop species-protection strategies to set aside relevant parcels or provide conservation easements for credits that can be sold to other parties whose activities might result in the incidental taking of habitat. In 2004, credit prices ranged from $3,000 to $125,000/acre. These differences reflected variation in the quality of habitat provided in the credit and whether or not the parcel was part of a larger protected area. Accordingly, suppliers of credits transform a potential legal liability under the ESA into a financial asset, a credit that they can sell to

subsidies available under the Conservation Reserve Program that limit farmer participation. Available at http://webarchives.cdlib.org/sw1vh5dg3r/http://ers.usda.gov/AmberWaves/May07SpecialIssue/Features/Environmental.htm.

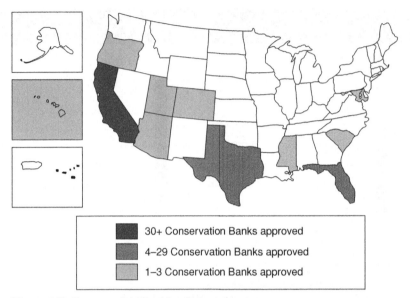

Figure 6.8. Conservation Banking States.
Source: Approved USFWS conservation banks, U.S. Fish and Wildlife Service
(2013), *Endangered Species Program*, 1. http://www.fws.gov/endangered/land-
owners/conservation-banking.html. Approved California conservation banks
are described in http://www.dfg.ca.gov/habcon/conplan/mitbank/catalogue/.

buyers. The existence of a credit bank provides for a rapid, legitmate,
and cost-effective mitigation option for other landowners who seek to
develop their properties without compromising ESA objectives.

California first set up conservation banks in 1995 under the ESA
for parcels of land protected and managed to conserve listed species.
Throughout the United States, 133 conservation banks currently protect more than 100,000 acres benefitting more than ninety listed
species. Banks range in size from twenty-five acres to 27,000 acres.[28]
The current status of conservation banking is shown in Figure 6.8. It is
limited to a handful of states.

There is a relatively modest amount of banking, given the numbers
of listed species, their geographic spread, and the potential benefits
of greater use of environmental markets. The main impediments are

---

[28] Scarlett and Boyd (2011, 56). See also Jessica Fox and Anamaria Nino-Murcia (2005),
     "Status of Species Conservation Banking in the United States," *Conservation Biology*
     19(4): 996–1007.

bureaucratic and political restrictions arising from multiple federal and state agencies involved in establishing conservation banks and in determining the mitigation provided by each credit in exchange for lost habitat (the credit ratio).

The creation of mitigation credits or the establishment of a conservation credit bank requires hiring biologists and legal consultants and often a long negotiation process with regulatory agency officials. Further, there is the risk as noted above that in providing habitat, a private landowner may reveal a previously unrecognized endangered species, leading to greater ESA regulation. Additionally, because markets are thin, there are difficulties in locating buyers and sellers for market exchange.[29]

TRADABLE DEVELOPMENT RIGHTS

Tradable development rights (TDRs) are another example of conservation credits. They can protect open space or agricultural lands near urban settings[30] and allow density to be transferred from one property to another while meeting overall open-space objectives. The property owner who purchases TDRs develops the land more densely than is permitted under baseline zoning rules and the property owner who sells TDRs maintains the land as less-developed and is compensated for doing so through the sale of TDRs. About 140 such programs are found throughout the United States. Their advantages are that they allow for voluntary exchange of development density and that those property owners who forego more commercial activities have incentives to provide open space or rural amenities.

The baseline zoning rule sets the development cap under which the TDRs are exchanged and its level is critical for setting a TDR market. If the cap is set too high, then the TDRs have little value because development can occur without them. Similarly if the zoning cap is near the

---

[29] Fox and Nino-Murcia (2005, 1001–1006).

[30] For a discussion see Keohane and Olmstead (2007, 201–202); Virginia McConnell and Margaret Walls (2009), "U.S. Experience with Transferable Development Rights," *Review of Environmental Economics and Policy* 3(2): 288–303; and Margaret Walls and Virginia McConnell (2007), *Transfer of Development Rights in U.S. Communities: Evaluating Program Design, Implementation, and Outcomes*, Washington D.C.: Resources for the Future.

desired level for the overall community and there is no demand for additional housing or commercial density, then there will be too little demand for TDRs to stimulate a market. Additionally, if the cap is too restrictive, TDR prices may be driven so high that development is driven elsewhere. Local governments may differentially zone areas that supply TDRs relative to areas that might require them in order to create a market in development rights. Accordingly, open, rural areas may have a low-density zoning rule, whereas regions near an urban fringe may have less-restrictive zoning to allow higher density but less than that which would be necessary for further urban expansion. The purchase of TDRs from the rural selling area to the more urban receiving area allows for development beyond the zoning limit, reimbursing land owners in rural areas for keeping the open character of their lands and the amenities those actions provide.

ECOSYSTEM SERVICE TRANSACTION COSTS

All of the markets for ecosystem services described here offer prospective benefits for achieving environmental quality, and amenity values are lower cost than more direct, command-and-control regulation because they elicit the incentives of users. They become a direct part of the solution by converting liabilities into opportunities and assets. At the same time, all of the examples appear to under-achieve their potentials. Here we summarize some of the transaction costs encountered in creating and expanding these environmental markets.

- Creating credit banks – To start a credit bank, the party must have up-front capital to purchase and restore the environmental asset for which a credit will be issued. As with any nascent investment, risk makes it more difficult to obtain capital. Moreover, it takes time to create a banking agreement that delays a return on investment. A survey by Fox and Nino-Murcia (2005, 1001) found that 67 percent of credit bank owners and managers reported technical and political challenges with state and federal agencies. Prior to regulatory reforms in 2008, agreement with the USFWS took an average of 2.18 years, ranging from 8 months to 6 years with a median of 2 years (Fox and Nino-Murcia, 2005, 1002). After 2008 when processes were streamlined, mitigation bank numbers grew from eighty-nine new banks in 2009 to 104 in 2010, despite the down economy.

- Certifying credits – To ensure that the resource conservation is actually occurring to offset destruction of endangered species habitat, wetlands, or other environmental values, a governmental agency must certify the credits that are issued. Agencies have considerable discretion in determining what will be certified, and discretion varies across jurisdictions. For example, habitat conservation credits can be issued under federal wetland agreements, ESA habitat conservation plans, ESA safe harbor agreements (whereby species protection is provided voluntarily, but not at the same level as more specific endangered habitat designation), and federal and state agency memoranda of understandings. All of these certification processes take time and resources.

- Establishing the exchange rate between the easement and the credit – There is seldom a one-to-one correlation between the resource destroyed and the one created or restored. Between 1993 and 2000, the Institute for Water Resources reported that permits were issued for the development of 24,000 acres of wetlands, but 42,000 acres were required for mitigation (Bonds and Pompe, 2003, 963). On the other hand, if the mitigation value of a parcel is high, the ratio is much lower. In the Wright Preservation Bank with 178.8 acres in California, for example, one habitat credit was issued for every 0.01 acre conserved because there were multiple endangered species on the the the site, including the Sebastopol meadowfoam, Burke's goldfields, and California tiger salamander.[31] There is also the question of the service area to which the credit applies, and the farther a mitigation bank is from the destroyed habitat or wetland, the lower the ratio of credits to acres mitigated.

- Monitoring the conservation easement – Conservation easements must be monitored to be effective. This includes evaluating compliance to ensure production consistent with credit authorization, determination of goals and performance toward meeting those goals, and provision of feedback information especially when there are exogenous environmental changes, such as climate. There must also be a dispute resolution process for cases where the credit owner

---

[31] http://us.speciesbanking.com/pages/dynamic/banks.page.php?page_id=7289.

and the agency disagree. To ensure continuous production and monitoring of conservation values, banking agreements often include some form of bonding, which adds to the capital costs.

- Establishing a price – The newness and diversity of conservation markets contributes to the cost of pricing conservation credits. On the demand side, there can be wide differences in the value and willingness to pay for land being disturbed. Shopping centers and housing developments were willing to pay more prior to the economic downturn, and transportation agencies received added funding from the federal government in 2009 as part of the stimulus program. On the supply side, mitigation near urban areas is more expensive than in rural areas, and restoration of endangered species habitat can be expensive if major vegetative changes are necessary. Prices are also more difficult to determine in thin markets, which was especially true in the early days of conservation trading. As these markets grow, however, prices will become more transparent and stable.
- Contiguity – This complicates matters for any of these tradable conservation credits, as several adjacent parcels may have greater environmental value than a checkerboard-patterned landscape.

Ecosystem service markets illustrate the importance of political processes for transaction costs. These markets got their start as a result of regulations that capped environmental degradation. Such caps lowered the transaction costs of determining the quantity that would be produced, even if there is no guarantee that the cap coincides with efficiency. Bureaucratic rules and discretionary changes, on the other hand, can raise transaction costs. Many landowners are unprepared to bear the financial burden of land management and property taxes during the interim negotiation time. After the agreement is signed, additional hardships can often develop as regulatory changes occur and new conservation standards have to be met on already developed land. If agencies can arbitrarily change the terms of credits or the requirements for permitting, conservation markets will be less successful. This is an example of regulatory risk. We have noted this issue above, but there is always the potential for regulatory agencies to tighten the cap when private parties set aside or recover habitat to provide credits within an existing cap. Such regulatory risk reduces the value of participation in ecosystem service markets because landowners who voluntarily provide credits may be made worse off if regulations are extended to include restrictions on land use, for which they are not compensated.

In conclusion, markets for ecosystem services offer considerable benefits in lowering the cost of achieving environmental goals when political factors do not increase transaction costs. These added costs may explain why tradable development rights, for example, have not been used as frequently as many experts expected.[32] Only by limiting regulatory interventions, posting offer prices in a centralized location, and otherwise helping to broker exchanges between potential sellers and buyers of conservation credits can governments can promote their use.

RECLAIM

RECLAIM was inaugurated in 1993 by the South Coast Air Quality Management District (SCAQMD). The region had high levels of nitrogen oxides (NO_x) and sulfur oxides (SO_x), mainly SO_2, contributing to Los Angeles' famous smog. In light of the failure of past regulation to significantly improve air quality at an acceptable resource and political cost, a new pollution trading approach was implemented. RECLAIM replaced some 130 specific control measures that had been required under previous regulation. A key problem under those regulations was the lack of information on site emissions as well as high compliance costs that varied significantly across regulated facilities.

RECLAIM built on the ideas developed much earlier by economists Thomas Crocker (1966) and J.H. Dales (1968) that were already being used elsewhere in the country, for national SO_2 pollution control.[33] Under RECLAIM, total annual emissions caps for the gases were set and then reduced each year to lower NO_x releases by 75 percent and SO_2 by 60 percent from regulated facilities by 2003. The objective was to bring the South Coast air basin into compliance with national

---

[32] McConnell and Walls (2009, 300–302).

[33] Thomas D. Crocker (1966), "The Structuring of Atmospheric Pollution Control Systems," in H. Wolozin, ed., *The Economics of Air Pollution*, New York: W.W. Norton, 61–68; J.H. Dales (1968), *Property and Prices*, Toronto: University of Toronto Press.

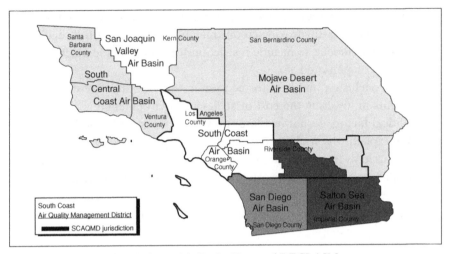

Figure 6.9. The South Coast Air Basin, Home of RECLAIM.
Source: Environmental Protection Agency (2006), "An Overview of the Regional Clean Air Incentives Market (RECLAIM), Staff Paper, Washington DC: EPA Clean Air Markets Division, August 14: 2.

air quality standards by 2010.[34] Annual allowable emission permits were distributed to more than 300 major fixed sources of pollutants (utilities and refineries held 90 percent of the permits) based largely on past peak production. Facilities had to hold credits equal to their actual emissions, but could buy or sell permits within a year. They were not bankable across years. Firms that could reduce their emissions below their allocations and held excess credits could sell them to firms that could not meet their pollution targets. This trading option theoretically provided incentives for firms to develop technologies to lower emissions and free up allowances for trade.[35] The provisions also allowed the overall regional airshed to achieve a given air quality goal at lower cost than without trade, even if marginal abatement costs were not fully equated.

---

[34] Environmental Protection Agency (2006). See also the EPA's 2002 report on RECLAIM at http://www.epa.gov/region09/air/reclaim/.

[35] The allowances are use rights to emit pollutants and not, strictly speaking, more secure property rights. We will see the outcome of this later in SO_2 markets and fishing share quotas in the U.S. and Canada. See Tom Tietenberg (2007), "Tradable Permits in Principle and Practice," in Jody Freeman and Charles D. Kolstad, eds., *Moving to Markets in Environmental Regulation: Lessons from Twenty Years of Experience*, New York: Oxford University Press, 63–94, 78.

The potential for the program, however, was narrowed because small, new sources of pollution were exempted, although monitoring costs may have made inclusion of most of these impractical. The narrow range of firms involved, however, meant that the market was thin, making it difficult for potential buyers and sellers to locate one another, raising transaction costs.[36] Additionally, there were criticisms of initial over-allocation of allowances, regulatory complexities, some localized "hot spots" of pollution, and a failure to achieve annual total emission targets especially during the 2000–2001 energy crisis in California, in which unprecedented electricity demand led to the use of power plants that were not equipped with NO_x emission control devices.[37]

Even so, RECLAIM generally has been viewed as a success, compared to the alternative of command-and-control regulation.[38] RECLAIM may have lowered costs by 46 percent relative to achieving the same aggregate reductions under the prior air quality management program that involved fixed emissions caps and no trades.[39] As shown in Figure 6.10 emissions have fallen for both NO_x and SO_x through fairly active markets.

NO_x allowance average prices ranged from a low of $1,200 per ton for 2004 to $9,730 per ton for 2008 to $10,193 per ton for 2010. For SO_x, average 2004 prices ranged from $1,400 per ton to around $4,450 per ton by 2007.[40] There was a spike in NO_x permit prices in 2000–2001 to up to $90,000 per ton. With sharp rises in energy demand requiring permits to cover older generating plants in the Los Angeles Basin Allowance, prices rose. Had allowance banking been feasible, market prices would have been less volatile.[41] In the next section, we

---

[36] Lata Gangadharan (2000), "Transaction Costs in Pollution Markets: An Empirical Study," *Land Economics* 76(44): 601–614.

[37] Anne Egelston and Maurie J. Cohen (2004): California RECLAIM's Market Failure: Lessons for the Kyoto Protocol, *Climate Policy* 4:4, 427–444.

[38] Meredith Fowlie, Stephen P. Holland, and Erin T. Mansur (2011), "What Do Emissions Markets Deliver and to Whom? Evidence from Southern California's NOx Trading Program," Working Paper, March 28. http://nature.berkeley.edu/~fowlie/fowlie_holland_mansur_reclaim.pdf/.

[39] Lawrence H. Goulder (2013), "Markets for Pollution Allowances: What Are the (New) Lessons?" *Journal of Economic Perspectives* 27(1): 87–102.

[40] http://en.wikipedia.org/wiki/Regional_Clean_Air_Incentives_Market.

[41] There was also the temporary removal of some electric utility units from the cap-and-trade system and the imposition of mandates on those units to retrofit NO_x emission control devices. For a general discussion, see A. Denny Ellerman (2007),

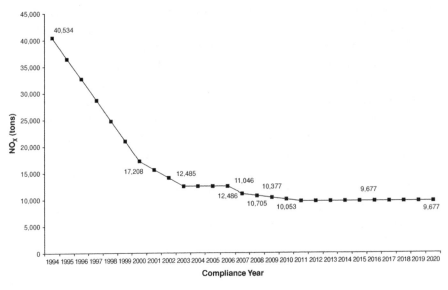

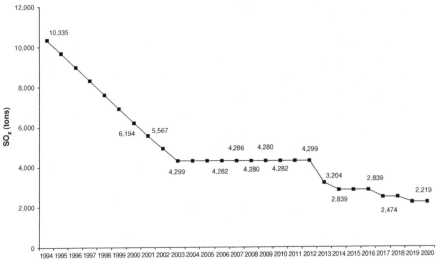

Figure 6.10. NO$_x$ and SO$_x$ Emission Levels of RECLAIM 1994–2020.
Source: South Coast Air Quality Management District (2013), *Annual RECLAIM Audit Report for the 2011 Compliance Year*, March 1, Diamond Bar, California. Figures 2.1, 2.2, page 2.6, available at https://aqmd.gov/hb/attachments/2011–2015/2013Mar/2013-Mar1–029.pdf.

also examine tradable emissions allowances, but at a broader scale with cross-state markets in sulfur dioxide (SO_2) emission permits. In this case, the record initially was one of much success in reducing abatement costs, but this environmental market has suffered from political and bureaucratic interventions.

SO_2 EMISSION PERMITS

This example of an environmental market is one of the most ambitious with the largest scope in the United States, the control of SO_2 through cap and trade.[42] SO_2 is a colorless gas emitted into the atmosphere from the burning of fossil fuels (coal and oil), which in high concentrations can have serious health effects, and its particulates contribute to the buildup of sulfur in soils and in waterways in regions distant from the source of emissions. This process, commonly known as acid rain, contributes to acidification of forests and lakes. Within the United States, SO_2 has long been regulated as a pollutant. As we discussed in Chapter 2, the high cost of command-and-control regulation of SO_2 emissions under the 1970 and 1977 Clean Air Act Amendments that set national concentration limits of the gas led to the adoption of a cap-and-trade system with 1990 Title IV of the 1990 Clean Air Act Amendments.[43] This was the first large-scale, long-term U.S. environmental program

---

"Are Cap-and-Trade Programs More Environmentally Effective than Conventional Regulation?" in Jody Freeman and Charles D. Kolstad, eds., *Moving to Markets in Environmental Regulation: Lessons from Twenty Years of Experience*, New York: Oxford University Press, 48–62, 56–58. The importance of allowance banking for the performance of cap-and-trade markets is discussed in Arthur G. Fraas and Nathan Richardson (2010), "Banking on Allowances: The EPA's Mixed Record in Managing Emissions-Market Transitions," Discussion Paper 10–42, Washington D.C.: Resources for the Future.

[42] As of January 2013, the California Air Resources Control Board (CARB) began regulating greenhouse gas emissions among 300 stationary sources via a cap-and-trade program. Whether the allowances will suffer the same outcome from political and regulatory intervention as occurred with the SO_2 permit program remains to be seen. For a discussion of the California cap-and-trade system see: www.edf.org/climate/AB32.

[43] Donald N. Dewees (1998), "Tradable Pollution Permits," in Peter Newman, ed., *The New Palgrave Dictionary of Economics and the Law*, Vol. 3, London: MacMillan, 596–601, 597–598; Paul L. Joskow and Richard Schmalensee (1998), "The Political Economy of Market-Based Environmental Policy: The U.S. Acid Raid Program," *The Journal of Law and Economics* 41(1): 37–83, 43–44.

Figure 6.11. SO$_2$ Emissions.
Source: Google Images: http://publicphoto.org/industries/coal-fired-power-plant-smoke-stack-emissions/attachment/coal-fired-power-plant_smoke-stack-emissions_55997/.

to rely on tradable emission permits, and they provided a precedent for their use in other cases.[44]

The program was introduced in two phases, with Phase I in 1995 affecting the 110 dirtiest coal-fired electricity-generating facilities, including about 363 generating units, mostly east of the Mississippi River and Phase II, in 2000, including all other coal-fired electricity-generating facilities with a capacity greater than

[44] Joskow and Schmalensee (1998, 38), 1990 CAAA, Public Law 101–549. Robert N. Stavins (2007), "Market-Based Environmental Policies: What Can We Learn from U.S. Experience (and Related Research)?" in Jody Freeman and Charles D. Kolstad, eds., *Moving to Markets in Environmental Regulation*, New York: Oxford University Press, 19–47, 23.

twenty-five megawatts, as well as smaller ones using fuel with a relatively high sulfur content, totaling about 3,200 generating units.[45]

Under the law, a utility was required to surrender one allowance for each ton of SO_2 emitted by its plants. Utilities could transfer allowances among facilities or to other firms or bank them for use in future years, including across the two phases. Allowances were allocated on the basis of energy input during a base period of 1985–1987 and calculated so that aggregated emissions equaled the fixed target cap. Unlike prescriptive technology-based regulation, whereby emissions could increase with greater overall production, cap-and-trade set aggregate emissions levels that were gradually tightened to lower overall SO_2 in the atmosphere. With trade of emission allowances, the marginal cost of compliance could be equalized across facilities and equal to the price of allowances. Utilities that had new technologies and capital equipment that released less SO_2 than their allowances authorized or that had access to low-sulfur coal could trade the excess to utilities with more polluting plants. Those firms would buy allowances so long as the allowance price was less than their cost of abatement. As they entered the market, the price of available allowances rose, giving them incentives to innovate in new technologies and fuels that released less SO_2. Meanwhile, those utilities that sold permits had incentives to innovate in order to sell more in the market. Because of variable demands for energy, such as those stimulated by unusually hot or cold weather, most utilities banked allowances for those times when older, mothballed plants and equipment that polluted more had to be brought into production to meet this demand.

The incentives provided by the SO_2 emission allowances for more efficient responses to pollution control are clear. Moreover, the allowance price provided information on the marginal cost of compliance because no utility would pay more to comply with SO_2 controls than it would pay for allowances. No utility would sell allowances for less than it had to pay to meet the restrictions. As a result, tradable emission allowances were the basis for environmental markets. What

---

[45] Richard Schmalensee and Robert N. Stavins (2013), "The SO_2 Allowance Trading System: The Ironic History of a Grand Policy Experiment," *Journal of Economic Perspectives* 27(1): 103–122, 104–105.

is less well recognized is that the performance of those markets and hence, the incentives for lower-cost environmental benefits depended on the security of the property right in emission allowances. The 1990 CAA Amendments, however, that established the SO_2 allowance program expressly stated that the pollution allowances would not be considered property rights, subject to takings protections under the U.S. Constitution.[46] The emission allowances were use privileges, and accordingly revocable or adjustable without compensation by government. This naturally made them potentially at risk, and we will see the impact of this situation. The lack of property rights security ultimately undermined the country's largest cap-and-trade market. The lesson is that for environmental markets to perform effectively over the long-term, the property right must be secure and protected from takings.

Emissions caps under the program produced substantial declines in power plant SO_2 releases. Total emissions in the first year of the program were 25 percent below 1990 levels and more than 35 percent below 1980 levels, and by 2000, emission levels were almost 40 percent below those of 1980.[47] The program's long-term Phase II goal to reduce the amount of nationwide utility emissions of SO_2 to 8.95 million tons annually was achieved by 2007 through the nationwide trading of emission allowances. It has been estimated that abatement costs would have been more than three times as high as they actually were to achieve this level of pollution reduction, $2.6 billion annually as compared to the actual program cost of $747 million.[48] These efficiency gains were also promoted by railroad transportation deregulation after 1976 that allowed for the shipment of low-sulfur coal from Wyoming

---

[46] CAA §403(f), 42 U.S.C. §7651b(f).

[47] Dallas Burtraw and Sarah Jo Szambelan (2009), "U.S. Emissions Trading Markets for SO2 and NO*x*," *Discussion Paper 09–04* Washington D.C.: Resources for the Future, October, 6.

[48] The political history and performance of the U.S. Acid Rain Program is described in A. Denny Ellerman, Paul L. Joskow, Richard Schmalensee, Juan-Pablo Montero, and Elizabeth M. Bailey (2000), *Markets for Clean Air: The US Acid Rain Program*, New York: Cambridge University Press. See also Tom H. Tietenberg (2006), *Emissions Trading Principles and Practice*, 2nd Ed., Washington D.C.: Resources for the Future; Nathaniel O. Keohane and Sheila M. Olmstead (2007), *Markets and the Environment*, Washington D.C.: Island Press, 183–190; Nathaniel O. Keohane (2007), "Cost Savings from Allowance Trading in the 1990 Clean Air Act: Estimates from a Choice Based Model," in Jody Freeman and Charles D. Kolstad, eds. (2007), 194–229.

and Montana to Upper Midwest and Northeastern utilities, displacing use of high-sulfur coal from the Midwest in power generation.[49]

Allowance trading was active, varying with the price of low-sulfur coal and natural gas that affected compliance costs, electricity demand, and regulatory changes. The latter turned out to be the major problem. In 2000 the volume of inter-firm trading reached nearly 15 million allowances, and by 2005 most trades were between economically unrelated firms, rather than across facilities.[50] This environmental market, however, was soon to face regulatory and judicial interventions that ultimately undercut it and its ability to reduce SO_2 releases at low cost. Moreover, the experience with the collapse of the SO_2 emissions allowance market potentially weakens confidence in the ability of environmental markets to perform on a wide scale for a long time without bureaucratic and political discretionary actions that are not held back by property rights guarantees. The problems began with efforts to expand regulation of fine particulate emissions associated with SO_2 releases from power plants.

By the late 1990s, there was also growing concern about fine particulate emissions from electricity generating units and their health effects. In 2002 the Bush Administration tried to amend the Clean Air Act to tighten controls on particulates with a Clear Skies and Global Climate Change Initiative, but the legislation did not pass Congress.[51] The EPA then attempted to implement administrative controls on particulates using its discretion within the existing SO_2 legislation as part of the earlier Clean Air Act Amendments. In 2005, the EPA introduced the Clean Air Interstate Rule (CAIR), which reduced the cap on SO_2 and nitrogen oxide (NO_x) emissions by 50 percent in CAIR Phase I and 65 percent in Phase II, and focused these more stringent restrictions on certain utility facilities with high particulate releases in twenty-eight states.[52] In this way the EPA sought to reduce particulate emissions, even though it did not have explicit congressional authorization to do so.

---

[49] Schmalensee and Stavins (2013, 110–112).
[50] Burtraw and Szambelan (2009, 9).
[51] Executive Office, "President Announces Clear Skies & Global Climate Change Initiatives," February 14, 2002.
[52] http://www.epa.gov/cair/index.htm.

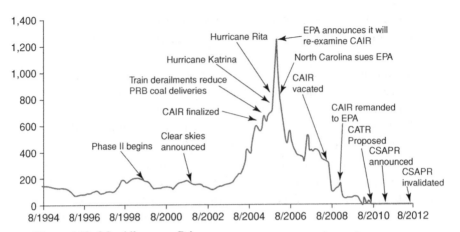

Figure 6.12. SO₂ Allowance Prices.
Source: Richard Schmalensee and Robert N. Stavins (2013), "The SO₂
Allowance Trading System: The Ironic History of a Grand Policy Experi-
ment," *Journal of Economic Perspectives* 27(1): 103–122, 110–112, 114.

In adopting the Clean Air Interstate Rule, the agency changed the
number of allowances that had to be surrendered for each ton of SO_2
emissions from a 1:1 ratio to 2:1 for 2010–2014 and from 2015 on to a
2.86:1 ratio for most polluting sources east of the Rocky Mountains.
These sources were contributing to violation of EPA's ambient air
quality standards for fine particulates in the eastern United States. This
action both reduced the cap on SO_2 significantly and, because different
exchange ratios were required in different parts of the country, added
uncertainty to the national SO_2 allowances trading market.[53] CAIR
did allow utilities to bank their SO_2 allowances to meet subsequent
tighter emissions standards that would be required to reduce particulate emission. Allowance banking would potentially help to smooth
the transition costs to more stringent controls. Initially, as shown in
Figure 6.12, allowance prices rose and became more volatile after 2004
in anticipation of the tighter cap and other regulatory actions, and the
effects of Hurricanes Katrina and Rita. After peaking in 2006, they
began a rapid decline, eventually trending to zero.

[53] http://www.hunton.com/files/Publication/5051a1df-52fc-44c9–9ee5–4116e8e79b5b/
Presentation/PublicationAttachment/bbb014cd-7082–4b7f-a2db-931942da09d0/
Fixing_CAIR_4.10.pdf, 13.

CAIR proved to be ineffective, demonstrating the problems of agency discretion when not endorsed by Congress and the fundamental weakness of an environmental market where the main instrument, in this case emission allowance permits, are not secure property rights. When the instrument is not a secure property right, regulatory agencies can engage in polices without weighing the private costs involved. There may be compelling reasons for regulatory adjustments, but they require congressional debate and authorization for national policy initiatives, including compensation for parties adversely affected. Without weighing full benefits and costs and considering the distributional implications of their actions, agency officials can go too far and make decisions that ultimately undermine the overall objective of environmental markets – the protection of the resource or provision of environmental quality in a cost-effective manner. This is what happened with the SO_2 allowance program.

CAIR was first challenged by North Carolina, other states, and some utilities in legal action against the EPA. The challenge alleged that interstate emission allowance trading allowed under CAIR (and the SO_2 market) was inconsistent with the Clean Air Act's provision that each state control emissions that affected downwind states' air quality. This judicial action rattled emissions markets. Eventually the case went to the D.C. Circuit Court of Appeals, where CAIR was struck down in 2008 and sent back to the EPA for policy redesign.[54] After considerable policy recalibration including consideration of a Clean Air Transport Rule (CATR), the EPA issued a new policy in 2011, the Cross-State Air Pollution Rule (CSAPR). This rule severely restricted interstate trading of allowances by setting state-specific SO_2 and NO_x emissions caps and allowing only intrastate trading (with limited exchanges between some states), disallowed the use of any allowances banked by utilities in anticipation of the implementation of CAIR and its tighter emissions controls, and effectively reinstated traditional technology-based, command-and-control emission restrictions.[55] Later in 2012,

---

[54] United States Court of Appeals FOR THE DISTRICT OF COLUMBIA CIRCUIT Decided July 11, 2008.
   No. 05–1244 STATE OF NORTH CAROLINA v. ENVIRONMENTAL PROTECTION AGENCY.

[55] http://epa.gov/airtransport/. For additional discussion of the EPA's actions that ultimately undermined the SO_2 trading system, see Mark Peters (2010), "Changes Choke

the Cross-State Air Pollution Rule itself was challenged, and the D.C. Circuit Court of Appeals sent it back to the EPA for review.[56]

The loss of banking for existing Title IV emission allowances is particularly instructive for the credibility of the assets created under cap-and-trade and for the incentives of firms to invest in them.[57] Some 12 million emission allowances that had been purchased and banked by firms were stranded, dramatically losing value with losses of an estimated $3 billion. Under the law, there were no takings protections.[58] With the EPA's regulatory fluctuations and the insecurity of any emissions allowance, the future of any interstate trading program to reduce air pollution is now questionable.[59]

The SO_2 allowance price pattern indicates the conflicts that exist between secure property rights, environmental objectives, and political and bureaucratic agendas, regardless of the merit of their motives. It is apparent that for markets to work for the environment, natural resources, and the users themselves, property rights must be defined and respected. With property rights security, owners can plan ahead with investment in pollution abatement technologies knowing that their benefits will be captured in saved allowances that can be banked. Security also makes the market work more effective by reducing volatility. When share or allowance prices jump or fall for some exogenous reason, shares or banked allowances can be sold (purchased) to smooth price patterns.

Finally, with secure property rights, regulators are restrained by the costs of taking property if new regulations reduce the value of the share or allowance. There may be reasons for regulatory change, but compensating owners for property and past investments reveals the opportunity cost of any policy change. Regulators then must seek

---

Cap-and-Trade Market," *Wall Street Journal* July 12, at http://online.wsj.com/article/ SB10001424052748704258604575360821005676554.html. See also Schmalensee and Stavins (2013).

[56] Matthew L. Wald, "Court Blocks E.P.A. Rule on Cross-State Pollution," *New York Times* August 22, 2012: A15; Ryan Tracy, "Court Voids Rule on Coal Pollution," *Wall Street Journal* August 21, 2012.

[57] For analysis and effects on the market, see Fraas and Richardson (2010).

[58] Fraas and Richardson (2010, 37, 43).

[59] For a discussion of this issue, see Kati Kiefer (2010), "A Missing Market: The Future of Interstate Emissions Trading Programs after North Carolina v. EPA," *Saint Louis University Law Journal* 54: 635–674.

funding through Congress or other means, and this in itself is a useful process because legislative negotiations reveal social preferences and the weighing of the costs and benefits of alternative budget priorities. Absent property rights security, regulators are much freer to adjust policies with little concern as to the costs involved because they are born by share and allowance holders. Further, the policy is subject to greater litigation challenge because the rights are not firm and with broader agency discretion, there is greater opportunity for other constituencies to seek to modify policies. More secure property rights with constitutional guarantees restrain litigious activity and promote greater stability in meeting environmental objectives.

We now turn to a final example of a cap-and-trade system, individual transferable quotas within an overall annual allowable catch. In the United States, ITQs have similar potential property rights weaknesses as exist with the SO_x allowance permits, although regulatory actions have not undermined them to the same degree.

INDIVIDUAL FISHERY QUOTAS

Ocean fisheries markets cover even larger spatial areas than conservation credits or air permits. The initial regulatory response to overexploitation, waste, and depletion of fish stocks has been to implement input and output controls. Because these have mostly been unsuccessful, rights-based practices, such as individual transferable quotas (ITQs), have been adopted to create shares in a total allowable catch. These were first adopted in 1986 and 1989 by New Zealand and Iceland, respectively, for improving fisheries management.[60] Even today, perhaps as little as five percent of the world's fish stocks have a property rights regime, leaving many others subject to serious depletion.[61]

---

[60] For a discussion of fishery management in these two countries, see Thorolfur Matthiasson and Sveinn Agnarsson (2010), "Property Rights in Icelandic Fisheries," in R. Quentin Grafton, Ray Hilborn, Dale Squires, Maree Tait, and Meryl J. Williams, eds., *Handbook of Marine Fisheries Conservation and Management*, New York: Oxford University Press, 299–309 and Robin Connor and Bruce Shallard (2010), "Evolving Governance in New Zealand Fisheries," in R. Quentin Grafton, et al. eds. (2010), 347–359.

[61] Ransom A. Myers and Boris Worm, (2003), "Rapid Worldwide Depletion of Predatory Fish Communities," *Nature* 423: 280–283; and Jennifer A. Devine, Krista D.

Figure 6.13. Congested Fishing with Regulated Seasons.
Source: Opening Day of Alaska Commercial Salmon Fishing, Google Images:
http://www.fishingplaces.org/2010/09/sitka-alaska-fishing/.

The use of ITQs and similar quotas requires political jurisdiction over the ocean, as was provided through the 200-mile exclusive economic zones (EEZs) and government enforcement of those limits. Iceland staked its fishery claims in 1975; the U.S. Congress did so in 1974, followed by Presidential Proclamation in 1983; and Canada acted in 1977.[62]

The strength of ITQ property right varies, however. In New Zealand, quota ownership is viewed as a perpetual right to fish, and the rights can serve as collateral in financial markets.[63] In contrast, ITQs in the United States have been controversial and are a weaker ownership right.[64] In 1996, a four-year moratorium was placed on new ITQs under the Magnuson-Stevens Act (U.S.C. 1801, 1996), and the law included specific language stating that quota shares "shall be considered a permit," that they "may be revoked, limited, or modified at any time," that they "shall not confer any right of compensation to the

Baker, and Richard L. Haedrich, (2006), "Fisheries: Deep-Sea Fishes Qualify as Endangered," *Nature* 439: 29.
[62] Hannesson (2004, 38, 107, 116).
[63] Corbett Grainger and Christopher Costello (2011), "The Value of Secure Property Rights: Evidence from Global Fisheries," NBER Working Paper 17019, Cambridge: NBER, where they examine the impact of insecure fishery quota rights on quota values across countries.
[64] Arnason (2002, 52–57).

holder... if it is revoked, limited, or modified," that they "shall not create, or be construed to create, any right, title, or interest in or to any fish before the fish is harvested by the holder," and that they "shall be considered a grant of permission to the holder of the quota share to engage in activities permitted by such... quota share."[65] In addition, there generally are constraints on transferability. For instance, in the Pacific Halibut fishery, political efforts to maintain a small-boat fishery and the economies of adjacent communities that support them brought limits on quota transfers to larger vessel owners. A single individual can own only 0.5 percent of the total quota, and the quota owner must be on board when fishing takes place as a way of preventing absentee ownership.[66]

Where property rights are weaker, sales values should be lower than in cases where rights are stronger, all else equal, and short-term lease prices should be higher. Comparing the ratio of quota lease prices to sales prices (the dividend price ratio) across United States, New Zealand, and Canadian fisheries, Grainger and Costello (2011) find that the ratios for the U.S. are significantly higher than in the other countries, supporting the perception that the U.S. has more uncertain property rights.[67] Figure 6.14 plots the ratio of lease to sales prices for the United States, Canada, and New Zealand.

In their analysis of the New Zealand fishery quota market Newell, Sanchirico, and Kerr (2005) find generally vibrant markets, although they vary according to fishery and number of quota holders. In general, between 1986 and 2000, the total number of quota holders declined, with some consolidation especially within inshore fisheries, which were subject to considerable overharvest.[68] Fishers tend to hold a portfolio

---

[65] Quoted in Grainger and Costello (2009, 3). The nature of property rights in U.S. fishery ITQs is described by see Mark Fina and Tyson Kade (2012), "Legal and Policy Implications of the Perception of Property Rights in Catch Shares," *Washington Journal of Environmental Law and Policy* 2: 283–328,

[66] Rajesh Singh, Quinn Weninger, and Matthew Doyle, (2006), "Fisheries Management with Stock Growth Uncertainty and Costly Capital Adjustment," *Journal of Environmental Economics and Management* 52(2): 582–599; 595. Other continuing threats to U.S. fishery property rights are described in Chameides (2011).

[67] More uncertain property rights, as indicated by sales prices that are driven down by weak property rights relative to short-term lease prices that are not affected as described by Grainger and Costello (2011).

[68] Newell, Sanchirico, and Kerr (2005, 444, 446).

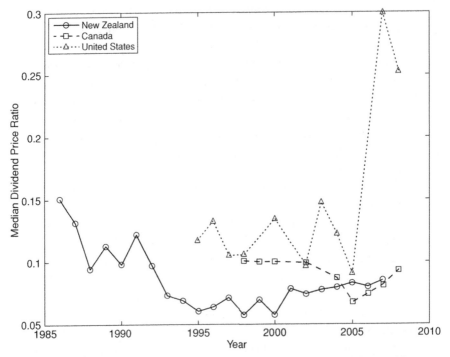

Figure 6.14. Dividend Price (Lease/Sales Ratio) for U.S., Canadian, and New Zealand Fishery Quotas.
Source: Corbett Grainger and Christopher Costello (2011), "The Value of Secure Property Rights: Evidence from Global Fisheries," NBER Working Paper 17019, Cambridge: NBER: 12. Downloaded from http://cbey.yale. edu/uploads/Environmental%20Economics%20Seminar/Property_Rights_March25c.pdf.

of quotas across in- and offshore fisheries. Quota market trades are handled through brokers for small and medium-sized quota owners, whereas large owners engage in bilateral trades. Brokers advertise quota prices and quantities for sale or lease in trade magazines, newspapers, and on the internet, and their fees and roles are similar to brokers in emission permit and real estate markets in the United States and New Zealand. Quota price dispersion has narrowed over time, consistent with the development of reasonably well-functioning markets, and the overall profitability of quota ownership has risen, indicating positive fish stock gains from the rights-based system.[69] Finally, in

[69] Newell, Sanchirico, and Kerr (2005, 445–448, 457, 459–460).

Table 6.1. *British Columbia Halibut Fishery*

Year	Season Length (Days)	Number of Active Vessels	Percent of Halibut Marketed as Fresh
1980	64	333	N/A
1981	58	337	
1982	61	301	
1983	24	305	
1984	22	334	
1885	22	363	
1986	15	417	
1987	16	424	
1988	14	435	
1989	11	435	42%
1990	6	435	
1991	214	433	94%
1992	240	431	
1993	245	531	
1994	245	313	N/A
1995	245	294	
1996	245	281	

Source: Table created from data presented in R. Quentin Grafton, Dale Squires, and Kevin J. Fox (2000, 685), and See also Christopher M. Dewees, Bruce R. Turris, and James E. Wilen (1995), "The Effects of Individual Vessel Quotas in the British Columbia Halibut Fishery," *Marine Resource Economics* 10: 211–30, 219.

contrast to the U.S. condition, sales prices have risen relative to lease prices.[70]

The data in Table 6.1 show the effects of tradable fishery shares in the British Columbia Halibut fishery on the number of vessels, season length, and share of fresh (high value) versus frozen product (low value). As we have discussed earlier, prior to the adoption of the ITQ program under regulation, there was a fishing derby, congestion, and a gradual shortening of the fishing season.[71] In 1990 it was only six days, which meant that all the halibut had to be caught at that time, frozen, and then shipped to market as less-valuable frozen halibut. After the ITQ program was implemented in 1990, the season expanded to 245 days, the number of vessels declined, and importantly, valuable

[70] Newell, Sanchirico, and Kerr (2005, 458).
[71] Technically, the BC Halibut program was an individual vessel quota or IVQ. We will use the more familiar ITQ term.

fresh halibut could be available for most of the year. The longer season also allowed for more careful handling of the fish and time for locating the best markets. As shown in the table, for two selected periods, the share of halibut marketed as fresh rose from 42 percent during a pre-quota period (1989–1990) to 94 percent in a quota period (1991–1993). Moreover, more recent research indicates that the halibut stock and fishing industry has continued to flourish under the quota regime.[72]

CONCLUSION

There are common threads running through the examples presented in this chapter. One is that the most successful environmental markets are local. This is because of the information requirements necessary for often heterogeneous assets to be exchanged, the limited numbers of buyers and sellers associated with a particular environmental problem, and the lower prominence of distributional conflicts that weaken property rights. Second, for markets to work on a wider scale, as they do in New Zealand for ITQs, the use rights associated with cap-and-trade systems must be secure property rights. If they are vulnerable to political and bureaucratic manipulation, the potential for environmental markets is undermined. Problems of meeting resource and environmental quality objectives are even greater at the global level, and in that case, the ability of markets to provide low-cost solutions may be more limited where many sovereign jurisdictions are involved, governance institutions vary in quality, and the rule of law is not always adhered to.

[72] Mark Herrmann and Keith Criddle (2006), "An Econometric Market Model for the Pacific Halibut Fishery," *Marine Resource Economics* 21: 129–158.

7

Tackling the Global Commons

In this chapter, we examine broader environmental and natural resource open-access problems that cross political jurisdictions. To get insights into what opportunities and challenges exist for the use of environmental markets, we examine case studies where multi-jurisdictional environmental markets have been implemented and where they have not. The nature of the underlying property rights helps to explain the differences in the potential for markets.

In earlier chapters, the analysis and examples indicated that environmental markets appear to work best when addressing more localized open-access problems that are narrow in scope, where property rights are secure, and where the parties involved share common incentives regarding resource conservation. Because immediate users often are both the source and the solution to the problem, they are more likely to internalize the costs and benefits of resolving it. At the local level, the costs of measuring and bounding environmental assets and demarcating property rights are generally lower. Moreover, confined open-access problems typically fall under a single political authority. In this situation, property rights, markets, and any distributional or administrative conflicts surrounding them are handled by politicians and bureaucratic officials who are at least loosely responsible to local political constituencies. Parties with more actual experience with the resource typically have the best information about it, the losses due to open access, the effects of human actions relative to more system-wide factors, and potential remedies.[1]

---

[1] For a discussion of the importance of local knowledge see Ronald N. Johnson (1995), "Implications of Taxing Quota Value in an Individual Transferable Quota Fishery," *Marine Resource Economics* 10(4): 327–340, 337 and Terry L. Anderson, Ragnar

We emphasize the importance of resolving environmental problems through the creation of property rights whenever it is cost-effective to do so. These property rights may come in the form of common property in cases where the resource is local and well defined, and the community using the resource is relatively small and homogeneous. Where the resource is more widely spread and where the population of users is larger and more heterogeneous, more formal private property rights and markets can be an important solution to the tragedy of the commons.[2] Differences in values and abatement costs that exist among larger groups of users provide a basis for exchange that may not exist in more confined settings.

To be effective, property rights require exclusion and durability, both of which add to transaction costs. Measurement and bounding are one such cost. All else equal, more stationary, observable resources are easier to measure and to control access to. Another source of transaction costs is the difficulty of determining who gets the property rights when those parties whose use practices must change are made worse off because they do not receive the rights. Even if the total gains from avoiding open-access losses could provide compensation from beneficiaries to losers,[3] distributional conflicts can increase the costs of making such payments to resolve conflicts and may block the emergence of property rights and markets. When there are many, heterogeneous parties claiming a resource, it is no easy matter to determine who should get the rights, who should receive compensation for being denied access, who should pay, and the level of payment. These are complex political economy problems for politicians and members of regulatory agencies when any allocation decision is made. Finally, there are the costs of reaching agreement on a property rights distribution when people have differential assessments of the benefits

---

Arnason, and Gary D. Libecap (2011), "Efficiency Advantages of Grandfathering in Rights-Based Fisheries Management," *Annual Review of Resource Economics* 3: 159–179, 166.

[2] Transaction costs for the assignment of property rights also increase with heterogeneity and group size. The key difference is that, once allocated, private property rights can be traded. This usually is less feasible in common property settings.

[3] One way to think of this is to consider overall social welfare like a pie. We can aim to maximize the size of the pie, which might mean that some individuals would get a smaller slice (or a smaller overall percentage). The alternative would be to have a smaller pie with equal shares. Under the former, compensation could make everyone better off.

and costs of closing access to the commons. Information asymmetries, and hence perceptions of benefits and costs, increase with size and sources of open-access losses and with the spatial distribution of the problem. Further, greater scientific uncertainty about the causes of the problem (e.g. for a fishery the problem is overfishing or changes in natural conditions) and its remedies make it harder to agree on a property rights solution. In many cases, opposition to perceived distributional outcomes may outweigh the expected benefits of taking action. As a result, no political consensus will emerge and little will be done to address the problem.

An environmental or resource crisis, however, such as the collapse of a fish stock or intense levels of air pollution, can narrow these distributional concerns. A crisis shows that the *status quo* is untenable and provides new information about open-access losses. In this event, political forces may line up for the adoption of property rights and environmental markets, especially if they appear to be the low-cost and most complete solution.

The costs we describe occur within a single political jurisdiction, but they are far more formidable when crossing political boundaries. Not only are measurement, bounding, and enforcement costs higher, but distributional conflicts and their impact on political decision making loom even larger when multiple governments and constituencies are involved. In this chapter we examine some of the costs encountered and their implications for the assignment of property rights and use of markets in addressing extensive open-access problems.

BARGAINING AND ENFORCEMENT ACROSS POLITICAL JURISDICTIONS

In Chapters 4 and 5 we examined bargaining both within groups and within single political jurisdictions to mitigate the losses of open access using property rights and markets. Successful collective action is influenced by the nature and value of the resource; the size and heterogeneity of the bargaining group; and the nature of the institution implemented, particularly with regard to the distribution of the net benefits of the arrangement.[4]

---

[4] The conditions for successful collective action that do not address underlying political economy issues are provided in Elinor Ostrom (1990), *Governing the Commons:*

When the value of the common resource is low or the transaction costs of addressing the problem are high or both, there is limited incentive or ability for collective efforts until values increase, costs fall, or both. Even when the resource is sufficiently valuable to warrant action, larger, more multifaceted groups, encountered when resource problems are broadly spread, bring higher bargaining and compliance costs. Free riding on the actions of parties that adhere to collective agreements encourages defection, undermining those efforts. Further, when the resource is geographically widespread, as with migratory species or the global atmosphere, only a very small part of it will be observed and understood by individual users. Individuals, therefore, are less likely to see how their sacrifices for mitigation bring about positive results. These challenges are amplified if the science is poorly understood, resource responses are uncertain, and reaction times are long – perhaps occurring across generations.[5] For example, climate change policy has been contentious in part because of the high level of uncertainty in projecting the damages of temperature change, especially at the regional level where parties determine the costs and benefits of taking remedial action and where politicians form their positions in multinational negotiations. When outcomes are uncertain, it is hard for constituencies under any political authority to determine their willingness to pay for possible remedies to the environmental

The Evolution of Institutions for Collective Action, Cambridge University Press, 88–101; Elinor Ostrom (1998), "Self-Governance of Common-Pool Resources," in Peter Newman, ed., *The New Palgrave Dictionary of Economics and The Law*, Vol. 3, New York: Macmillan, 424–432; Elinor Ostrom (2000), "Collective Action and the Evolution of Social Norms," *Journal of Economic Perspectives* 14(3): 137–158; and Elinor Ostrom (2011), "Beyond Markets and States: Polycentric Governance of Complex Economic Systems," *American Economic Review* 100(3): 641–672. A useful summary of her analysis is provided by Jean-Marie Baland and Jean-Philippe Platteau (1996), *Halting Degradation of Natural Resources: Is There a Role for Rural Communities?* Rome and Oxford: FAO and Oxford University Press, pp. 286–290. For a discussion of the politics involved see Libecap (1989, 17–19) and Sam Peltzman, 1976, "Toward a More General Theory of Regulation," *Journal of Law and Economics* 19(2): 211–240 and Gary S. Becker, 1983, "A Theory of Competition among Pressure Groups for Political Influence," *Quarterly Journal of Economics* 98(3): 371–400.

[5] This seems to be especially the case for GHG controls, where there is a great deal of uncertainty in estimating costs and effects of GHG buildup and their distribution across the planet. For a discussion of IPCC climate modeling, see http://www.ipcc-data.org/ddc_climscen.html.

problem.[6] Accordingly, it is difficult to develop a policy consensus on what action to take. Additionally, open-access problems are not uniformly distributed among populations and states. Some may view the asset as unthreatened or the problem of little consequence, whereas others view conditions in much more dire terms.

There also is the problem of leakage or migration of production from more-regulated to less-regulated locations. If this occurs, those who bear mitigation costs will see additional economic losses and possibly greater aggregate resource use, be it air emissions or fishery harvests. The relocation of economic opportunities and wealth, even if short term, are huge political issues in regions that mitigate, but lose out as others expand production.[7] If these conditions exist, constituencies in one jurisdiction may not see positive net benefits from confronting open-access problems. If the costs and benefits of mitigation are not shared more-or-less proportionately, then consensus is a less likely solution.[8] Actions will only be individually rational if the participants are made better off or no worse off with cooperation than without it.

These bargaining problems become exceedingly complex when agreement is required among representatives of different political jurisdiction, especially if those jurisdictions have different per capita incomes, different histories of resource use, and different governance institutions.[9] In such cases, cross-jurisdictional transfers may

---

[6] For example, see the low willingness to pay for global warming mitigation because of scientific uncertainty in Robert S. Pindyck (2012), "Uncertain Outcomes and Climate Change Policy," *Journal of Environmental Economics and Management* 63: 289–303.

[7] The limits of local, unilateral environmental action when broad enforcement costs are high and when economic migration or new entry are possible are discussed by Jonathan Baert Wiener (2007), "Think Globally, Act Globally; The Limits of Local Climate Change Policies," *University of Pennsylvania Law Review* 155: 101–119.

[8] The importance of the nature of the sharing rule is discussed in Gary D. Libecap and James L. Smith (1999), "The Self-Enforcing Provisions of Oil and Gas Unit Operating Agreements: Theory and Evidence," *Journal of Law, Economics and Organization* 15(2): 526–548; 532 and Steven N. Wiggins and Gary D. Libecap (1985), "Oil Field Unitization: Contractual Failure in the Presence of Imperfect Information," *American Economic Review* 75(3): 368–385.

[9] For a discussion of the transaction costs of cross-country bargaining, see Beth V. Yarborough and Robert M. Yarborough (1994), "International Contracting and Territorial Control: The Boundary Question," *Journal of Institutional and Theoretical Economics* 150(1): 239–264; James K. Sebenius (1984), *Negotiating the Law of the Sea*, Cambridge: Harvard University Press; Scott Barrett (1994), "Self-Enforcing International Environmental Agreements," *Oxford Economic Papers* 46: 878–894;

be required from expected beneficiaries to expected losers. These transfers are complex enough within a country and become far more complicated when they cross political boundaries because the amounts are typically larger, fairness criteria more controversial, and compliance more difficult to measure and enforce.[10] Under these circumstances, local politicians must decide if it is in the interest of their constituencies (and hence in their interest) to participate in any collective response. To illustrate the challenges involved, we examine transboundary efforts to address open access with increasing degrees of complexity.

REGIONAL GREENHOUSE GAS INITIATIVE

We begin with the case of an interstate effort to control emissions that potentially contribute to climate change, the Regional Greenhouse Gas Initiative or RGGI. RGGI is a cap-and-trade environmental markets program to reduce CO_2 emissions by 10 percent between 2009 and 2018. The initiative was laid out in 2003 by the Governors of nine Northeastern and Mid-Atlantic states – Connecticut, Delaware, Maine, Massachusetts, New Hampshire, New Jersey, New York, Rhode Island, and Vermont.[11] The details were finally agreed on in 2005, and the first compliance year began in 2009. Initially, there were two compliance periods of three years each, January 1, 2009 – December 31, 2011 and January 1, 2012 – December 31, 2014. Within each compliance period, member states establish CO_2 Budget Trading Programs that cap the total annual allowable emissions from their electric utilities within the aggregate RGGI target. From 2012 to 2014,

Scott Barrett (2003), *Environment & Statecraft*, New York: Oxford University Press; Scott Barrett (2007), *Why Cooperate: The Incentive to Supply Global Public Goods*, New York: Oxford University Press; and Charles Kolstad and Alastair Ulph (2008), "Learning and International Environmental Agreements," *Climatic Change* 89: 125–141.

[10] For a discussion of the politics of transfers see James M. Buchanan and Gordon Tullock (1962), *The Calculus of Consent*, Ann Arbor: University of Michigan Press; Mancur Olson (1965), *The Logic of Collective Action. Public Goods and the Theory of Groups*, Cambridge: Harvard University Press; Peltzman (1976); Becker (1983); and Ronald N. Johnson and Gary D. Libecap (2003), "Transaction Costs and Coalition Stability under Majority Rule," *Economic Inquiry* 41(2): 193–207.

[11] http://www.rggi.org/.

the RGGI cap is 165 million short tons of CO_2 per year. Beginning in 2015, the cap is to decrease by 2.5 percent per year, for a total reduction of 10 percent by 2018.[12] The caps affect 209 fossil fuel-fired power plants twenty-give megawatts or greater in size. Emission allowances are auctioned four times a year, and under a collaborative Model Rule, regulated utilities can use a CO_2 allowance issued by any other participating state to demonstrate compliance with their own states' program. In this manner, the state programs function as a single regional market for CO_2 emissions. Theoretically, utilities can sell unused allowances to companies that have higher observance costs or bank them across allowance periods and thereby achieve admission reduction targets at lower total cost.

Over the first three years of the Regional Greenhouse Gas Initiative, average annual emissions were 23 percent less than in the previous three years, although the economic downturn and greater use of natural gas played an important role in the reduction. Table 7.1 shows cumulative allowances and proceeds by compliance period and state.

Despite this apparent success, there have been problems in the cross-state effort, even with its relatively modest abatement objectives. Membership has been subject to political winds, indicating the potential fragility of such voluntary agreements. Massachusetts and Rhode Island withdrew by 2005 and rejoined in 2007 following new gubernatorial elections; Maryland also joined in 2007; and New Jersey withdrew as of 2012.[13] Reactions by state politicians to internal interests add uncertainty to the long-term security of allowance permits, the effectiveness of the market, and any financial return participating firms anticipate from purchasing and banking allowances. The SO_2 allowance market examined in Chapter 6 illustrates the potential hazards of cap-and-trade across political jurisdictions. Political shifts underscore the problem of designing cross-jurisdiction property rights and trading markets when there is no overriding enforcement mechanism. As states leave or join RGGI, the overall cap has to be recalculated within a new group of participants, affecting overall emission reductions and the value of allowances.

---

[12] http://www.rggi.org/docs/RGGI_Fact_Sheet.pdf.

[13] Mireya Navarro (2011), "Christie Pulls New Jersey From 10-State Climate Initiative," *New York Times* May 26, 2011.

Table 7.1. *Cumulative RGGI Allowances and Auction Proceeds by State through 2012*

State	Cumulative First Control Period Allowances Sold	Cumulative Second Control Period Allowances Sold	Cumulative Proceeds
Connecticut	22,953,057	6,703,016	$65,167,702.91
Delaware	9,952,619	3,598,987	$29,690,897.09
Maine	11,797,376	3,383,526	$34,246,621.95
Maryland	74,943,417	22,579,565	$219,115,648.80
Massachusetts	62,024,346	17,557,926	$178,921,781.07
New Hampshire	14,479,101	4,635,489	$42,452,628.87
New York	142,786,651	40,462,985	$410,586,619.96
Rhode Island	6,244,404	1,756,408	$17,977,844.73
Vermont	2,877,123	809,649	$8,284,461.54
Total for States Participating in Second RGGI Control Period	348,058,094	101,487,551	$1,006,444,206.92
New Jersey*	46,266,477	2,217,293	$113,344,551.27
TOTAL	394,324,571	103,704,844	$1,119,788,758.19

* New Jersey withdrew

Source: Regional Greenhouse Gas Initiative Auction Results, Cumulative Allowances and Proceeds by State (2013) http://www.rggi.org/market/co2_auctions/results.

Further, setting the regional (and hence, state) emissions cap and determining the number of allowances to be auctioned have been subject to competing constituent group pressures. Initially, the cap was set high. With a generous allocation of allowances and lower overall emissions levels than anticipated, auction prices trended toward the reserve price of $1.89/short ton. For example, as of June 8, 2012, they sold for $1.93 per allowance.[14] Many of the allowances have remained unsold. In 2012, governors of seven of the nine remaining states in RGGI – New York, Connecticut, Delaware, Maryland, Massachusetts, Rhode Island, and Vermont – announced that excess, unsold allowances would be retired. As of early 2013, there has been debate among the governors as to whether the cap should be raised above current emissions or lowered. There is concern about the impact

[14] http://www.platts.com/RSSFeedDetailedNews/RSSFeed/ElectricPower/6734973. http://www.rggi.org/market/co2_auctions/results.

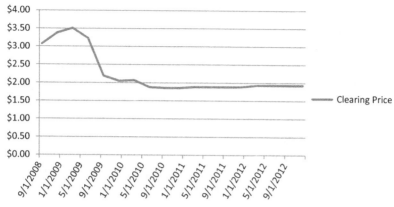

Figure 7.1. RGGI Auction Prices.
Source: Authors' calculations using data from http://www.monitoringanalytics
.com/reports/PJM_State_of_the_Market/2012/2012q2-som-pjm-sec7.pdf   and
http://www.rggi.org/market/co2_auctions/results.

of higher energy costs in the region and the migration of industry during a period of slow economic growth.[15] Finally, although the auction proceeds of more than $1 billion by early 2013 were to be used to fund energy efficiency and renewable energy, New Jersey devoted revenues to cover budget shortfalls. This experience also undermines the credibility of claims that auction funds will be used in a particular manner, when there are changing political incentives and no means of enforcing commitments across political jurisdictions and across time.[16]

Figure 7.1 plots RGGI allowance auction prices from September 2008 through 2012. As shown, they have not been very high, never reaching target prices of $20 to $30 per ton, figures that are thought to

[15] Mireya Navarro (2012), "Regional Cap-and-Trade Effort Seeks Greater Impact by Cutting Carbon Allowances," *New York Times* January 26, 2012; http://www.nytimes .com/2013/01/25/opinion/northeast-faces-stark-choice-on-climate-pollution.html. See also Yihsu Chen (2010), "Does a Regional Greenhouse Gas Policy Make Sense? A Case Study of Carbon Leakage and Emission Spillovers," working paper, Sierra Nevada Research Institute, UC Merced.

[16] In a well-known paper, Parry et al. argue that auction funds could reduce distortions in the economy if they are used to offset distorting income taxes. See Ian Parry, W.H., Robertson, C. Williams III, and Lawrence H. Goulder. (1999). "When Can Carbon Abatement Policies Increase Welfare? The Fundamental Role of Distorted Factor Markets," *Journal of Environmental Economics and Management* 37: 52–84. The political model by which long-term commitments are made and adhered to, however, requires more attention.

reflect the global cost of carbon. In the face of political uncertainties in this cross-state effort, reduced demand for electricity with slow economic growth, and a plentiful supply of allowances, the price may not induce long-term investment in abatement technologies.

Although RGGI represents a trans-jurisdiction effort for addressing CO_2 emissions, its efforts are not likely to have any measurable impact on global stocks. Accordingly, the costs and benefits of such actions are unlikely to result in a positive net benefit for RGGI electricity rate payers. Unless there is more concerted and effective international cooperation to address CO_2 emission controls, this and similar local or regional programs may not be politically durable as emission caps are further tightened and electricity rates rise, and global CO_2 emissions continue to increase. Voters and rate payers will realize the costs they bear are in the presence of free riding elsewhere. RGGI can serve as a template for other cap-and-trade programs. The experience of the SO_2 allowance market, however, serves as a caution.

EUROPEAN UNION EMISSIONS TRADING SYSTEM

The European Union Emissions Trading System (EU ETS) is an even more ambitious cross-jurisdictional cap-and-trade initiative. Because it includes multiple countries, its record may be indicative of what is or is not possible in other multilateral cases. It is important, though, to keep in mind that the EU ETS takes place within a relatively homogenous group of European countries – at least compared to a broader collection of countries across the world – and the participants are part of a broader governance system, the European Union, which binds their economies and political systems together.

The EU ETS covers more air pollution sources and has a higher total value of trading than either RGGI or the U.S. SO_2 trading program. It is the largest cap-and-trade program in the world.[17] Because its caps have been less tight and allowances more liberal than those of the SO_2 emissions trading market, it has reduced pollution releases by less.[18] Unlike RGGI, the EU ETS involves sovereign countries,

---

[17] http://ec.europa.eu/clima/policies/ets/linking/index_en.htm.

[18] A. Denny Ellerman and Barbara K. Buchner (2008), "Over-Allocation or Abatement? A Preliminary Analysis of the EU ETS, based on the 2005–06 Emissions Data," *Environment and Resource Economics* 41: 267–287.

which should make collective political action and environmental markets more difficult to implement. Although members of the European Union are subject to its mandates, internal political pressures have influenced the position of country politicians in setting caps and distributing allowances.[19]

The EU ETS began with ratification of the Kyoto Protocol by the European Union in 2002 and the commitment to have its fifteen Western European members reduce CO_2 emissions by 8 percent compared to 1990 levels by 2008–2012.[20] The EU ETS was designed to coordinate cutbacks across member countries that varied in economic activity and emissions. By 2007, the EU ETS included twenty-seven member countries (new Eastern and Southern European EU members) plus three non-members with the aim of lowering CO_2 emissions by at least 20 percent by 2020 relative to 1990.[21]

The EU ETS is a CO_2 emissions cap-and-allowance trading system that affects iron and steel, certain mineral industries including cement, electric power facilities, refining, and pulp and paper for about 46 percent of the EU's CO_2 discharges.[22] Most of the initial focus was on

---

[19] The acrimony that can take place even within the EU has been clearly evidenced by the continuing efforts within the EU to protect the Euro in the face of potential debt defaults by Greece, Ireland, Portugal, Spain, and Italy, as well as by the differential stands taken by the UK, Germany, and France. One of many sources is http://money .cnn.com/2011/10/10/news/international/merkel_sarkozy_euro_debt_crisis/index.htm.

[20] Austria, Belgium, Denmark, Finland, France, Germany, Greece, Ireland, Italy, Luxembourg, the Netherlands, Portugal, Spain, Sweden, and the United Kingdom. The Kyoto Protocol was drafted at the Committee of Parties (COP) 3 meeting in 1997. Kyoto Protocol to the United Nations Framework Convention on Climate Change, http://unfccc.int/resource/docs/convkp/kpeng.html.

[21] Poland, the Czech Republic, Slovakia, Hungary, Malta, Cyprus, Estonia, Latvia, Lithuania, Bulgaria, Romania, Slovenia plus Iceland, Norway, and Liechtenstein. For a discussion see A. Denny Ellerman and Paul L. Joskow (2008), *European Union's Emissions Trading System in Perspective*, Arlington, Virginia: Pew Center on Global Climate Change and Committee on Climate Change (2011), *Meeting Carbon Budgets – 3rd Progress Report to Parliament*, London.

[22] Joseph Kruger, Wallace E. Oates, and William A. Pizer (2007), "Decentralization in the EU Emissions Trading Scheme and Lessons for Global Policy," *The Review of Environmental Economics and Policy* 1(1): 112–133. About 50 percent of emissions are not covered (transportation, household) for political and cost reasons, so that the EU may not meet its aggregate targets. For a discussion and evaluation of the European Union trading scheme, see Frank J. Convery and Luke Redmond (2007), "Market and Price Developments in the European Union Emissions Trading Scheme," *The Review of Environmental Economics and Policy* 1(1): 88–111; A. Denny A. Ellerman and Barbara K. Buchner (2007), "The European Union Emissions Trading Scheme: Origins, Allocation, and Early Results," *The Review of*

the electricity utility sector, which did not directly face international competition. Moreover the costs could be passed on to consumers with relatively inelastic electricity demands.

There are three trading periods, Phase I, 2005–2007, Phase II, 2008–2012, and Phase III, 2013–2020, with progressively lower caps. The European Commission administers the overall CO_2 target and in the first two phases, member countries devise national allocation plans (NAPs) that define their individual caps and allocate emission allowances to regulated firms that are tradable across the EU.[23] The Commission registers traders, trades, and credits or offset purchases used by companies within member countries to meet CO_2 targets. Most offsets are through credits achieved under the Clean Development Mechanism that allows for emission reduction investments in developing countries.[24] Tradable allocations are largely grandfathered to regulated facilities in the first two phases, but with more to be auctioned in Phase III. Each member country maintains its own registry, monitoring, reporting, and verification system.

At the end of each year during the trading period, the facilities surrender allowances equivalent to their emissions at one allowance per one ton of CO_2 released. Those with emissions below their allowances sell or bank the surplus, and those with excess emissions buy allowances. Companies trade directly with each other; employ a broker; or use a formal exchange. Originally a fine of €40 ($57) per excess ton of CO_2 emitted was imposed on plants exceeding their targets, which rose to €100 ($143) in 2008 to encourage use of the trading scheme, when allocation prices fluctuated at much lower levels.[25]

The European Commission has regulatory jurisdiction over member country emissions within the overall EU Kyoto target. The

---

Environmental Economics and Policy 1(1): 66–87 and A. Denny Ellerman and Paul L. Joskow. (2008), *The European Union's Emissions Trading System in Perspective*, Washington, DC: Pew Center on Global Climate Change.

[23] The Commission can modify a country's NAP if it is not consistent with the overall EU cap. The process is to be more centralized under the Commission in phase three.

[24] The Kyoto Protocol authorized the use of clean development mechanism (CDM), joint implementation (JI) and international emissions trading for developed countries to meet their targets. CDM allows companies to undertake projects in developing countries to reduce emissions and gain credits, certified emissions reductions (CERs); JI similarly allows companies to undertake similar projects within developed countries and gain credits, emissions reduction units (ERUs).

[25] $1.43 per euro in July 2011.

commission defines allocations uniformly as a common commodity for trade across the EU, whose members already are intricately bound economically and politically. In this regard, the EU ETS and the RGGI are loosely consistent with the conditions for successful collective action as outlined in Chapter 4. As it has expanded, however, EU members have become more heterogeneous in historical experiences, economic development, and institutions for supporting markets, collecting data, and enforcing contracts. These differences would have been a greater challenge for coordinated action had not most Eastern European countries received national caps in Phase I that exceeded their actual emissions, allowing them to sell and become net beneficiaries in the scheme. More stringent targets were assigned to larger, developed Western European countries with a longer stake in the EU, such as Germany and the United Kingdom.[26]

Figure 7.2 shows the patterns of weekly emission permit futures prices for those trading during Phase I through 2007 with delivery December 2007 and Phase II with delivery December 2009. Although there could be banking within periods, there was no banking across periods so that the two trading sessions are separate. Phase I prices collapsed after April 2006 and then trended to zero by October 2007. The variation in Phase I prices was due to initial over-allocation of allowances as a result of political pressures and uncertainty as to how many allowances to distribute, as well as the inability of companies to bank them after 2007. Because there was no past trading of carbon allocations, there were no historical price data for benchmarking, and there was limited reliable emissions information at the facility level for grandfathering.

Subsequent price fluctuations during Phase II occurred as a result of shifts in demand for energy from weather and deteriorating macroeconomic conditions after 2008. Trading volumes steadily increased from a

---

[26] See country caps and actual emissions from the European Commission as reported in Ellerman and Joskow (2008) and discussed in Per-Olov Marklund and Eva Samakovlis (2007), "What is driving the EU Burden-Sharing Agreement: Efficiency or Equity?" *Journal of Environmental Management* 85(2): 317–29. There was a decline in carbon emissions and economic activity during the transition to market economies in Eastern Europe and much less information about past discharges for setting allocations. And, as is often the case, politics played a role in enticing new members into the scheme.

EU ETS Allowance Prices

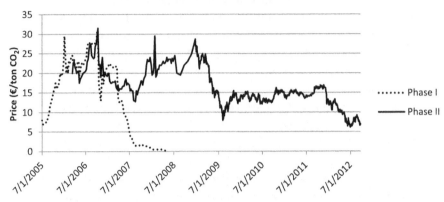

Figure 7.2. EU ETS Emissions Allowance Futures Prices, 2005–2012.
Source: Authors' calculations using nominal prices. January 2005-December 2007 estimated from http://www.c2es.org/docUploads/EU-ETS-In-Perspective-Report.pdf, p. 13: January 2008–July 2012, from Christian de Perthuis and Raphaël Trotignon (2013) "Governance of CO_2 Markets: Lessons from the EU ETS," Paris-Dauphine University CDC Climat Working Paper 2013–07, p. 10.

monthly average of about 10 million units in the first quarter of 2005 to around 100 million from the first quarter of 2007 onward. Over-the-counter exchanges account for about two-thirds of all trading activity, and exchange markets account for the other third.[27]

An oversupply of Phase II permits caused prices to fall from €30 ($43) in 2008 to less than €10 ($14.30) by the end of 2011. A general economic slowdown in Europe reduced demand for electricity and emission allowances, and the EU in 2012 sold an additional 300 million permits to fund green energy projects, which further reduced prices. Finally, the EU introduced new command-and-control regulations on energy efficiency to lower emissions further, a factor not considered in setting the cap. If effective, the new regulations will reduce demand for permits. By 2020, the EU ETS could have a surplus of 845 million permits against a planned cap for that year of 1.8 billion. This condition will not only keep allowance prices low, but reduce incentives for firms to invest in emission-reduction technologies in lieu of purchasing (cheap) permits. The EU is considering intervening into

[27] Ellerman and Joskow (2008).

the market by withholding enough permits to raise the price.[28] At the same time while the decline in permit prices reduces incentives of regulated firms to reduce emissions, fewer permits, a tighter cap, and higher energy prices are resisted by countries in the EU suffering from stagnant economic growth and loss of international competitiveness. A tug of war is developing between EU climate policy and the European Commission and political leaders in member countries concerned with deteriorating economic outcomes.[29]

All of this is indicative of a potentially insecure cap-and-trade market, subject to political and bureaucratic interventions that can undermine its effectiveness in a somewhat similar manner to what has occurred with the U.S. SO_2 market. Adjusting the cap requires negotiations among EU members, and high emitters, such as Poland, resist further cap reductions. These political moves probably cannot be avoided, suggesting that the cap will be set higher than would be the case if firms were more homogeneous and located in a single political jurisdiction.

The EU ETS has achieved some abatement success, but according to the International Energy Agency, overall world CO_2 emissions have continued to rise. This suggests that a much tighter EU ETS cap would be required to reduce the buildup of global concentrations, unless other countries cut back more.[30] The European Commission is not directly accountable to member country citizens. This political autonomy allows the Commission to issue costly regulations to meet CO_2 emission targets. Whether or not this authority is politically sustainable in the face of difficult economic conditions within the European Union and continued global free riding on CO_2 is unclear.

RGGI and the EU ETS are cap-and-trade programs that involve exchange of permits to emit. The incentives to participate arise from

---

[28] Longyearbyen (2012), "Carbon Prices: Breathing Difficulties: A Market in Need of a Miracle," *Economist* March 3.

[29] See Sean Carney, "Europe's Emissions Plan Hits Turbulence: Crisis Hampers Program Aimed at Fighting Global Warming, as Economic Recovery Efforts and Environmental Goals Clash," February 20, 2013, A10, http://online.wsj.com/article/SB10001424127887323764804578314130143612990.html.

[30] http://www.iea.org/index_info.asp?id=1959. Emissions by country are provided the UN in thousand metric tons, in http://mdgs.un.org/unsd/mdg/SeriesDetail.aspx?srid=749&crid=. See also http://www.global-greenhouse-warming.com/IPCC-greenhouse-gas-emission-trends.html.

the value of the permit relative to the cost of abatement. The overall objective is to provide a global public good in the form of reduced CO_2 emissions. Participating organizations do not necessarily capture any private benefits from the reductions other than reduced abatement costs. In the following cases, however, the cap-and-trade programs involve the right to fish, individual transferable quotas (ITQs). In these examples, the objective is to create rents in a larger stock and the property rights holders are in a position to capture some of those returns. This changes the nature of the cap-and-trade program in a manner we explore in Chapter 8. To begin, it is instructive to see how they operate in a multijurisdictional setting. The first case involves parallel (ITQ) programs in the United States and Canada.

THE PACIFIC NORTHWEST HALIBUT FISHERY IN THE UNITED STATES AND CANADA

Transboundary fisheries are an example of a resource that can benefit from a market solution. In the case of fisheries, using a two period data set, 1994 and 2002 for 200 fish stocks, some of which migrate across jurisdictional boundaries, McWhinnie (2009) finds that those that are shared among many countries on the high seas are systematically over-exploited, controlling for other factors. The probability of overharvest increases with the number of countries utilizing the stock. For example, if two countries are fishing a single stock, it is nine percent more likely to be overharvested and 19 percent more likely to be depleted than a fishery that is solely within one country. If the stock is shared by five countries, it is 36 percent more likely to be overfished and 82 percent more likely to be depleted. It does not matter how much of a country's waters are involved (the portion within its exclusive economic zone or EEZ). Cross-country access appears to be a key determinant of overharvest. Further, higher-valued, slower-growing stocks are most at risk.[31]

The Pacific Northwest halibut fishery offers an excellent example of how a property rights solution can be applied to a fishery for which

---

[31] Stephanie F. McWhinnie (2009), "The Tragedy of the Commons in International Fisheries: An Empirical Examination," *Journal of Environmental Economics and Management* 57: 321–333; 328–329.

two countries share a single stock, exclusion is possible, and each has a rights-based system. Canada adopted an individual transferable quota system by vessel (IVQ) in 1990, and the United States adopted a similar, individual fishery quota (IFQ) in 1995. The benefits of both were evidenced by increases in season length, reduction in vessel numbers, and growth in the share of fresh halibut sold.[32] The question is how have these two separate cap-and-trade programs cooperated and performed? Has a cross-jurisdiction market emerged?

Following the criteria for successful collective action outlined in Chapter 4, we might anticipate cooperation. Only two countries are involved, there is a long-standing history of collaboration and trust, and the fisheries are bounded within the EEZs of the two countries. Although there are numerous fishers in both countries, those with quotas have incentives to protect the stock within their own fishing areas.

The United States and Canada cooperate on the management of halibut under the Halibut Convention of 1923, which also created the International Pacific Halibut Commission (IPHC), a scientific body that conducts stock assessments and recommends conservation measures. In 1976 the IPCH's jurisdiction was extended to include the EEZs of both countries. The United States and Canada are responsible for management within their respective areas, but each country's fishers are to stay within the total harvest quotas set by the IPHC for its 10 regulatory areas as part of the overall Total Allowable Catch (TAC).

As shown in Figure 7.3, the areas covered in the IPHC's jurisdiction include the Pacific Northwest, the Gulf of Alaska, the Aleutian Islands, and the Eastern Bering Sea. Since the introduction of rights-based systems in both countries, halibut stocks have improved.[33] There also are strong ex-vessel revenues, driven by the sale of fresh halibut, and there are proposals to extend the season from 245 to 321 days. Average

---

[32] Christopher M. Dewees, Bruce R. Turris, and James E. Wilen (1995), "The Effects of Individual Vessel Quotas in the British Columbia Halibut Fishery," *Marine Resource Economics* 10: 211–30; R. Quentin Grafton, Dale Squires, and Kevin J. Fox (2000), "Private Property and Economic Efficiency: A Study of a Common-Pool Resource," *The Journal of Law and Economics* 43(2), 679–713; Mark Herrmann and Keith Criddle (2006), "An Econometric Market Model for the Pacific Halibut Fishery," *Marine Resource Economics* 21: 129–158.

[33] Recent (2012) assessments in the U.S. fishery, however, have raised concerns about just how large the stock is.

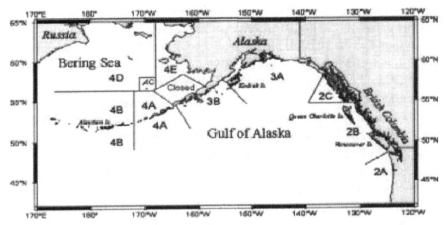

Figure 7.3. IPHC Regulatory Areas[34]
Source: Mark Herrmann and Keith Criddle (2006), "An Econometric Market Model for the Pacific Halibut Fishery," *Marine Resource Economics* 21: 129–158, 130.

ex-vessel prices are virtually identical across the two countries, indicating the degree to which the market is integrated.[35]

In this case, international cooperation and a market involving two separate cap-and-trade systems perform well. Within the overall U.S. and Canadian rights system, use rights as IVQs and IFQs have been relatively secure, even without formal property rights guarantees, with no apparent serious intervention by the regulatory agency or politicians to undermine them. In part, this may be because the fishery stock is so vigorous and revenues so high that the parties have organized to protect them.[36] At the same time, Canadian and U.S. fishers are excluded from one another's territories. This effectively precludes a cross-jurisdictional market. Political resistance to integration prevents cross-country exchanges.

ATLANTIC BLUEFIN TUNA CONSERVATION

Overfishing of Atlantic bluefin tuna illustrates the problem for creating secure property rights in wild ocean fisheries when entry

[34] IPHC objectives, policies, and programs are described at http://www.iphc.int/.
[35] Hermann and Criddle (2006, 130–154).
[36] There have been some distributional impacts on processors, especially those less able to respond to the new fresh fish market. No significant redistribution that weakens the quota shares is apparent.

cannot be prevented. The losses associated with highly-migratory, open-ocean fisheries are generally greater than with more territorial species, such as halibut.[37] They cross the 200-mile exclusive economic zones of coastal states, recognized by the United Nations Convention on the Law of the Sea (UNCLOS), and travel the high seas.[38] Accordingly, highly-migratory stocks are subject to competitive fishing by vessels from multiple countries, and many stocks have declined significantly. Capacity and vessel numbers are increasing as developing countries with little fishing history expand fleets or provide flags of convenience to distant water fishing nations.

Perhaps no fishery better reflects problems involved with highly-migratory species than the Atlantic bluefin tuna *Thunnus thynnus*. Bluefin tuna are the world's most valuable fish by weight. Prices are often greater than $100,000 per fish, and a 489-pound tuna sold for $1.78 million at Tokyo's Tsukiji fish market in January 2013.[39] The International Commission for the Conservation of Atlantic Tunas for the Atlantic (ICCAT) is one of five Regional Fishery Management Organizations (RFMOs) that are charged with the management of the world's bluefin tunas and other fish.[40] RFMOs are organizational structures to bring countries together to manage fish that roam in and out of multiple countries' exclusive economic zones and into the open ocean that is owned by no country. The ICCAT's territory covers the Atlantic, the Mediterranean, and the Gulf of Mexico. Figure 7.4 illustrates ICCAT's management area, the eastern and western stocks within its jurisdiction (divided by ICCAT along the 45°W meridian), and their perceived migratory patterns and spawning grounds. Stocks in the eastern and western Atlantic have steadily declined from historic levels, and current harvests appear unsustainable.

One might think that with such a valuable fishery property rights and effective management would develop along the lines described

[37] UNCLOS Annex 1 lists Highly-Migratory Species United Nations (1982). *United Nations Convention on the Law of the Sea*. U.N. Doc. A/Conf. 62/122.
[38] The UN Convention on the Law of the Sea followed from the third UN Conference on the Law of the Sea (UNCLOS III) adopted in 1982.
[39] http://en.mercopress.com/2013/01/12/bluefin-tuna-opens-2013-with-record-auction-price-at-tsukiji-1.78-million-dollars. These very high January prices are ceremonial compared to the average sale.
[40] International Convention for the Conservation of Atlantic tunas opened for signature May 14, 1966, 673 U.N.T.S. 63, 20 U.S.T. 2887.

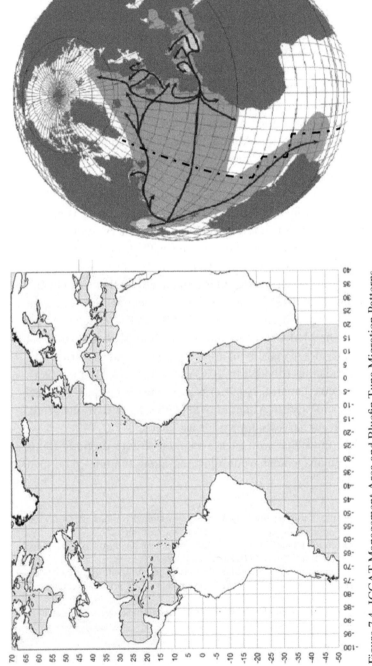

Figure 7.4. ICCAT Management Area and Bluefin Tuna Migration Patterns.
Source: ICCAT Convention Area http://www.iccat.int/en/convarea.htm. Map of the spatial distribution of Atlantic bluefin tuna, main migration routes and spawning grounds. The vertical dashed line depicts the stock delimitation between the two current ICCAT management units (modified after Jean-Marc Fromentin and Joseph Powers (2005), "Atlantic Bluefin Tuna: Population Dynamics, Ecology, Fisheries and Management," *Fish and Fisheries* 6(4), 281–306).

by Demsetz (1967).[41] But this has not occurred. A major problem in gaining consensus on management to conserve the stock is the lack of exclusion. RFMOs such as the ICCAT generally set an annual total allowable catch (TAC) consistent with maximum sustainable yield or other criteria and allocate the TAC across members. Member countries, in turn, distribute their quota among their fishing fleets. These are a property right to fish. New countries entering a fishery, however, are to be included in the management organization following Articles 8, 10, and 11 of the 1995 FAO Code of Conduct for Responsible Fisheries, and the 1995 UN Agreement on the Conservation and Management of Straddling Fish and Highly Migratory Fish Stocks (UNFSA).[42] Bringing new fishing states into the conservation scheme as required by international conventions, however, dilutes existing member countries' shares of the overall TAC and any stock improvements brought about by their harvest restraints. In the case of bluefin tuna, the number of ICCAT members grew from nine in 1970 to forty-eight in 2008 with most new members being developing countries.[43] Table 7.2 shows the nature of entry into the fishery.[44]

Coastal states have sole authority within their exclusive economic zones, and although ICCAT prohibits the sale of TAC quotas, developing countries without an established industry circumvent this restriction by selling flags of convenience to fleets from other nations. With new entry there are disputes over the property rights associated with

[41] Harold Demsetz (1967), "Toward a Theory of Property Rights," *American Economic Review* 57: 347–359.

[42] A summary of UNCLOS is available here: http://www.un.org/Depts/los/convention_agreements/convention_historical_perspective.htm. The 200-mile EEZ resulted from the third United Nations Conference on the Law of the Sea (UNCLOS III), held between 1973 and 1982, and UNCLOS came into force on November 16, 1994. The 1995 *Code of Conduct for Responsible Fisheries* is described at FAO (1995) and ftp://ftp.fao.org/docrep/fao/005/v9878e/v9878e00.pdf, and the 1995 *Agreement for the Implementation of the Provisions of the United Nations Convention on the Law of the Sea of 10 December 1982 Relating to the Conservation and Management of Straddling Fish Stocks and Highly Migratory Fish Stocks* http://www.un.org/Depts/los/convention_agreements/texts/fish_stocks_agreement/CONF164_37.htm.

[43] A list of ICCAT Contracting Parties is available online: http://www.iccat.int/en/contracting.htm.

[44] ICCAT maintains an online database of vessels authorized to fish actively for bluefin tuna in the eastern Atlantic and the Mediterranean Sea: http://www.iccat.int/en/vesselsrecord.asp.

Table 7.2. *Summary of Entry into the Eastern Atlantic Bluefin Tuna Fishery*

Country Group	Year Joined ICCAT	Number of Active Vessels	1980 Harvest Share (%)	2008 Harvest Share (%)
Developed[1]	1970–2004	356	85.5	59.2
Developing[2]	1969–2007	656	14.5	41.8

[1] Developed countries include: European Union (France, Spain, Italy, Greece, Malta, Cyprus, Portugal, Ireland, and Denmark), Norway, Japan, Iceland, and Korea.
[2] Developing countries include: Morocco, Croatia, Tunisia, Libya, Turkey, Algeria, China, Egypt, Syria, Yugoslavia, Panama, and Chinese Taipei.
Source: Authors' calculations based on the following data: Year joined: http://www.iccat .int/en/contracting.htm; Vessels: http://www.iccat.int/en/vesselsrecord.asp; Harvest data are from International Commission for the Conservation of Atlantic Tunas (ICCAT). (2011). "Report of the 2010 Atlantic Bluefin Tuna Stock Assessment Session (Madrid, Spain – September 6 to 12, 2010)," *ICCAT Collective Volume of Scientific Papers* 66(2): 505–714, 614–617.

existing ICCAT TAC assignments. Allocation on the basis of historical catch disadvantages new members and countries whose fisheries traditionally used smaller vessels or less advanced equipment. Many coastal states have only small tuna fleets, but want to take advantage of the valuable fishery with a greater share of the TAC. Between 1983 and 1991, TAC distributions were heavily weighted by historical harvest, but at the insistence of new members since that time, more weight has been given to coastal state proximity to the fishery and consideration for developing-country industries. This TAC distribution encourages entry, and support for major TAC reductions among new RFMO members is limited. Current members resist quota reductions below historical catch, whereas new members oppose grandfathering allocations.[45]

Bluefin and other tunas fare better in another RFMO, the Western and Central Fisheries Commission.[46] Established in 2004, WCPFC

[45] R. Quentin Grafton, Rögnvaldur Hannesson, Bruce Shallard, Daryl R. Sykes, and Joseph Terry (2010), "The Economics of Allocation in Tuna Regional Fisheries Management Organizations," in Robin Allen, James Joseph and Dale Squires, eds., *Conservation and Management of Transnational Tuna Fisheries*, Oxford, UK: Wiley-Blackwell, 155–162 and Seth Korman (2011), "International Management of a High Seas Fishery: Political and Property-Rights Solutions and the Atlantic Bluefin," *Virginia Journal of International Law* 51(3): 697–748, 742.
[46] WCPFC, www.wcpfc.int/.

is more successful because of effective cooperation among four-teen Pacific island countries and eight territories whose exclusive economic zones overlap much of the relevant tuna area. This setting allows for exclusion and more closely meets Scott's (1955) sole ownership condition. The countries in the WCPFC are comparatively homogeneous in their economic development, do not have significant domestic fleets but have processing industries, and eight of the countries coordinate management through the Parties to the Nauru Agreement of 1982. The organization has effectively moderated harvest and prevented rent dissipation, at least for some tuna stocks.[47]

Creating a cap-and-trade market for tuna is difficult because secure quota assignments require entry constraints under conditions where there are differential incentives for existing and potential fishing nations to support such restrictions. For developed countries with established fleets, adjustable TACs and quota reallocations transfer rents achieved from conservation to entrants from developing countries. For developing countries, entry controls prevent expansion of their fishing industries. These differences make it difficult for political leaders to agree on limiting entry into an RFMO and associated participation in its TAC. Conceivably, developing countries could purchase the right to fish from fishers in developed countries who hold shares of the TAC, but these exchanges are prohibited by international conventions, such as UNCLOS provisions requiring that the high seas be open to nationals of all countries.[48] Moreover, such trading would involve payments from poorer developing countries to fishers in richer developed ones. Equity norms typically run counter to such transfers. As a result, it may be impossible to reach agreement on a property rights distribution that satisfies the objectives of both groups while protecting the stock.

WHALE CONSERVATION

A final example, whale conservation, is similar to tuna, but may be more amenable to a market solution because there are few incumbent

---

[47] Robert Gillett (2010), *Marine Fishery Resources of the Pacific Islands*, FAO Fisheries and Aquaculture Technical Paper, No. 537, Rome, FAO and Tom McClurg (2012). "A Case Study of High Seas Fisheries Governance: The PNA Agreement," paper presented at *Tackling the Global Fisheries Challenge*, PERC, Bozeman, MT, November 14–15.

[48] Convention on the Law of the Sea Article, 116, Dec. 10, 1982, 1833 U.N.T.S. 397.

Figure 7.5. Early Whaling When the Odds Were More Even.
Source: Google Images: http://sanctuaries.noaa.gov/maritime/whaling/.

fishing fleets. Historically, whales have been extremely valuable for meat, spermaceti, oil for use in cosmetics, and even more for oil as a light source and lubricant. Because whales have been and still are so valuable, open access to their harvest has brought serious declines in many of the world's whale populations.

To reverse the overharvest of whales, the International Whaling Commission (IWC) was established in 1946. The purpose of the IWC is "safeguarding for future generations the great natural resources represented by the whale stocks." This is a voluntary agreement and member countries can join or drop out as they wish. The IWC began with fifteen whale-hunting nations, but by 2011 there were eighty-nine members with many having no history of whaling. Indeed, some are landlocked, such as Switzerland and Mongolia. Since 1986, there has been a ban on commercial whaling under the IWC's moratorium. In a dramatic switch, the United States has gone from being one of the world's great whaling nations to being one of the most ardent supporters of the ban.

Not all countries agree that the moratorium is justified for all species. Japanese fleets have harvested whales under "scientific permits," since 1986, which are allowed by the IWC, but is condemned for doing so. Russia opposed the moratorium, Canada withdrew from the IWC in 1982 to protest prohibitions on small-scale whaling, and Norway and Iceland persist in whaling in limited numbers under their own quotas. The IWC allows limited annual aboriginal "subsistence" harvest quotas that citizens of the United States, Denmark, and Russia use. Anti-whaling non-governmental organizations, such as Greenpeace, charge that whaling continues to draw down stocks. Overall, documented whaling accounts for annual harvests of about 2,000 whales per year, and there likely are more unreported harvests.[49]

The IWC also allows intergovernmental organizations and non-governmental organizations, primarily environmental groups, to attend the meetings and to be represented by observers if they meet certain requirements. The expansion in IWC membership reflects the growing politicization of whale conservation as the anti-whaling movement has grown since the 1970s. Pro-and anti-whaling countries and groups campaign for their respective positions at annual IWC meetings. The United States incorporated the IWC policies into domestic law in the 1971 Pelly Amendment to the Fisherman's Protective Act of 1967. This amendment authorizes the Secretary of Commerce to notify the president if any country's fishing is diminishing the effectiveness of an international fishery conservation program (including the IWC's program). The president then has discretion to limit fish imports from that country. The United State has threatened sanctions under the Pelly Amendment as well as restrictions on access to U.S. fishing grounds under the 1979 Packwood-Magnuson Amendment to the Fishery Conservation and Management Act of 1976 to gain support for its position in IWC votes. In contrast, fishers from coastal countries, such as Iceland, argue that some whales are predators of their fish stocks and should be harvested.[50]

Internal politicking within the IWC creates a contentious, adversarial atmosphere that offers little for developing scientific evidence about the true conditions of whale stocks or, importantly, for enlisting incentives to protect those species that require it. Misinformation, moralizing, and emotion are used by both sides. It is a zero sum game,

[49] Calculated from figures in Christopher Costello, Leah R. Gerber, Steven Gaines (2012), "A Market Approach to Saving the Whales," *Nature* 481: 12 January: 139–140.

[50] A summary of some of the politics involved is provided in http://en.wikipedia.org/wiki/International_Whaling_Commission.

possibly for some whale stocks as well. There is no consensus as to the appropriate benchmark for maintaining or ending the moratorium on harvest for each species. Should it be preindustrial harvest levels or should it be an estimate of the stock necessary to sustain the species? The former objective may be unachievable, and the second requires considerable scientific information, much of which may not exist. Experience in fishery management, however, reveals that involving fishers, who depend on a species, know it well, and traverse its habitat frequently, is an invaluable tool for obtaining such information.[51] The current hostile setting generates little incentive or means for cooperation on information generation and sharing.

Financial considerations cannot be weighed in an informed manner. Large amounts are spent annually by the IWC and other organizations to gather data on whales, analyze and discuss it in yearly meetings, and to police the moratorium. Anti-whaling groups raise funds to support their efforts to impede whaling vessels, an action that also is dangerous for both parties. The economies of communities, especially those in Japan that have depended on whaling decline. Unfortunately, the opportunity costs of the moratorium for each species are unknown. Given the evidence on stocks, some whales might be harvested in particular areas with little damage. Even discussion of removing some successfully-rebounding species, such as the humpback whale from endangered status, however, meets intense opposition.[52] A movement within the IWC to review the ban on whaling and to allow for regulated harvest under a Revised Management Scheme is stalled.[53]

The data shown in Table 7.3 are drawn primarily from the IWC, and many whale populations are not known with precision. The IWC has a scientific committee that collects data and algorithms to estimate what populations are required to meet sustainable stock levels. Further some stocks are very local whereas others are widely dispersed

[51] Terry L. Anderson, Ragnar Arnason, and Gary D. Libecap (2011), "Efficiency Advantages of Grandfathering in Rights-Based Fisheries Management," *Annual Review of Resource Economics* 3: 159–179; 166.

[52] http://online.wsj.com/article/SB125745793337231859.html http://wiki.answers.com/Q/What_are_the_humpback_whales_current_population_status.

[53] The politics is quite evident from reading IWC meeting descriptions and resolutions http://www.iwcoffice.org/meetings/resolutions/resolutionmain.htm.

Figure 7.6. A Dangerous Confrontation between Whalers and Their Adversaries.
Source: http://www.mnn.com/earth-matters/translating-uncle-sam/stories/are-endangered-whales-still-in-danger.

and migrate over wide ranges. Stock estimates also are affected by other environmental factors, such as food supply, accident mortality (colliding with ships, by catch in fishing), and water quality. Assessing the "fitness" of the population (reproductive success, growth trends) for any harvest, however, has been very controversial.

The data in Table 7.3 suggest that some whale stocks have rebounded nicely and limited whaling might be feasible. At the same time, the discussion of the command-and-control moratorium of the IWC, wherein control depends on lobbying, publicity, and harassing whaling vessels, indicates little consensus for effective collective action. A tradable quota system with a more collaboratively determined cap for each species offers a potentially viable and attractive alternative. This arrangement builds on one described recently by Costello, Gerber, and Gaines (2012). It draws on successful management of many fisheries through the setting of total annual allowable catches and their distribution as tradable shares among fishermen (usually ITQs). These are typically assigned through past catch histories and in New Zealand and Iceland are strong long-term property rights, giving fishermen a stake in the survival of the stock, and an ability to trade quotas and consolidate or diversify as economic conditions warrant. Moreover, catch

Table 7.3. *Whale Stock Estimates*

Species	Population Estimate
Minke Whales	
Southern Hemispheres	761,000
North Atlantic	174,000
West Greenland	10,800
Northwest Pacific and Okhotsk Sea	25,000
Blue Whales	
Southern Hemisphere (Excluding Pygmy Blue)	2,300
Fin Whales	
North Atlantic (Central and Northeastern)	30,000
West Greenland	3,200
Grey Whales	
Eastern North Pacific	26,300
Western North Pacific	121
Bowhead Whales	
Bering-Chukchi-Beaufort Seas	10,500
West Greenland	1,230
Humpback Whales	
Western North Atlantic	11,600
Southern Hemisphere	42,000
North Pacific	10,000+
Right Whales	
Western North Atlantic	300
Southern Hemisphere	7,500
Bryde's Whales	
Western North Pacific	20,500
Pilot Whales	
Central and Eastern North Atlantic	780,000
Sperm Whale	100,000's

Source: http://iwcoffice.org/conservation/estimate.htm and B.L. Taylor, R. Baird, J. Barlow, S.M. Dawson, J. Ford, J.G. Mead, G. Notarbartolo di Sciara, P. Wade, and R.L. Pitman (2008), *Physeter macrocephalus.* In: IUCN (2011*). IUCN Red List of Threatened Species*, Version 2011.2. <www.iucnredlist.org>. Downloaded on 27 March 2012.

shares have an empirical record of changing incentives and improving the stock.[54]

The market would work as follows. Annual maximum catches would be determined for each whale stock that was designated as healthy.

---

[54] Christopher Costello, Steven D. Gaines, and John Lynham (2008), "Can Catch Shares Prevent Fisheries Collapse?" *Science* September 19, 321(5896): 1678–1681.

This of course would require collaboration between whalers and scientists, but in a new environment, such cooperation is more likely. With a value attached to whales, as outlined below, opportunity costs emerge for banning whaling, encouraging the selection of a reasonable benchmark for determining a species' stock status and setting a corresponding algorithm for setting annual harvests.

With a total harvest set, quotas would be distributed to member countries of the IWC, who could then distribute them among their citizens in any manner they chose or retire them. The initial allocation would be weighted toward countries with historical catch histories, but some quota would be granted to countries with no past whaling record. These distributed quotas would be fully useable or tradable to anyone – whalers themselves as well as to pro- or anti-whaling countries or groups. To reduce uncertainty, fully engage incentives, and limit regulatory interventions as occurred in the U.S. SO_2 market, the quotas would be recognized property rights, held in perpetuity. The number of whales ultimately hunted would depend on who owned the quota.

Costello, Gerber, and Gaines estimate that the per-whale values or costs to those wishing to engage in or reduce harvest likely range from \$13,000 (abundant Minke) – \$85,000 (less abundant Fin).[55] Such market trades could allow for all parties to be made better off and harvests for some species to be reduced to zero, whereas others could have "legal" and unimpeded whaling. When conservationists purchase shares from whalers, they benefit from the increased whale populations, and whalers benefit from receiving compensation. This is not only a win-win opportunity, but it depoliticizes whaling and creates a framework for protecting species that requires it and allows some harvest for others whose stocks appear vibrant.[56]

CONCLUSION

Broad, cross-jurisdiction, open-access problems are very difficult to address through the assignment of property rights and use of environmental markets because of the high transaction costs involved.

---

[55] Costello, Gerber, and Gaines (2012, 140).
[56] Costello, Gerber, Gaines (2012, 140).

There are not only resource costs in measurement and bounding, but political costs in distributing and enforcing property rights and market exchanges. Politicians have short-time horizons and political constituencies to consider. Bureaucrats have agency mandates and prerogatives to protect. Rights-based arrangements, however, reduce the options for both. But they have the merit of actually promoting environmental and natural resource stock improvements. As Coase pointed out in 1960, the challenge is to align private and public incentives and more complete property rights and trade allow for this alignment.[57]

There clearly are challenges. The initial allocation of property rights is contentious because it involves a distribution of wealth and political influence, and to reduce the losses of the commons some parties must be denied. Hence, there are difficult distributional outcomes and political risks affecting politicians and citizens across countries. Further, agency officials are always tempted to intervene with regulatory mandates that are often counterproductive with the performance of the market and reduce confidence in property rights. These problems exist within *single* political jurisdictions, but they are amplified in a multiple jurisdiction context. More constituencies, more politicians, and more bureaucrats, often with differential interests and certainly with different allegiances, are involved.

Pre-emptive command-and-control regulation, however, may even be more problematic. Enforcement and compliance costs could end up higher than with markets for achieving the same environmental objective. If exclusion is possible, markets involve locals, as a more bottom-up institution, and enlist their incentives. Regulation, especially at the cross jurisdiction and international levels, necessarily involves a heavy dose of top-down decrees. The experience with regulated open access in other settings reveals that costs actually are driven up and goals missed when affected parties compete on unrestricted margins for rents.[58] And because they are not owners, they have little ability to

---

[57] Ronald Coase (1960), "The Problem of Social Cost," *Journal of Law and Economics* 3: 1–44.

[58] Frances R. Homans and James E. Wilen (1997), "A Model of Regulated Open Access Resource Use," *Journal of Environmental Economics and Management* 32: 1–27, make regulation endogenous and show how rent dissipation can be higher

forestall the aggregate negative effects on the stock.[59] Property rights must be secure ~~to avoid this tragedy~~. Some of the cases described in this chapter, however, indicate that the costs involved may be too high for property rights and markets to be used in a collaborative manner across countries, at least until a resource or environmental crisis appears.

under regulated open access than pure open access. This is another form of cost not generally considered.

[59] Steven N.S. Cheung (1970), "The Structure of a Contract and the Theory of a Non-Exclusive Resource," *Journal of Law and Economics* 13(1): 49–70.

8

Property Rights and Environmental Markets

In a nutshell, this book has made the case for environmental markets based on well-defined, enforced, and transferable property rights. If all three exist, owners have an incentive to consider the full effects of their actions as they engage in Coasean bargaining to mitigate the losses of open access. Property rights – informal or formal, individual or group – help reduce the tragedy of the commons by assigning the costs and benefits of decisions, making the opportunity costs clear, limiting the race to capture rents, and allowing owners to reallocate resources across uses and across time. Property rights identify the relevant people who have a stake in the resource and who can engage in negotiation and contracting. Without them, there is little basis for bargaining. Absent exclusivity, any party can enter and compete for resource rents regardless of any agreement made by an initial group of users. Because everyone knows this potential, bargaining for environmental quality cannot gain much traction.

Property rights define expectations regarding entitlements from resource use, investment, coordination, and cooperation, relative to nonowners. They provide incentives for considering long-time horizons and for long-lasting collaboration. This certainly is necessary because most environmental and natural resource challenges involve the long term, require exclusion, and necessitate teamwork for solution. Secure property rights economize on the transaction costs of decision making, allowing market exchange, investment, and experimentation to take place quickly in response to new information regarding the environmental and natural resource asset. Given the limited scientific knowledge that often accompanies many open-access problems, the information generation and flexibility of markets are particularly critical.

We do not view property rights as a bundle of sticks with each stick referring to a particular attribute, such as exclusivity, transferability, durability, distinct use rights, and so forth. This notion of property implies that the sticks or attributes can be peeled away in the regulatory process without undermining the property right. But this view is incorrect. As use rights are stripped from rights holders, the role of the property institution in promoting efficiency in environmental and resource use gradually is lost. If legislators, regulatory agency officials, and judges can arbitrarily remove these "sticks" without due process and compensation, then there is little to constrain such actions. Costs are born by owners (and society) and not directly by agency officials or advocacy groups, for instance, who seek to limit the range of actions owners can take.[1] Opportunity costs are not weighed, and as rights are abridged, the gaps between social and private benefits and costs in use decisions and investment, often critical for the resource, are widened. The tragedy of the commons ensues.

Of course, property rights are never complete because of transaction costs, which can make definition, enforcement, and exchange too costly. Transaction costs are the costs of establishing and maintaining property rights, and they include costs of collecting, measuring, and analyzing information about the net benefits of mitigating open-access losses and their distribution across populations, costs of negotiation among individual claimants and politicians for recognition and definition, and costs of enforcement.[2] Even environmental economists who criticize command-and-control regulation recognize the potential for market failure as a result of transaction costs – in this case, the high costs of bargaining over the use of air, fish, or other resources, too little information and too few parties for competitive trades, limited supply

---

[1] Thomas W. Merrill and Henry E. Smith (2010), *Property*, New York: Oxford University Press, 1–13 argue this point, that property rights are not a bundle of sticks, but full ownership of the asset.

[2] Transaction costs, as they are used here, are defined by Douglas W. Allen (1991), "What are Transaction Costs?" *Research in Law and Economics* 14: 1–18 and Douglas W. Allen (2000), "Transaction Costs," in Boudewijn Bouckaert and Gerrit De Geest, eds., *The Encyclopedia of Law and Economics*, Vol. 1, Cheltenham: Edward Elgar, 893–926.

options creating market power, and free riding on public goods. This criticism begs three questions – why are transaction costs so high, can they be reduced, and if not, can resource management and environmental quality be improved using alternative institutions, essentially collective action through government?

Given the ubiquity of centralized environmental regulations, we began in Chapter 2 addressing the last question – what is the efficacy of environmental regulation? Since the 1970s, with the creation of the Environmental Protection Agency, the adoption of sweeping new amendments to the Clean Air and Clean Water Acts, and the enactment of the Endangered Species Act, environmental protections have largely become top-down regulatory processes, centralized by the federal government.[3] Overarching environmental and resource concerns have become more amenable to the imposition of categorical prohibitions (uniform technology and performance standards), rather than being addressed through the weighing of alternatives in a cost-effective manner on a case-by-case basis and a balancing of marginal benefits and costs. As a consequence, there is far greater reliance on statutes and administrative rulings than on adjudication of conflicts under the common law by state and local government actions to address environmental or resource dilemmas or by the further definition or refinement of property rights – individual or group – to directly confront the source of the problem.[4] This pattern of centralized regulation is driven both by an exogenous growth in popular demands for environmental quality and natural resource conservation that often cross jurisdictional boundaries as well as by endogenous demands from the regulatory institutions themselves and the political constituents linked to them.[5]

Also, since the 1970s, the concept of the environment has grown to encompass an expansive and eclectic array of issues, including clean

---

[3] Endangered Species Act: 7 U.S.C. § 136, 16 U.S.C. § 1531 *et seq.* (1973); Clean Air Act 42 U.S.C. §7401 *et seq.* (1970); and Clean Water Act: 33 U.S.C. § 1251 *et seq.* (1972).

[4] Steven J. Eagle (2008), "The Common Law and the Environment," *Case Western Law Review* 53(3): 583–620.

[5] Robert N. Stavins (2007), "Market-Based Environmental Policies: What Can We Learn from U.S. Experience (and Related Research)?" in Jody Freeman and Charles D. Kolstad, eds., *Moving to Markets in Environmental Regulation*, New York: Oxford University Press, 25; Nathaniel O. Keohane, Richard L. Revesz, and Robert N. Stavins (1998), "The Choice of Regulatory Instruments in Environmental Policy," *The Harvard Environmental Law Review* 22: 313–345.

air, water, and soil; vibrant fish and wildlife populations; expanded natural habitats, both for people and for non-humans; recreational access; biodiversity; ecosystem services; and so on. Meeting this collection of demands would be challenging even if there were a clear sense of prioritization, an understanding of the tradeoffs required in meeting them, and a nesting of spatial dimensions that allowed for determination of problem ranges, identification of the parties affected, and political jurisdictions. But none of these conditions exist. The current regulatory process does not encourage ranking, weighing of alternatives, or defininition of requisite problem and political boundaries.[6] As a result, there is an overlapping myriad of regulatory agencies at the federal and state level (EPA, U.S. Fish and Wildlife Service, NOAA's National Marine Fishery Service, U.S. Forest Service, U.S. Bureau of Land Management, U.S. National Park Service, for the federal government alone) with potentially conflicting jurisdictions, objectives, and aligned constituents.

As public choice analysis has shown, government failure stands at least side-by-side with market failure.[7] Constituent group politics, political incentives, and bureaucratic agendas determine policies, and

---

[6] For example, consider the politics of the Clean Air Act as discussed in Paul L. Joskow and Richard Schmalensee (1998), "The Political Economy of Market-Based Environmental Policy: The U.S. Acid Rain Program," *Journal of Law and Economics* 41 (April): 37–83; Robert W. Hahn (1990), "The Politics and Religion of Clean Air," *Regulation* (Winter): 21–30; and Bruce Ackerman and William T. Hassler (1981), *Clean Coal/Dirty Air: or How the Clean Air Act Became a Multibillion-Dollar Bail-Out for High-Sulfur Coal Producers*, New Haven: Yale University Press.

[7] The classic works on interest groups and interest group politics in economics are Mancur Olson (1965), *The Logic of Collective Action* Cambridge, MA: Harvard University Press; James M. Buchanan and Gordon Tullock (1962), *The Calculus of Consent*, Ann Arbor, MI: University of Michigan Press; Becker (1983); Peltzman (1976); and George J. Stigler (1971), "The Theory of Economic Regulation," *Bell Journal of Economics and Management* 2: 3–21. In political science, see Harold D. Lasswell (1936), *Politics: Who Gets What, When, How?* New York: McGraw Hill; Barry Weingast and William Marshall (1988), "The Industrial Organization of Congress; or, Why Legislatures, Like Firms, are not Organized as Markets," *Journal of Political Economy* 96 (February): 132–168; Kenneth Shepsle and Barry Weingast (1982), "Institutionalizing Majority Rule," *American Economic Review* 72: 367–371; Kenneth Shepsle and Barry Weingast (1987), "The Institutional Foundations of Committee Power," *American Political Science Review* 81: 85–104; and McNollgast (Mathew McCubbins Roger Noll, Barry Weingast (2007), "The Political Economy of Law," in A. Mitchell Polinsky and Steven Shavell, eds., *Handbook of Law and Economics*, Vol. 2, Elsevier, 1652–1738.

these are unlikely to coincide with broad public concerns,[8] and they may be more costly than a market.[9] Accordingly, selecting an alternative to environmental markets requires weighing of the costs and benefits of regulation.

In this political environment, the aim of the primary interest groups involved is to influence government policy at the top toward specific objectives of concern to them and to spread that policy across the broadest range of sub-political jurisdictions.[10] There is little consideration of opportunity costs or of broader economy-wide effects when single-interest policies are promoted, even in the name of public goods, such as environmental quality. This advocacy process involves lobbying, campaign contributions and voting pressures, appearing at regulatory and budget hearings, and in court challenges of regulatory agency actions.[11] It is a costly practice and perhaps only a small portion of the overall electorate has any involvement or understanding of the resource and budget exchanges implicitly made or of the aggregate direction of environmental policy.[12] This approach is inefficient and possibly not durable over the long run if the aggregate costs imposed become too high in a world of competitive economies where employment is scarce and not all country competitors devote the same resources to environmental quality and resource protection.[13]

---

[8] As the Gallup Polls reveal, there often is less concern with global warming than with other local environmental issues. For example, see this Gallup Poll at http://www .gallup.com/poll/146810/water-issues-worry-americans-global-warming-least.aspx.

[9] Frances R. Homans and James E. Wilen (1997), "A Model of Regulated Open Access Resource Use," *Journal of Environmental Economics and Management* 32: 1–27.

[10] Richard L. Revesz (1996), "The Control of Interstate Environmental Externalities in a Federal System," *University of Arizona Law Review* 38: 883–900; Barry Weingast (1995), "The Economic Role of Political Institutions: Market-Preserving Federalism and Economic Development," *Journal of Law, Economics, & Organization* 20(1): 1–31.

[11] Ronald N. Johnson and Gary D. Libecap (2001), "Information Distortion and Competitive Remedies in Government Transfer Policies: The Case of Ethanol," *Economics of Governance* 2(2): 101–134.

[12] For example, see this Gallup Poll at http://www.gallup.com/poll/146810/water-issues-worry-americans-global-warming-least.aspx.

[13] Scott Barrett (2007), *Why Cooperate: The Incentive to Supply Global Public Goods* New York: Oxford University Press; Dieter Helm (2008), "Climate-Change Policy: Why Has so Little Been Achieved?" *Oxford Review of Economic Policy*, 24(2): 211–238.

Because the science behind many environmental and natural resource problems often is incomplete, effective regulation, subsidization, or taxation policy, in the tradition of A.C. Pigou, requires information that local resource users are more likely to have than are regulators. Therefore, effective policy necessitates motivating local users to gather and act on such information, and property rights, unlike uniform performance and technology standards, provide that motivation. The contrast between command-and-control acid rain regulation and its replacement, the national SO_2 emissions permit market,[14] illustrates the substantial cost savings and flexibility that were generated by creating tradable pollution allowances to meet sulfur emission targets.

If actual users cannot be motivated to generate and use local information, they are likely to resist top-down regulations that set harvest or extraction levels, fishing season lengths, air pollution emissions, and land use regulations. Under these circumstances, regulations become a game of users against the state, not a game in which the environment or the economy wins.[15] This is basically what has happened with recent changes in the sulfur emission permit market, where the trading system has been undermined by regulatory and judicial intervention in the presence of weak property rights, as we discussed in Chapter 6.

Chapter 3 built on the work of Ronald Coase to make the case for more extensive use of environmental markets based on secure property rights. By emphasizing that transaction costs determine the extent to which bargaining over competing resource uses can take place, Coase diverts our attention away from market failure and focuses it on the sources of missing markets. Environmental markets are often absent because of unclear or unenforced property rights or because of legal restrictions on the assignment or transfer of rights. The policy question then becomes one of how to lower transaction costs so as to promote the definition of rights and the expansion of markets, rather than crafting more elaborate regulatory regimes.

---

[14] Hahn (1990); Peter B. Pashigian (1985), "Environmental Regulation: Whose Self-Interests are Being Protected?" *Economic Inquiry* 23(4): 551–584; Ackerman and Hassler (1981); and Bruce A. Ackerman and Richard B. Stewart (1985), "Reforming Environmental Law," *Stanford Law Review* 37: 1333–1365.

[15] See discussion of disagreement between regulators and fishers in New England, Meridian Institute (2010), *Catch Shares in New England*, February, Washington D.C.

One of Coase's most relevant points for understanding the potential for environmental markets is that all costs are reciprocal. A farmer's diversion of river water for irrigation imposes a cost on the person who wants the water for fish habitat just as much as the fisher's demand for instream flows to protect fish habitat imposes a cost on the farmer. The direction of causality cannot be determined until property rights are defined and enforced. If the transaction costs of defining, enforcing, and exchanging property rights are sufficiently low, Coase showed that bargaining leads to efficient resource allocation regardless of which competing users has the rights. Importantly, however, the assignment does affect the distribution of wealth which is one of the reasons that defining rights is politically difficult.

Conventional regulatory approaches, of the type discussed in Chapter 2, ignore the important questions of why property rights do not exist and whether they can be created by collective action. Greater attention to lowering the costs of defining and enforcing informal and formal property rights and the ability to use them as the basis for resource management and exchange opens the way for a broader use of common-property regimes. In Chapter 4 we examined common property and community-based institutions that have emerged to resolve competition for resources that dissipates rents. The work of Elinor Ostrom and her colleagues shows that common-property regimes have been overlooked as an option for addressing the problem of social cost. Common property typically works best in relatively tightly-knit, small communities with clear leadership, norms of behavior, repeat exchanges and trust among the membership that constrains group members in resource use. To be effective, these institutions also require that the resource is bounded, that entry is restricted, use is observed, and the resource is of comparatively low value.

As with markets and regulation, common property has limitations. It is vulnerable to exogenous shocks, especially those that increase resource values or lower extraction or use costs, because these invite entry, bringing parties that are not part of the original community contract. These shocks increase incentives for defection among original group members. Moreover, common-property regimes are susceptible to neglect or override by governments in response to influential constituencies. Indeed, common property may be more exposed than private property to such intervention and expropriation because individual ownership and responsibilities are more diluted than with private property. Although individual owners bear the full costs of regulatory overstep or expropriation, with common property, these costs are spread among all group members. Common property also may have higher internal decision-making costs because of the transaction costs involved in achieving consensus. Such consensus building may preclude entrepreneurship and innovation for enhancing resource values that nevertheless create group instability by upsetting *status quo* rankings and resource uses. Because effective common property regimes rely on homogeneity, they are not well suited for larger, heterogeneous groups with diverse demands on resources. This diversity of values, however, is the basis for exchange. In these cases, private property rights and markets are better suited for mitigating the losses of the tragedy of the commons.

Because transaction costs limit the potential for property rights, whether they are formal or informal, there is potential for government to lower transaction costs by helping to define and enforce rights through its police and adjudication powers and through the provision of new information about the resource and its dimensions. This role is especially important when resources are mobile, unobservable, and cross political boundaries, and when there are multiple conflicting demands over it.

Chapter 5 focused on the interface between property rights and politics. Because property rights assign ownership and wealth and typically rely on the monopoly of power held by the state for enforcement, they necessarily are political institutions. There are a variety of ways in which political processes can assign property rights. We discuss direct political distribution, such as grants by politicians to key political cronies as is often the case in less-developed economies where the rule-of-law is weak and governments are corrupt,[16] uniform allocation rules whereby all parties have an equal chance for receipt, such as with lotteries, auction, whereby resource rents go to the auctioneer (usually the state), and grandfathering or first possession, whereby rights

---

[16] Daron Acemoglu and James Robinson (2012), *The Origins of Power, Prosperity, and Poverty: Why Nations Fail*, New York: Crown and Douglass C. North, John Joseph Wallis, and Barry R. Weingast (2009), *Violence and Social Orders: A Conceptual Framework for Interpreting Recorded Human History*, New York: Cambridge University Press.

are granted on the basis of prior use. If transaction costs are low, the distribution of rights will not matter for efficiency because the rights can be traded, but of course, as we have argued, allocation does matter for the overall distribution of income.

Regardless of the option used, the political costs of assigning property rights are affected by the size and heterogeneity of the jurisdictions and constituencies involved who compete for the asset, associated distributional conflicts, and information about the costs of open access and the gains from establishing property rights to address it. Moving from open access or even regulated open access requires denying entry to some and changing production processes. Not all parties will be made better off unless there are compensating transfers from gainers to losers and these may or may not be forthcoming. Politicians respond to multiple constituencies and balance the relevant costs and benefits of assigning property rights to certain parties and of defining the range of options included in those rights. Accordingly, property rights may or may not end up being well defined. Politicians with short-time horizons are unlikely to bear the aggregate economic costs of a weak property rights system, but they may benefit from immediate concessions to influential parties.[17]

For this reason, many of the examples of successful environmental markets build on established property rights to land or water to achieve environmental goals. Incumbent owners can be a formidable constituency to protect environmental property rights. In contrast, newly-created use rights in cap-and-trade are more exposed to political manipulation. There usually is no existing constituency with a history of informal, but recognized ownership, and the new open setting in which rights are being defined allows for many parties to compete for resource rents and constraints on the new rights granted. Any political compromises made in this process, however, affect the nature and security of the property rights assigned.

This latter issue is one of critical importance because of the growing consideration of cap-and-trade regimes in air pollution control, fisheries management, and habitat protection. Not all cap-and-trade programs are the same nor will they have the same potential for

---

[17] Gary D. Libecap (2008), "Open Access Losses and Delay in the Assignment of Property Rights," *Arizona Law Review* 50(2), 379–408.

success. Outcomes, importantly, depend on the nature and security of the property rights that are integral to the institution. This point has not received enough attention.[18] Further, it has not been considered in the legislative and administrative processes, particularly in the United States, where new use rights have been weakened, along with the ability of cap-and-trade arrangements to function effectively to address environmental problems. Caps or total allowable emissions, harvests, or land uses in a particular area typically are set by agency officials. Shares are assigned to those caps. Whether or not actual users contribute information for determining the cap and have confidence in it, and whether or not the shares can instill incentives to provide environmental benefits and have market value (can be traded and banked), depends on the rights system. Property rights are the essential element to cap-and-trade, just as they are essential to addressing the overall problem of social cost. Shares that are not considered to be property rights reduce the potential for environmental markets to function, as we show happened with the sulfur emission trading market.

In the case of natural resource cap-and-trade systems, such as for fisheries, users are granted shares in the cap that often is set with their direct input. The cap is lower than open-access production levels to conserve the stock. Any rents that result are captured in part by shareholders as private gains. The value of the shares depends on the vibrancy of the stock. Accordingly, shareholders have incentive to organize and be vigilant in setting the correct cap, policing enforcement, and protecting their property rights from encroachment by regulatory agencies or the claims of other parties. In the case of cap-and-trade for environmental goods, such as clean air, conditions and incentives are fundamentally different. Each party has a share in the cap, and to the extent that the cap is effective in improving air quality, a public good is provided. The shareholder may receive little direct benefit, however, other than lower abatement costs achievable through exchange or banking of permits. Because of the public- good nature of the environmental good and the potential complexity of science involved, the regulatory agency staff determines the cap. The

---

[18] Corbett Grainger and Christopher Costello (2011), "The Value of Secure Property Rights: Evidence from Global Fisheries," NBER Working Paper 17019, Cambridge: NBER is an exception.

regulated entities may play little role other than lobbying to expand it in order to reduce compliance costs. As a result, cap-and-trade shareholders have less at stake in the share as a property right and are more vulnerable to arbitrary agency or judicial modification of it. These are key differences in cap-and-trade across the two resource types and they likely explain why fishery use rights have remained relatively more secure and have been more successful in terms of long-term outcomes than is the case with pollution emission use rights or conservation credits.

We concluded in Chapters 5 and 6 with two key points:

- The most successful environmental markets are quite local because of the information requirements necessary for addressing idiosyncratic resource problems, the limited numbers of buyers and sellers involved in a particular environmental problem, and the relatively lower prominence of distributional conflicts that weaken property rights.
- Broader environmental markets can work, as they do for ITQs in New Zealand, for example, but the use rights associated with cap-and-trade systems must be secure property rights. Otherwise they are vulnerable, as we have seen, to political and bureaucratic manipulation.

Creating property rights and markets for transboundary and global natural resources is even more difficult, as we described in Chapter 7. Transboundary issues require intergovernmental collaboration, which is much more difficult than creating property rights within single jurisdictions. The internal and cross-jurisdictional distributional conflicts, arbitration, and enforcement challenges are far greater because the distribution of the costs and benefits of the problem and its solution differ. Moreover, outcomes are often uncertain, making it difficult for constituencies in different regions to determine how they will be affected by cross-jurisdictional efforts. When this is the case, they are unlikely to support broad collective action. And measurement of the environmental problem and any response to collaboration is more complex when the spatial scope is expanded across wide areas. These problems must be addressed in order to have cross-jurisdictional cooperation, whether it be across U.S. states or countries of the world.

Negotiation and enforcement costs involving sovereign units can be formidable. The resulting high transaction costs of transboundary collaboration inhibit the development of an expansive property rights and market system. To illustrate our points we provided several examples in Chapter 7 demonstrating varied degrees of success.

WHY MARKETS NOW?

Increased demand for environmental amenities and competition over natural resources has brought new conflicts, which in turn require an extensive array of institutional arrangements including environmental markets. The dominant institution has been centralized regulation. Although regulation has had successes, especially in reducing air and water pollution and regulating land use, it has appeared where the benefits have been high and the mitigation costs low. Forty years since the enabling legislation was enacted, many of the low-hanging fruits, however, have been picked. Marginal abatement costs via centralized regulation are now high, but demand for further environmental quality and effective resource use continues.

As the disputes and costs rise, especially as we noted earlier, in light of slower economic growth in developed economies and greater global economic competition, more cost-effective policies are needed. Top-down regulation is likely to become even more contentious, costly, and ineffective in the future. Centralized regulation becomes an avenue for promoting the agendas of particular interests, including those of politicians and agencies, but not necessarily one for addressing the environmental open-access problem. Command-and-control approaches rely on uniform restrictions and do not meet the equal-marginal rule, whereby marginal abatement costs equal marginal abatement benefits and lead to cost-effective means of meeting environmental objectives. Further, they do not encourage experimentation and entrepreneurship because these activities disrupt regulatory arrangements and alliances. They encounter high enforcement costs because they are not incentive compatible with actual users. Moreover, command-and-control regulation does not generate opportunity costs for alternative approaches addressing the losses of open access, and there are few pressures for defining appropriate baselines for setting and evaluating goals. It is no surprise that command-and-control regulation may not be successful in achieving environmental and natural resource objectives, at least in a cost-effective, durable manner.

Property rights and markets, on the other hand, can address many of these shortcomings – at least in situations where the transaction costs of establishing and enforcing rights and exchange regimes are lower than those associated with more centralized regulation. However, to be effective, property rights must be secure. With security, owners can plan ahead with investment in technologies and new ways of doing things that promote the environment or the resource stock. They will internalize the net benefits of doing so. They can trade their rights when new opportunities develop or use property as collateral for loans and other investment funds.

Improving our environment ultimately will depend on entrepreneurship – recognizing the value of natural resources as assets and developing the technology and institutions that encourage resource users to consider the opportunity costs and benefits of their actions – making them residual claimants to new, higher values. If property rights are not secure, it will appear that markets fail when the essential ingredient – property rights – for markets is missing. Making further gains will require encouraging entrepreneurship to change existing institutions in order to lower transaction costs and stimulate environmental markets and the potential they provide.

Index

Abler, David G., 36n36
Acheson, James M., 12n25, 28n16, 55–6n6, 94n5
acid rain, and air quality regulation, 47–8
Ackerman, Bruce, 47, 207n6
aggregate demand, 24
Agnarsson, Sveinn, 167n60
Agrawal, Arun, 97n9
agriculture. *See* horticulture; livestock industry
air pollution: and competition for use of environmental goods, 1–2; and European Union Emissions Trading System, 182–8; and examples of government regulation, 18, 45–8; and RECLAIM program, 155–9; and Regional Greenhouse Gas Initiative, 131n50, 178–82; and sulfur dioxide emission permits, 159–67; tradable emission permits and use of property rights to reduce, 114
Air Quality Act of 1967, 46
Air Resources Board, 46
Alaska: and conflict between development of oil/gas deposits and environment, 6; and fishery cooperatives, 109–11; and Prudhoe Bay oil deposit, 85; and regulation of fishing industry, 45
Alaska Board of Fisheries, 110, 111
Alexander, Barbara, 98n11
Allen, Douglas W., 5n9, 205n2
allocation rule, for mineral claims, 103

allowance banking, and air pollution, 157, 159n41, 161, 164, 166
Alston, Lee J., 75n55
Anderson, C. Leigh, 102n18
Anderson, Terry L., 7n14, 13n26, 15n30, 52n82, 61n19, 69n36, 75–6n57, 79n64–5, 83n70, 86n78, 130n47, 132n53, 132n56, 173–4n1
Ando, Amy Whritenour, 49n78, 125–6
Arnasson, Ragnar, 13n26, 43, 52n82, 79n64, 132n56, 173–4n1
auctions, and allocation mechanisms for property rights, 130–1
automobile industry, and fuel efficiency standards, 4n7

Bachman, S., 15n30
Bailey, Elizabeth M., 162n48
Baland, Jean-Marie, 21–2n2, 53n2, 95n6, 97n9, 176n4
bargaining: community support for political, 125; and enforcement of property rights across political jurisdictions, 175–8; and Mono Lake controversy, 121n21; property rights and cost of, 66, 84; and reduction of hold-out potential, 89. *See also* trading
Barrett, Scott, 177–8n9
Barzel, Yoram, 74n53
Bator, Francis, 35
Becker, Gary S., 41, 94n5, 176n4, 178n10
bees and pollination services, in horticulture, 67–8
Berkes, Fikret, 55–6n6

Berthoud, Patrick, 126n40
Big Thompson Water Project
    (Colorado), 36n35, 139–43
bilateral trades, and water pollution
    trading regimes, 147
bison (buffalo), 26, 81
Bitterroot River (Montana), 115–17
Bleakley, Hoyt, 129n46
Blomquist, William, 92
boundaries: and costs of definition of
    property rights, 79–84; and examples of
    transboundary situations in fishery
    management, 188–90
Boyd, James, 143n17, 145n20
Brewer, Jedidiah R., 15n30, 83n70,
    142n14
British Columbia, and regulation of
    fishing industry, 44–5, 124, 171–2
British Petroleum, 85
Buchanan, James M., 11n19, 61n18,
    125n37, 178n10, 207n7
Buchner, Barbara K., 68n33, 183–4n22
Bureau of Reclamation (BOR), 139, 140,
    141
Bush, George H., 148
Bushnell, James B., 38n41

CAFE standards, 4n7
California: and conflicts over water
    rights, 70–2, 82n69, 117–21; and
    conservation banks, 150; and Gold
    Rush of 1848, 101; "no-trawl" zones on
    coast of, 126–7; and RECLAIM
    program, 155–9; smog and local air
    quality regulation in, 46–7
California Air Resources Control Board
    (CARB), 159n42
California Gold Rush of 1848, 101
California State Water Project, 71
Canada: and fur trade, 75; and
    International Whaling Commission,
    196–7; and regulation of fisheries, 45,
    169, 188–90. *See also* British Columbia
cap-and-trade programs: compared to
    traditional regulation, 22–3; in
    fisheries, 15–16, 190, 195, 213, 214; and
    markets for ecosystems services,
    144n18
carbon dioxide, and regulation of air
    quality, 46

carbon tax, 37–8
Carney, Sean, 16n32
cattlemen's associations, and history of
    livestock industry, 87, 105–7
causality, and property rights, 57
certified emissions reductions (CERs),
    and Kyoto Protocol, 184n24
certifying credits, 153
Chameides, Bill, 122n25
Cheung, Steven N. S., 27n15, 30n21,
    58n12
Chignik Fishery Cooperative (Alaska),
    109–11
chlorofluorocarbons (CFCs), 46
Christy, Francis, 107, 113
claims, and history of mining industry,
    103–4
Clay, Karen, 102n18
Clean Air Act: and costs of coal use for
    energy production, 11; and point
    sources of pollution, 36n36; and
    regulation of air quality, 46; and sulfur
    oxide emissions, 4n8, 113n1, 159, 163
Clean Air Interstate Rule (CAIR),
    163–5
Clean Air Transport Rule (CATR), 165
Clean Development Mechanism (CDM),
    184
Clean Water Act, 146
Clear Skies and Global Climate Change
    Initiative, 163
climate change, and leakage in
    regulation, 38. *See also* global warming;
    greenhouse gases; Hurricanes Katrina
    and Rita
coal industry, and air pollution, 11, 47,
    160–1, 162–3
Coase, Ronald, 14, 25, 27n15, 53, 54, 57,
    58–64, 66, 68, 73, 122, 209–10
collective action, conditions for
    successful, 94–9
Colorado, and water allocation and
    management, 120, 139–43
Colorado River. *See* Big Thompson
    Project
command-and-control regulation, and
    markets for ecosystems services,
    144n18
common property resource management
    (CPRM): and conditions for successful

Olmstead, Sheila M., 21n2, 34n30, 53n2,
  57n11, 146n21, 151n30
Olson, Mancur, 97n9, 125n37, 178n10,
  207n7
open access: centrality of in controversies
  on ownership of environment, 2–17;
  and common property resource
  management, 93; and examples from
  global commons, 173–203, 214–15. *See
  also* property rights; tragedy of the
  commons
opportunity costs, and whale
  conservation, 201
Oregon, and water rights, 69–70, 135–9
Oregon Water Trust (OWT). *See*
  Freshwater Trust
Ostrom, Elinor, 31n22, 55–6n6, 93, 94,
  96n7, 99, 100, 101, 108, 135, 175–6n4,
  210
overproduction, environmental problems
  related to, 6
ownership, of environment: centrality of
  open access in controversy on, 2–17;
  and government regulation, 17–18;
  reciprocal nature of problem, 1–2. *See
  also* property rights

Packwood-Magnuson Amendment
  (Fishery Conservation and
  Management Act), 197
Palo Verde Irrigation District
  (California), 72
Parker, Dominic P., 98n12, 124n33
Parker, T. K., 15n30
Parry, Ian, 181n16
Pelly Amendment, 197
Peltzman, Sam, 11n19, 41, 94n5, 125n37,
  176n4, 207n7
permits, and assignment of use privileges,
  18
Peters, Mark, 165–6n55
Pigou, Arthur Cecil, 12, 33–5, 39–40, 48,
  51–2, 73, 209
Pindyck, Robert S., 177n6
Platteau, Jean-Philippe, 21–2n2, 53n2,
  95n6, 97n9, 176n4
point sources, of pollution, 36n36
policy: and concept of "double dividend,"
  5n11, 130–1n48; distributional impacts
  of environmental, 5–6; and federal

lands in nineteenth century, 101, 105–6;
  influence of interest groups on
  environmental, 208. *See also*
  regulation; taxation
politics: and centrality of open access to
  discussions of ownership of
  environment, 11; and conflicts over
  property rights, 115–21; definition and
  enforcement of property rights, 57n10,
  58n14; and influence of interest groups
  on environmental policy, 208; interface
  between property rights and, 211–12;
  and mechanisms for allocation of
  property rights, 128–33; and political
  economy of property rights, 121–8;
  Regional Greenhouse Gas Initiative
  (RGGI) and state, 179
Polluter Pays Principle, 58n14
pollution. *See* air pollution; water
  pollution
positive analysis, as distinct from
  normative analysis in discussions of
  open access, 5
prices: for air pollution allowances, 157;
  for conservation easements, 154; and
  water trading, 142. *See also* cost(s)
prior appropriation, of water rights,
  69n36
prisoners' dilemma games, 99
property rights: as alternative to
  government regulation, 113; and
  centrality of open access to controversy
  on ownership of environment, 13–17;
  characteristics of effective, 174–5; and
  conclusions on role of in environmental
  markets, 204–16; costs of defining,
  enforcing, and trading, 72–86; creation
  of through legislation, 10; and
  cross-border fisheries management in
  Pacific Northwest, 188–90; framework
  for discussion of, 55–8; government and
  transaction costs, 86–91; introduction
  to concepts of, 53–5; land trusts and
  conservation easements, 145; political
  economy of, 121–8; politics of conflicts
  over, 115–21; politics of mechanisms
  for allocation of, 128–33; requirement
  for government recognition and
  enforcement of, 114–15; and resolution
  of conflicting uses, 68–72; strategic

Made in the USA
Coppell, TX
10 March 2022